Constructing Knowledge Societies: New Challenges for Tertiary Education

THE WORLD BANK
Washington, D.C.

Cover illustration: Gennady Kurbat/Getty Images.

ISBN 0-8213-5143-5

Library of Congress Cataloging-in-Publication Data
Constructing knowledge societies : new challenges for tertiary education.
    p. cm. — (Directions in development)
    Includes bibliographical references.
    ISBN 0-8213-5143-5
    1. Education, Higher—Economic aspects—Developing countries. 2. Educational assistance—Developing countries. I. World Bank. II. Directions in development (Washington, D.C.)
LC67.68.D44 C66 2002
378.172'2—dc21

200266388

*This document is dedicated to the memory of
Tom Eisemon, in appreciation of his intellectual
leadership and innovative contributions to the
World Bank's work in higher education.*

Contents

4 The Changing Nexus: Tertiary Education Institutions,   67
the Marketplace, and the State

5 World Bank Support for Tertiary Education   99

Appendixes

Bibliography   197

Boxes

Figures

Tables

Foreword

Tertiary education is more than the capstone of the traditional education pyramid; it is a critical pillar of human development worldwide. In today's lifelong-learning framework, tertiary education provides not only the high-level skills necessary for every labor market but also the training essential for teachers, doctors, nurses, civil servants, engineers, humanists, entrepreneurs, scientists, social scientists, and myriad personnel. It is these trained individuals who develop the capacity and analytical skills that drive local economies, support civil society, teach children, lead effective governments, and make important decisions which affect entire societies. Universities are clearly a key part of all tertiary systems, but the diverse and growing set of public and private tertiary institutions in every country—colleges, technical training institutes, community colleges, nursing schools, research laboratories, centers of excellence, distance learning centers, and many more—forms a network of institutions that support the production of the higher-order capacity necessary for development.

The World Bank has been active since 1963 in supporting the growth and diversification of tertiary education systems in developing countries and in promoting essential policy reforms to make the sector more efficient, relevant, equitable, transparent, and responsive. In 1994, after three decades of involvement in tertiary education reforms, the World Bank published an analysis of its endeavors, *Higher Education: Lessons of Experience*. This book has served as an important policy framework and reference for continued World Bank involvement in tertiary education—through projects, research, sector studies, training, and technical assistance—over the past eight years.

Since the publication of *Higher Education,* knowledge has become, more than ever, a primary factor of production throughout the world economy. The recent transformations in the world and in tertiary education have made necessary a reexamination of policies and assumptions to inform our work in a rapidly changing environment. Indeed, the pace of change and innovation has intensified markedly: product development cycles are being compressed, services are becoming a larger proportion of economic output worldwide, computer power and capacity continue to rise and hardware prices to fall, data transmission costs are declining, and communication technology (as evidenced by the spread of the Internet and of cellular phone usage worldwide) is expanding, particularly in developing countries. Tertiary education, in its training, research, and informational role, is vital if countries are to adapt to these far-reaching changes.

The recent World Bank study *Globalization, Growth, and Poverty: Building an Inclusive World Economy,* by David Dollar and Paul Collier, describes how 24 developing countries that integrated themselves more closely into the global economy experienced higher economic growth, a reduced incidence of poverty, a rise in the average wage, an increased share of trade in gross domestic product, and improved health outcomes. These countries simultaneously raised their rates of participation in higher education. Indeed, the countries that benefited most from integration with the world economy achieved the most marked increases in educational levels. In addition, there is growing evidence that tertiary education, through its role in empowering domestic constituencies, building institutions, and nurturing favorable regulatory frameworks and governance structures, is vital to a country's efforts to increase social capital and to promote social cohesion, which is proving to be an important determinant of economic growth and development.

A look at World Bank lending for education over the past three decades shows that about a quarter of the entire education portfolio has consistently been dedicated to projects in tertiary education. Before 2000, borrowers for tertiary education tended to be middle-income countries, with clients such as Argentina, China, and Indonesia receiving some of the largest loans for this purpose. Then, in 2000, the World Bank and the United Nations Educational, Scientific, and Cultural Organization (UNESCO) published *Higher Education in Developing Countries: Peril and Promise,* a report by the independent Task Force on Higher Education and Society. World Bank President James D. Wolfensohn wholeheartedly endorsed the conclusions of the report—that tertiary education is important in building capacity and reducing poverty. Largely in response to growing requests from low-income countries for tertiary education projects, the World Bank has been active in expanding stakeholder dialogues on tertiary education reform and in the preparation of new loans, including initiatives in South Asia and Africa. The Bank recognizes the need to embrace a more balanced, holistic approach to investments and to encourage improvements in the entire lifelong education system, irrespective of a country's income level.

Although there has been much growth and many improvements in tertiary education systems in developing and transition countries and broader use of foreign and distance education providers, the evolving nature of the knowledge economy highlights the rigidities and weaknesses that prevent certain tertiary education systems from maximizing their potential to build local capacity. Developing countries are at the greatest risk of exclusion from the dynamics of the world economy. This marginalization not only promotes human capital flight ("brain drain") from the countries that can least afford it but also raises the likelihood that local concerns will be overlooked, ignored, and postponed. Among these concerns are HIV/AIDS and other public health issues, lagging agricultural production, environmental degradation, lack of institutional capacity, a dearth of the research and innovation that could help a country tap into the growing stock of global knowledge, and problems such as the digital divide between and within countries.

This report reviews and analyzes not only World Bank experience in tertiary education but also the experiences of the many actors in the subsector outside the framework of Bank activity. A large number of stakeholders, government officials, practitioners, academics, and administrators worldwide were consulted in the preparation of this report. Their valuable stories, experiences, and viewpoints are broadly reflected in the comprehensive set of examples from which the main points of analysis are drawn.

Underlying the diverse array of problems and solutions is the notion that tertiary education confers important public goods that are essential to development and poverty reduction—goods that must be accessible to all strata, to all peoples, and to both men and women. The report also emphasizes that tertiary education can no longer be viewed as a discrete subsector of education. Rather, it must be seen as but one critical element that buttresses a holistic system of education—a system which must become more flexible, diverse, efficient, and responsive to the knowledge economy. This study recognizes that context is vital to understanding problems and that stakeholder consultation is imperative in designing solutions.

Mamphela Ramphele
Managing Director (Human Development)
The World Bank

Acknowledgments

This report was prepared by a team led by Jamil Salmi in close collaboration with members of the Bank's tertiary education thematic group (COREHEG), including Benoît Millot, David Court, Michael Crawford, Peter Darvas, Fred Golladay, Lauritz Holm-Nielsen, Richard Hopper, Andrei Markov, Peter Moock, Hena Mukherjee, William Saint, Shashi Shrivastava, Francis Steier, and Rosita van Meel. Special thanks are due to Richard Hopper for his invaluable contributions to the entire document, to William Saint for extensive work on the executive summary and the strategy for low-income countries and small states, to Lauritz Holm-Nielsen and Michael Crawford for taking the lead on the national innovation framework, to Shashi Shrivastava for mobilizing written comments in South Asia, to Birgit Zischke for excellent research assistance, and to Lorelei Lacdao and Julie Wagshal for their dedication and careful production of the final report. The team worked under the general guidance of Ruth Kagia, director of the Education Department, and Jo Ritzen, vice president of the Human Development Network.

The team sought advice at the beginning of the process from a group of distinguished scholars, including Philip Altbach, José Joaquin Brunner, Elaine El-Khawas, Carmen García Guadilla, Daniel Levy, and Alan Wagner. Warm thanks are extended to them. Extensive consultations on the various drafts were also carried out within and outside the World Bank. In addition to review meetings with education sector staff and other staff members in the Bank's operational regions, stakeholder consultations were organized to seek the views of the tertiary education community in all regions where the Bank is active. The list of those who participated in these review and consultation meetings and of those who generously offered written comments would be too long to permit recognition of the contributions of each individual. The team would like to make special mention, however, of the thoughtful comments offered by Ralph Harbison a few weeks before his sudden death. While the team expresses its appreciation to all colleagues, within and outside the World

Bank, for their insightful observations and suggestions on various aspects of the report, it bears the ultimate responsibility for any short-comings, errors, or misinterpretations.

Abbreviations

AERC	African Economic Research Consortium
APL	Adaptable program loan
GDP	Gross domestic product
IBRD	International Bank for Reconstruction and Development
ICT	Information and communication technologies
IDA	International Development Association
IDF	Institutional Development Fund
IFC	International Finance Corporation
ILO	International Labour Office/International Labour Organization
IT	Information technology
LIL	Learning and innovation loan
MBA	Master of business administration degree
MDGs	Millennium Development Goals of the United Nations
MIS	Management information system
MIT	Massachusetts Institute of Technology
NIS	National information system
OECD	Organisation for Economic Co-operation and Development
PRSC	Poverty reduction strategy credit
R&D	Research and development
S&T	Science and technology
SMEs	Small and medium-size enterprises
TAL	Technical assistance loan
TFP	Total factor productivity
UNAIDS	Joint United Nations Programme on HIV/AIDS
UNESCO	United Nations Educational, Scientific, and Cultural Organization
WTO	World Trade Organization

Executive Summary

Developing and transition economies face significant new trends in the global environment that affect not only the shape and mode of operation but also the very purpose of tertiary education systems. Among the most critical dimensions of change are the convergent impacts of globalization, the increasing importance of knowledge as a main driver of growth, and the information and communication revolution. Knowledge accumulation and application have become major factors in economic development and are increasingly at the core of a country's competitive advantage in the global economy. The combination of increased computing power, diminishing prices of hardware and software, improvement of wireless and satellite technologies, and reduced telecommunication costs has all but removed the space and time barriers to information access and exchange.

Both opportunities and threats arise from these changes. On the positive side, the role of tertiary education in the construction of knowledge economies and democratic societies is more influential than ever. Indeed, tertiary education is central to the creation of the intellectual capacity on which knowledge production and utilization depend and to the promotion of the lifelong-learning practices necessary to update individual knowledge and skills. Another favorable development is the emergence of new types of tertiary institutions and new forms of competition, inducing traditional institutions to change their modes of operation and delivery and to take advantage of the opportunities offered by the new information and communication technologies (ICT). But on the negative side, this technological transformation carries the real danger of a growing digital divide between and within nations.

Even as these new opportunities and challenges emerge, most developing and transition countries continue to wrestle with difficulties stemming from inadequate responses to long-standing problems facing their tertiary education systems. Among these unresolved challenges are the need to expand tertiary education coverage in a sustainable way, inequalities of access and outcomes, problems of educational quality and relevance, and rigid governance structures and management practices.

Purposes and Findings of This Report

The World Bank has actively supported tertiary education reform efforts in a number of countries. Nevertheless, there is a perception that the Bank has not been fully responsive to the growing demand by clients for tertiary education interventions and that, especially in the poorest countries, lending for the subsector has not matched the importance of tertiary education systems for economic and social development. The Bank is commonly viewed as supporting only basic education; systematically advocating the reallocation of public expenditures from tertiary to basic education; promoting cost recovery and private sector expansion; and discouraging low-income countries from considering any investment in advanced human capital. Given these perceptions, the rapid changes taking place in the global environment, and the persistence of the traditional problems of tertiary education in developing and transition countries, reexamining the World Bank's policies and experiences in tertiary education has become a matter of urgency.

This report describes how tertiary education contributes to building up a country's capacity for participation in an increasingly knowledge-based world economy and investigates policy options for tertiary education that have the potential to enhance economic growth and reduce poverty. It examines the following questions: What is the importance of tertiary education for economic and social development? How should developing and transition countries position themselves to take full advantage of the potential contribution of tertiary education? How can the World Bank and other development agencies assist in this process?

The report draws on ongoing Bank research and analysis on the dynamics of knowledge economies and on science and technology development. Using this background, it explores how countries can adapt and shape their tertiary education systems to confront successfully the combination of new and old challenges in the context of the rising significance for tertiary education of internal and international market forces. It examines the justification for continuing public support of tertiary education and the appropriate role of the state in support of knowledge-driven economic growth. Finally, it reviews the lessons from recent World Bank experience with support of tertiary education, including ways of minimizing the negative political impact of reforms, and makes recommendations for future Bank involvement.

Although this report expands on many of the themes developed in the first World Bank policy paper on tertiary education, *Higher Education:*

The Lessons of Experience (1994), it emphasizes the following new trends:

- The emerging role of knowledge as a major driver of economic development
- The appearance of new providers of tertiary education in a "borderless education" environment
- The transformation of modes of delivery and organizational patterns in tertiary education as a result of the information and communication revolution
- The rise of market forces in tertiary education and the emergence of a global market for advanced human capital
- The increase in requests from World Bank client countries for financial support for tertiary education reform and development
- The recognition of the need for a balanced and comprehensive view of education as a holistic system that includes not only the human capital contribution of tertiary education but also its critical humanistic and social capital building dimensions and its role as an important global public good.

Briefly, the main messages of this document are as follows:

- Social and economic progress is achieved principally through the advancement and application of knowledge.
- Tertiary education is necessary for the effective creation, dissemination, and application of knowledge and for building technical and professional capacity.
- Developing and transition countries are at risk of being further marginalized in a highly competitive world economy because their tertiary education systems are not adequately prepared to capitalize on the creation and use of knowledge.
- The state has a responsibility to put in place an enabling framework that encourages tertiary education institutions to be more innovative and more responsive to the needs of a globally competitive knowledge economy and to the changing labor market requirements for advanced human capital.
- The World Bank Group can assist its client countries in drawing on international experience and in mobilizing the resources needed to improve the effectiveness and responsiveness of their tertiary education systems.

Tertiary Education Policy in the Context of the World Bank's Development Strategy

As this study shows, support for tertiary education programs contributes to the Bank's overall strategic framework and goals, as outlined below.

Poverty Reduction through Economic Growth

Tertiary education exercises a direct influence on national productivity, which largely determines living standards and a country's ability to compete in the global economy. Tertiary education institutions support knowledge-driven economic growth strategies and poverty reduction by (a) training a qualified and adaptable labor force, including high-level scientists, professionals, technicians, teachers in basic and secondary education, and future government, civil service, and business leaders; (b) generating new knowledge; and (c) building the capacity to access existing stores of global knowledge and to adapt that knowledge to local use. Tertiary education institutions are unique in their ability to integrate and create synergy among these three dimensions. Sustainable transformation and growth throughout the economy are not possible without the capacity-building contribution of an innovative tertiary education system. This is especially true in low-income countries with weak institutional capacity and limited human capital.

Poverty Reduction through Redistribution and Empowerment

Tertiary education supports the opportunity and empowerment dimensions outlined in *World Development Report 2000/2001*. Access to tertiary education can open better employment and income opportunities to underprivileged students, thereby decreasing inequity. The norms, values, attitudes, ethics, and knowledge that tertiary institutions can impart to students constitute the social capital necessary to construct healthy civil societies and socially cohesive cultures.

Fulfillment of Millennium Development Goals

It is doubtful that any developing country could make significant progress toward achieving the United Nations Millennium Development Goals (MDGs) for education—universal enrollment in primary education and elimination of gender disparities in primary and secondary education—without a strong tertiary education system. Tertiary education supports the rest of the education system through the training of teachers and school principals, the involvement of specialists from tertiary education institutions in curriculum design and educational research, and the establishment of admission criteria that influence the content and methods of teaching and learning at the secondary level. A similar argument applies to the contribution of postsecondary medical education, especially the training of medical doctors, epidemiologists, public health specialists, and hospital managers, to meeting the basic health MDGs.

The State and Tertiary Education

Research on the dynamics of knowledge-driven development has identified the converging roles of four contributing factors: a country's macroeconomic incentive and institutional regime, its ICT infrastructure, its national innovation system, and the quality of its human resources. Of these, the contribution of tertiary education is vital with respect to the national innovation system and the development of human resources.

In this context, continued government support of tertiary education is justified by three important considerations: the existence of externalities from tertiary education, equity issues, and the supportive role of tertiary education in the education system as a whole.

Externalities

Investments in tertiary education generate major external benefits that are crucial for knowledge-driven economic and social development. Private investment in tertiary education can be suboptimal because individuals do not capture all the benefits of education. A few examples will illustrate how education yields benefits to society as a whole.

Technological innovations and the diffusion of scientific and technical innovations lead to higher productivity, and most of these innovations are the products of basic and applied research undertaken in universities. Progress in the agriculture, health, and environment sectors, in particular, is heavily dependent on the application of such innovations. Higher skill levels in the labor force—an outcome of increased educational levels—and the qualitative improvements that permit workers to use new technology also boost productivity.

Tertiary education facilitates nation building by promoting greater social cohesion, trust in social institutions, democratic participation and open debate, and appreciation of diversity in gender, ethnicity, religion, and social class. Furthermore, pluralistic and democratic societies depend on research and analysis that are fostered through social sciences and humanities programs. Improved health behaviors and outcomes also yield strong social benefits, and higher education is indispensable for training the needed health care professionals.

Equity

Imperfections in capital markets limit the ability of individuals to borrow sufficiently for tertiary education, thereby hindering the participation of meritorious but economically disadvantaged groups. Although more than 60 countries have student loan programs, access to affordable loans frequently remains restricted to a minority of students. Moreover, these loans are not necessarily available to the students with limited resources who most need financial aid. Very few countries have national programs reaching more than 10 percent of the student population, and these exceptions are rich countries such as Australia, Canada, Sweden, the United Kingdom, and the United States. In addition, where they do exist, student loans are not always available for the whole range of academic programs and disciplines.

Support for Other Levels of the Education System

Tertiary education plays a key role in supporting basic and secondary education, thereby buttressing the economic externalities produced by these lower levels. Improved tertiary education is necessary for sustainable progress in basic education. The supply of qualified teachers and school leaders, capacity for curriculum design, research on teaching and learning, economic analysis and management—these and many more components of basic education reform are hampered by weak tertiary education systems. A comprehensive approach to the development of the education sector is required, along with a balanced distribution of budgetary resources to ensure that countries invest appropriately in tertiary education, with attention to their progress toward the Millennium Development Goals.

When looking at the public benefits of tertiary education, it is important to note the existence of joint-product effects linked to the complementarity between tertiary education and the lower levels of education, as described above, and between undergraduate and postgraduate education. While many undergraduate and professional education programs can be offered in separate institutions (business and law are examples), high-cost activities such as basic research and various types of specialized graduate training are more efficiently organized in combination with undergraduate training. Cross-subsidization across educational disciplines, programs, and levels leads to public-good effects that are valuable but are difficult to quantify. In addition, there are economies of scale that justify public support of expensive programs such as basic sciences that are almost natural monopolies.

Determining Appropriate Investment Levels

Notwithstanding the methodological difficulties involved in measuring externalities, the existence of these important public benefits indicates that the costs of insufficient investment in tertiary education can be very high. These costs can include reduced ability of a country to compete effectively in global and regional economies; a widening of economic and social disparities; declines in the quality of life, in health status, and in life expectancy; an increase in unavoidable public expenditures on social welfare programs; and a deterioration of social cohesion. Sustainable transformation and growth throughout the economy cannot be achieved without an innovative tertiary education system to help build the absorptive capacity that is required if private sector investment and donor resources are to have a lasting productive impact.

At the same time, the development of a holistic education system calls for a comprehensive approach to resource allocation. Certain guidelines can be applied to ensure a balanced distribution of budgetary resources and an appropriate sequencing of investment across the three education subsectors in relation to a country's level of education development, pattern of economic growth, and fiscal situation. Based on the experience of industrial countries that have emphasized the role of education in supporting economic growth and social cohesion, it would seem that an appropriate range for the overall level of investment in education as a share of gross domestic product (GDP) would be between 4 and 6 percent. In this context, expenditures on tertiary education would generally represent between 15 and 20 percent of all expenditures on public education. Developing countries that devote more than 20 percent of their education budget to tertiary education, especially those that have not attained universal primary education coverage, are likely to have a distorted allocation that favors an elitist university system and does not adequately support basic and secondary education. Similarly, countries that spend more than 20 percent of their tertiary education budget on noneducational expenditures such as student subsidies are likely to be underinvesting in materials, equipment, library resources, and other inputs that are crucial for quality learning.

The Evolving Role of the State: Guidance through an Enabling Framework and Appropriate Incentives

As their direct involvement in the funding and provision of tertiary education diminishes, governments rely less on the traditional state control model to make reforms happen. Instead they promote change by guiding and encouraging tertiary education institutions through a coherent policy framework, an enabling regulatory environment, and appropriate financial incentives.

1. Countries and tertiary education institutions willing to take advantage of the new opportunities presented by the knowledge economy and the ICT revolution must be proactive in fostering innovations and launching meaningful reforms in a coherent policy framework. Although there is no blueprint that is valid for all countries, a common prerequisite seems to be a clear vision for the long-term development of a comprehensive, diversified, and well-articulated tertiary education system. Student mobility can be encouraged by developing open systems that offer recognition of relevant prior experience, degree equivalencies, credit transfer, tuition exchange schemes, access to national scholarships and student loans, and a comprehensive qualifications and lifelong-learning framework.

2. The regulatory environment should be one that encourages rather than stifles innovations in public institutions and initiatives by the private sector to expand access to good-quality tertiary education. Rules for the establishment of new institutions, including private and virtual ones, should be restricted to outlining minimum quality requirements and should not constitute barriers to entry. Other regulatory considerations should be the development of quality assurance mechanisms (evaluation, accreditation, national examinations, rankings, and publication of information), financial controls to which public institutions are required to conform, and intellectual property rights legislation.

3. Although public funding remains the main source of support for tertiary education in most countries, it is being channeled in new ways and is being increasingly supplemented by nonpublic resources. Both of these changes bring market forces to bear in ways heretofore uncommon in the financing of public institutions. New financing strategies have been put in place in the public sector to generate revenue from institutional assets, to mobilize additional resources from students and their families, and to encourage donations from third-party contributors. Many governments have also encouraged the creation of private institutions as an effective approach for easing pressures on the public purse and satisfying pent-up demand.

World Bank Support for Tertiary Education

In the 1970s and 1980s much of the support provided by World Bank tertiary education projects was piecemeal, with a narrow focus on the establishment of new programs or on discrete quality improvement measures for existing teaching and research activities. These projects sometimes created well-equipped academic oases—which tended to become unsustainable over time. The Bank was rarely able to offer the type of long-term comprehensive support for tertiary education that is required for successful reform and effective institution building.

An internal review of implementation experience with tertiary education projects undertaken in 1992 and an assessment of recent and ongoing interventions in this subsector have offered critical insights into more productive ways of supporting tertiary education reforms and innovations. Three vital lessons emerge from past and current tertiary education projects, as outlined below.

Comprehensive reforms can be more effective than piecemeal ones. Interventions integrated into a broad reform program based on a global change strategy are more likely to bear fruit than isolated efforts. Financing reforms, especially the introduction of tuition fees and the expansion of private tertiary education, are difficult to implement successfully without equity measures to help disadvantaged students gain access to and afford tertiary education. They also require significant devolution of government control in matters affecting institutional costs, as well as incentives for institutions to engage in cost-saving and income-generating activities.

The preference for comprehensiveness does not mean that all aspects of a reform should be packed into a single operation. Sequencing provides the tools for responding to and adjusting to evolving challenges. Long-term involvement through a series of complementary operations, as occurred in China, Indonesia, the Republic of Korea, and Tunisia, has proved essential for ensuring structural change that is sustainable.

Attention to the political-economy aspects of reform is vital. Until the beginning of the 1990s, little attention was paid to the political economy of tertiary education reforms, on the assumption that a technically sound reform program and agreement with top government officials were all that was needed for change to succeed. But when it came to actual implementation, political reality often proved stronger than the technocratic vision. In many countries various interest groups have resisted proposed reform programs. Launching and implementing tertiary education reforms has been more successful when decisionmakers have managed to build a consensus among the various constituents of the tertiary education community.

Reliance on positive incentives to promote change can be pivotal. The extent to which projects rely on positive incentives rather than mandatory edicts to stimulate change has a great influence on outcomes, as institutions and actors tend to respond more readily to constructive stimuli. The World Bank has had positive experience with such policy instruments as competitive funds, accreditation mechanisms, and management information systems. Well-designed competitive funds and incentives encourage better performance by tertiary education institutions and can be powerful vehicles for transformation and innovation, as demonstrated by the positive results of projects in Argentina, Chile, the Arab Republic of Egypt, Guinea, and Indonesia.

Directions for Future Bank Support

Investment in tertiary education is an important pillar of development strategies that emphasize the construction of democratic, knowledge-based economies and societies. The World Bank can play a central role by facilitating policy dialogue and knowledge sharing, supporting reforms through program and project lending, and promoting an enabling framework for the production of the global public goods crucial to the development of tertiary education.

Facilitating Policy Dialogue and Knowledge Sharing

Reform proposals that are likely to affect established practices and vested interests are always met with fierce resistance and opposition from those groups most affected by the intended redistribution of power and wealth. Under the right circumstances, the Bank may play a catalytic role by encouraging and facilitating the policy dialogue on tertiary education reforms. This can often be accomplished through preemptive information sharing and analytical work in support of national dialogue and goal-setting efforts, as well as through project preparation activities aimed at building stakeholder consensus during the project concept and appraisal phases. The Bank can bring to the same table stakeholders who would not normally converse and work together. It can also share information on a great variety of national and institutional experiences that can nourish the debate in any country and that offer objective reference points for analysis of the local situation and assessment of the range and content of policy options worth considering. This type of dialogue can assist in the formulation of a long-term vision for the country's tertiary education system as a whole and in the preparation of strategic plans at the level of individual institutions.

The World Bank's comparative advantage in relation to other donor agencies in supporting policy dialogue in client countries stems from two related factors. First, the Bank has access to worldwide experiences that can be shared with interested counterparts and stakeholders. Second, it can tie reform of tertiary education to economywide reform. The comprehensive nature of the Bank's work allows it to adopt a systemwide approach linking sectoral issues to the overall development framework and public finance context of any country, rather than focus on isolated interventions in support of specific institutions.

Supporting Reforms through Program and Project Lending

In supporting the actual implementation of tertiary education reforms, the World Bank gives priority to programs and projects that can bring about positive developments and innovations by:

- Increasing institutional diversification (growth of nonuniversity and private institutions) to expand coverage on a financially viable basis and establish a lifelong-learning framework with multiple points of entry and multiple pathways
- Strengthening science and technology research and development capacity in selected areas linked to a country's priorities for the development of comparative advantages
- Improving the relevance and quality of tertiary education
- Promoting greater equity mechanisms (scholarships and student loans) intended to create and expand access and opportunities for disadvantaged students
- Establishing sustainable financing systems to encourage responsiveness and flexibility
- Strengthening management capacities, through such measures as introduction of management information systems, to promote improved accountability, administration, and governance and more efficient utilization of existing resources
- Enhancing and expanding information technology and communications capacity to reduce the digital divide (complementing existing global initiatives by the World Bank such as the Global Development Learning Network, the African Virtual University, the Global Development Network, and World Links).

The lessons of recent experience show that Bank support to client countries should be:

- Appropriate to a country's specific circumstances
- Predicated on strategic planning at national and institutional levels
- Focused on promoting autonomy and accountability
- Geared toward enhancing institutional capacity and facilitating the cross-fertilization of relevant regional experiences

- Sequenced, with a time horizon consistent with the long-term nature of capacity enhancement efforts
- Sensitive to local political considerations affecting tertiary education reform.

The relative emphasis and mix of interventions appropriate for any given country are linked to its specific political and economic circumstances both at the macroeconomic level and in tertiary education. Income level, country size, and political stability are all important factors. In setting priorities for the appropriate mix of lending and non-lending services in a given country, the Bank will be guided by the following criteria: (a) the need to change (the gravity of the issues and the urgency of reform) and (b) willingness to reform, as reflected in the government's commitment to implementing meaningful change and its ability to mobilize major stakeholders in support of the reform agenda.

In countries where the need for reform is acute, the choice of lending instrument should be guided by the following considerations:

- Adaptable program loans (APLs) are preferred in countries with a strategic framework and expectations of political stability, as they facilitate a systemwide, holistic, long-term approach. When necessary, the first phase of the APL could focus on consolidating the strategic framework for reform and on building consensus among all stakeholders.
- Budget support can be extended in the context of programs for the education sector as a whole in countries where the tertiary education reform agenda is a high priority and where there is a clear commitment from all stakeholders to support the proposed reforms.
- Technical assistance loans (TALs) or learning and innovation loans (LILs) are appropriate where there is government interest in initiating change in the tertiary education sector but the conditions for implementing a reform are not fully met (that is, when there is high need but low political will). Countries should use TALs to help formulate a comprehensive reform strategy and build a national consensus around it. LILs should be used to pilot innovations before they are replicated on a larger scale.
- International Finance Corporation (IFC) loans and guarantees in support of individual private institutions can be extended to complement International Bank for Reconstruction and Development (IBRD) loans in countries that have established a positive regulatory and incentives framework to promote private tertiary education. IBRD lending that involves private tertiary education would focus on systemwide interventions for quality improvement and accreditation (using competi-

tive funding) or for the establishment of student loan schemes for the entire private sector.

Most of the options outlined above are directly relevant to middle-income countries. Important distinctions are warranted, however, for three groups of World Bank clients: transition countries, low-income countries, and small states. Such countries operate under special conditions that require a different focus and set of priorities.

- The leading options for improving tertiary education in the transition countries of Eastern Europe and Central Asia include introducing more flexible and less specialized curricula, promoting shorter programs and courses, creating a more adaptable regulatory framework, and establishing systems of public funding that encourage institutions to respond to market demands for quality and diversity. Other important options include improving access through the provision of financial aid to students, requiring external participation in governance, and professionalizing university administration. Public investments are needed to build capacity for academic and management innovation, to expand the breadth of course offerings at individual institutions, and to create new programs in response to evolving demand-driven areas of learning.
- Directions for tertiary education development for low-income countries would have three priorities: (a) building capacity for managing and improving the basic and secondary education system, including capacity for training and retraining teachers and principals; (b) expanding the production of qualified professionals and technicians through a cost-effective combination of public and private nonuniversity institutions; and (c) making targeted investments in fields of advanced training and research in chosen areas of comparative advantage. In countries that rely on poverty reduction strategy credits, the focus should be on resource rationalization measures to ensure balanced development of the entire education sector; on an effective contribution by tertiary education to the country's Education for All program, especially through the teacher training institutions; and on the capacity-building role of tertiary education to promote the achievement of the other MDGs (agriculture, health, environment) and facilitate economic diversification efforts.
- In addressing the tertiary education needs of small states, the top priorities are (a) subregional partnerships with neighboring small states to establish a networked university; (b) strategically focused tertiary education institutions that address a very limited proportion of the nation's critical human skill requirements; (c) negotiated franchise partnerships between the national government and external

providers of tertiary education; and (d) government-negotiated provision of distance education by a recognized international provider.

Promoting an Enabling Framework for Global Public Goods

Globalization and the growth of borderless education raise important issues that affect tertiary education in all countries but are often beyond the control of any one national government. Among these challenges are new forms of human capital flight ("brain drain") that result in a loss of local capacity in fields critical to development; the absence of a proper international accreditation and qualifications framework; the absence of accepted legislation regarding foreign tertiary education providers; the lack of clear intellectual property regulations governing distance education programs; and barriers to access to information and communication technologies, including the Internet. The World Bank is uniquely positioned to work with its partners in the international community to promote an enabling framework for the global public goods that are crucial for the future of tertiary education.

Brain drain issues. The following measures could be envisaged for dealing with brain drain: (a) increased reliance on joint degrees; (b) inclusion in donor-funded scholarships of allocations for purchasing the minimum equipment and materials needed by returning scholars and for travel to update knowledge; (c) a preference for sending grantees to top-quality training institutions in other developing countries that possess an oversupply of skilled labor, such as India; and (d) creation of a favorable local work environment for national researchers and specialists.

International quality assurance framework. In addition to the support provided through accreditation components in specific country projects, the World Bank will contribute toward the goal of establishing an international qualifications framework through consultations with donors and specialized professional associations, as well as through the Development Grant Facility. Two sets of complementary initiatives will be considered: (a) technical and financial assistance to groups of small countries that wish to set up a regional quality assurance system in lieu of separate national ones and (b) support for global quality assurance initiatives on a thematic basis.

Trade barriers. The World Bank will work at both international and national levels to help define rules of conduct and appropriate safeguards designed to protect students from low-quality offerings and fraudulent providers, without allowing these mechanisms to constitute rigid entry barriers. Governments, licensing bodies, and tertiary education institutions could apply the following criteria to evaluate foreign providers that are not yet accredited by an internationally recognized agency: (a) minimum infrastructure, facilities, and staffing requirements; (b) appropriate, transparent, and accurate information on the policies, mission statements, study programs, and feedback mechanisms of foreign providers, including the channels for complaints and appeals; (c) capacity-building partnerships between foreign providers and local institutions; and (d) comparable academic quality and standards, including the full recognition in the home country of the degrees and qualifications delivered by foreign providers in a developing country.

Intellectual property rights. The World Bank will play a brokering role to help create and nurture dissemination partnerships among publishing companies, universities in advanced nations, and tertiary education institutions in developing countries. This could be done along the lines of the decision by the Massachusetts Institute of Technology to offer all its courses free of charge on the Web, or the recently announced agreement among six leading publishers of medical journals to give free access to their journals to more than 600 institutions in the 60 poorest countries.

Bridging the digital gap. As part of its strategic commitment to global public goods, the World Bank will contribute to decreasing the digital divide between industrial and developing countries by supporting investments in ICT infrastructure for tertiary education within countries or even in multiple countries, as is happening under the Millennium Science Initiative.

In conclusion, the Bank aspires to apply its extensive knowledge base and financial resources toward increased efforts in the tertiary education sector. Strengthening the capacity of tertiary education institutions to respond flexibly to the new demands of knowledge societies will increase their contribution to poverty reduction through the long-term economic effects and the associated welfare benefits that come from sustained growth.

Overview and Main Findings

It is not the strongest of the species that survive, nor the most intelligent, but the one most responsive to change.

Charles Darwin

As the 21st century opens, tertiary education is facing unprecedented challenges, arising from the convergent impacts of globalization, the increasing importance of knowledge as a principal driver of growth, and the information and communication revolution.[1] But opportunities are emerging from these challenges. The role of education in general, and of tertiary education in particular, is now more influential than ever in the construction of knowledge economies and democratic societies. Tertiary education is indeed central to the creation of the intellectual capacity on which knowledge production and utilization depend and to the promotion of the lifelong-learning practices necessary for updating people's knowledge and skills. At the same time, new types of tertiary institutions and new forms of competition are appearing, inducing traditional institutions to change their modes of operation and delivery and take advantage of the opportunities offered by the new information and communication technologies.

The State of Tertiary Education in Developing and Transition Countries

In response to these momentous and converging trends in the environment, a number of countries have undertaken significant transformations of their tertiary education systems, including changes in patterns of financing and governance, growing institutional differentiation, the creation of evaluation and accreditation mechanisms, curriculum reforms, and technological innovations. But progress has been uneven, and sharp contrasts remain between and within tertiary education systems worldwide. Most developing and transition countries continue to wrestle with difficulties arising from inadequate responses to existing challenges. Among these unresolved issues are the expansion of tertiary education coverage in a sustainable way, the reduction of inequalities of access and outcomes, the improvement of educational quality and relevance, and the introduction of effective governance structures and management practices. Even though tertiary-level enrollments have grown significantly in virtually all countries in the developing world, the enrollment gap between the most advanced economies and developing countries has widened. In addition, tertiary education systems continue to be elitist as regards access and the socioeconomic composition of the student body. Financial resources have been insufficient to sustain growth of enrollment and improve quality. In many countries rigid governance models and management practices are preventing tertiary education institutions from embracing change and launching reforms and innovations.

In this context, developing and transition countries are confronted with a dual task. On the one hand, there is a pressing need to overcome the existing coverage, equity, quality, and governance problems that have beset their tertiary education systems. On the other hand, developing and transition countries, like industrial countries, are exposed to the new challenges arising from the construction of knowledge-based economies and democratic societies. A key concern is whether developing and transition countries can adapt and shape their tertiary education systems to confront successfully this combination of old and new challenges.

Purposes of This Report

Even though the World Bank has actively supported tertiary education reform efforts in a wide variety of countries for many years, there is a perception that the Bank has not been fully responsive to the growing demand for tertiary education interventions by clients and that lending for the subsector has not matched the growing importance of tertiary education for economic and social development, especially in the poorest developing countries. It thus became necessary to revisit the Bank's policies and experience regarding tertiary education in the light of the changes in the world environment and the persistence of the traditional problems of tertiary education in developing and transition countries.

This World Bank report on tertiary education describes the role of tertiary education in building up a country's capacity for participation in an increasingly knowledge-based world economy and investigates policy options that have the potential to enhance economic growth and reduce poverty. The report examines the following questions:

- What is the importance of tertiary education for economic and social development?
- How should developing and transition countries position themselves to take full advantage of the potential contribution of tertiary education?
- How can the World Bank and other development agencies assist in this process?

The report has two complementary goals. The first is to provide information and insights that reflect current knowledge about successful reforms and effective implementation and that are applicable to World Bank tertiary education lending practices. The second is to engage client countries and the international community in a dialogue on the role of tertiary education in the context of overall World Bank strategies and policies, the justification for investing in the subsector, and ways of minimizing the negative political impact of tertiary education reforms.

The report builds on previous World Bank policy research and analysis, notably *Higher Education: The Lessons of Experience* (1994); *Education Sector Strategy* (1999a); and the report of the independent Task Force on Higher Education and Society set up jointly by the World Bank and the United Nations Educational, Scientific, and Cultural Organization (UNESCO), *Higher Education in Developing Countries: Peril and Promise* (2000). It also draws on recent work by the Organisation for Economic Co-operation and Development (OECD), UNESCO, and the regional banks, as listed in the Bibliography in this volume. In addition, it links knowledge about tertiary education with the findings of recent *World Development Reports—The State in a Changing World* (1997), *Knowledge for Development* (1999c), and *Entering the 21st Century* (2000e)—and with ongoing Bank analytical and strategic work on the dynamics of knowledge economies and on science and technology development.

This study expands on many of the themes developed in the first World Bank policy document on the subsector, the 1994 volume *Higher Education*. Nevertheless, it contains significant differences, stemming from the radical changes that have transformed the external environment in which tertiary education systems operate. Foremost among these changes are the emerging role of knowledge as a major driver of economic development, the appearance of new providers of tertiary education in a "borderless education" environment, and the transformation of modes of delivery and organizational patterns in tertiary education in response to the information and communication revolution. Other important changes in the past few years are the rise of market forces in tertiary education and the emergence of a global market for advanced human capital. There has also been a notable increase in requests from World Bank client countries for financial support for tertiary education reform and development, often as a consequence of their rapid progress in basic and secondary education coverage. The report emphasizes the need for a balanced and comprehensive view of education as a holistic and global system that includes not only the human capital contribution of tertiary education but also its critical humanistic and social capital building dimensions and its role as an important international public good. This perspective leads to new recommendations for tertiary education policy.

Although the World Bank is but one of many donor agencies working in the tertiary education subsector, it can make a significant contribution in at least two important areas. First, the World Bank is in a unique position to introduce a comparative global perspective on recent tertiary education developments and reform while engaging in policy dialogue in a large number of developing and transition countries. Second, extensive technical and practical experience with tertiary education projects over the past 20 years provides the World Bank with relevant and concrete implementation lessons from successful and less successful reforms in a variety of national and institutional contexts.

Tertiary Education Policy in the Context of Overall World Bank Strategy

The findings of this report demonstrate how improvements in tertiary education contribute to the World Bank's overall strategy, including its work in support of the United Nations Millennium Development Goals.

Poverty Reduction through Economic Growth

The Bank's analytical framework for studying and explaining the dynamics of knowledge-driven development identifies the converging roles of four contributing factors: the macroeconomic incentive and institutional regime, the information and telecommunication infrastructure, the national innovation system, and the quality of human resources. In this framework, the contribution of tertiary education is acknowledged as vital because it exercises a direct influence on national productivity, which largely determines living standards and a country's ability to compete and participate fully in the globalization process. More specifically, tertiary education institutions support knowledge-driven economic growth strategies and poverty reduction by (a) training a qualified and adaptable labor force, including high-level scientists, professionals, technicians, teachers in basic and secondary education, and future government, civil service, and business leaders; (b) generating new knowledge; and (c) providing the capacity to access existing stores of global knowledge and adapt this knowledge to local use. Tertiary education institutions are unique in their ability to integrate and create synergy among these three dimensions. Sustainable transformation and growth throughout the economy are not possible without the capacity-building contributions of an innovative tertiary education system, especially in low-income countries with weak institutional capacity and limited human capital.

Poverty Reduction through Redistribution and Empowerment

World Development Report 2000/2001 emphasizes a poverty reduction strategy based on empowerment, opportunity, and security. The role of tertiary education is linked to the opportunity and empowerment dimensions. Tertiary education can offer better opportunities and life chances for low-income and minority students, thereby increasing their employability, income prospects, and social mobility and decreasing income inequality. The norms, values, attitudes, ethics, and knowledge that tertiary institutions can impart to students contribute to the social capital necessary for constructing healthy civil societies and socially cohesive cultures, achieving good governance, and building democratic political systems.

Fulfillment of Millennium Development Goals

Tertiary education institutions play an essential role in support of basic and secondary education. The training of teachers and school principals, from preschool to the upper secondary level, is the primary responsibility of tertiary education institutions. Education specialists with tertiary education qualifications participate in curriculum design and educational research for lower levels. The linkage between tertiary education and the other levels of schooling has the potential to stimulate a virtuous circle of capacity building because the quality of tertiary education affects the quality of primary and secondary school education and is in turn directly influenced by the quality of secondary school graduates.

Outline and Principal Messages of the Report

This volume is organized into five chapters, supplemented by data and information appendixes. Chapter 1 analyzes recent changes in the global environment that constitute new challenges for tertiary education institutions. In Chapter 2 the implications of these changes are examined from the viewpoint of the contribution of tertiary education to economic and social development. Chapter 3 looks at the present state of tertiary education in developing and transition countries and assesses progress toward overcoming the traditional problems of access and coverage, equity, quality and relevance, and governance. Chapter 4 discusses the evolving nature of the relationship between tertiary education institutions, the marketplace, and the state; the justification for continuing public support of tertiary education; and the appropriate role of the state in support of knowledge-driven economic growth. Finally, Chapter 5 evaluates recent Bank experience with assistance to tertiary education and proposes a framework for future Bank involvement.

Briefly, the main messages of the report are as follows:

- Social and economic progress is achieved principally through the advancement and application of knowledge.
- Tertiary education is necessary for the creation, dissemination, and application of knowledge and for building technical and professional capacity.
- Developing and transition countries are at risk of being further marginalized in a highly competitive world economy because their tertiary education systems are not adequately prepared to capitalize on the creation and use of knowledge.
- The state has a responsibility to put in place an enabling framework that encourages tertiary education institutions to be more innovative and responsive to the needs of a globally competitive knowledge economy and the changing labor market requirements for advanced human capital.
- The World Bank Group can assist its client countries in drawing on international experience and mobilizing the resources needed to improve the effectiveness and responsiveness of their tertiary education systems.

1
The Changing Global Environment

All things change. Yet nothing is extinguished . . . there is nothing in the whole world which is permanent. Everything flows onwards and all things are brought into being with a changing nature. The ages themselves glide by in constant movement, for still waters will never reach the sea.

Ovid

The last decade of the 20th century saw significant changes in the global environment that, in one way or another, bear heavily on the role, functions, shape, and mode of operation of tertiary education systems all over the world, including those in developing and transition countries. As Table 1.1 shows, some of these trends offer opportunities while others constitute potential threats. Among the most influential changes are the increasing importance of knowledge as a driver of growth in the context of the global economy, the information and communication revolution, the emergence of a worldwide labor market, and global sociopolitical transformations. This chapter examines each in turn.

Knowledge as a Key Factor in Development

The ability of a society to produce, select, adapt, commercialize, and use knowledge is critical for sustained economic growth and improved living standards. Knowledge has become the most important factor in economic development.[1] A recent study by the OECD on the determinants of growth concluded that "underlying long-term growth rates in OECD economies depend on maintaining and expanding the knowledge base" (OECD 1998b: 4). *World Development Report 1998/1999* concurred, stating that "today's most technologically advanced economies are truly knowledge-based . . . creating millions of knowledge-related jobs in an array of disciplines that have emerged overnight" (World Bank 1999c: 16). The real growth of value added in knowledge-based industries has consistently outpaced overall growth rates in many OECD member countries

Table 1.1 Opportunities and Threats Stemming from Changes in the Global Environment

Change factor	Opportunities	Threats
Growing role of knowledge	• Possibility of leapfrogging in selected areas of economic growth • Resolution of social problems (food security, health, water supply, energy, environment)	• Increasing knowledge gap among nations
ICT revolution	• Easier access to knowledge and information	• Growing digital divide among and within nations
Global labor market	• Easier access to expertise, skills, and knowledge embedded in professionals	• Growing brain drain and loss of advanced human capital
Political and social change • Spread of democracy • Violence, corruption, and crime • HIV/AIDS	• Positive environment for reform	• Growing brain drain and political instability • Loss of human resources

Note: ICT = information and communication technologies.

over the past two decades. Growth of value added for the 1986–94 period was 3.0 percent for knowledge industries versus 2.3 percent for the business sector as a whole.[2] Between 1985 and 1997, the share of knowledge-based industries in total value added rose from 51 to 59 percent in Germany, from 45 to 51 percent in the United Kingdom, and from 34 to 42 percent in Finland (OECD 2001).

The process of globalization is accelerating this trend because knowledge is increasingly at the core of a country's competitive advantage (Porter 1990). Comparative advantages among nations come less and less from abundant natural resources or cheap labor and increasingly from technical innovations and the competitive use of knowledge—or from a combination of the two, as is illustrated by the success story of Bangalore, the capital of the Indian software industry. The proportion of goods in international trade with a medium-high or high level of technology content rose from 33 percent in 1976 to 54 percent in 1996 (World Bank 1999c: 28).

Today, economic growth is as much a process of knowledge accumulation as of capital accumulation. In OECD countries, investment in the intangibles that make up the knowledge base—research and development (R&D), education, and computer software—is equaling or even exceeding investment in physical equipment. Firms devote at least one-third of their investment to knowledge-based intangibles such as training, R&D, patents, licensing, design, and marketing. In this context, economies of scope, derived from the ability to design and offer different products and services while using the same technology, are becoming a powerful factor in expansion. In high-technology industries such as electronics and telecommunications, economies of scope can be more of a driving force than traditional economies of scale (Banker, Chang, and Majumdar 1998).

A new type of enterprise—the producer services company, which provides specialized knowledge, information, and data in support of existing manufacturing firms—has begun to prosper. Experts see such companies as the principal source of created comparative advantage and significant value added in highly industrialized economies (Gibbons 1998). In the knowledge economy, advances in microelectronics, multimedia, and telecommunications give rise to important productivity gains in many sectors and are also key components of a multitude of new products in a wide range of industrial and service activities. At the same time, the rapid acceleration in the rhythm of creation and dissemination of knowledge means that the life span of technologies and products becomes progressively shorter and that obsolescence sets in more quickly.

Developing and transition economies are affected by these transformations but are not yet reaping all of the potential benefits. Indeed, the capacity to generate and harness knowledge in the pursuit of sustainable development and improved living standards is not shared equally among nations. There are striking disparities between rich and poor countries in science and technology (S&T) investment and capacity. It was estimated in 1996 that OECD member countries accounted for 85 percent of total investment in R&D; China, India, Brazil, and the newly industrialized countries of East Asia for 11 percent; and the rest of the world for only 4 percent. Among the reasons for the divergence in agricultural productivity between industrial and developing countries are that advanced economies spend up to five times more on agriculture-related R&D than do their counterparts in developing countries and that they possess the critical combination of infrastructure, expertise, and organizational and incentive structures that allows these investments to be productive. Members of the exclusive group of advanced economies enjoy the fruits of a virtuous circle in which the concrete benefits of research help produce the wealth and public support needed to continue the investigation of the frontiers of science (Romer 1990).

By contrast, the large majority of countries in the developing world have neither articulated a development strategy linking the application of knowledge to economic growth nor built up their national S&T capacity. A key indicator is the ratio of foreign patent applications to local patent applications, which measures, in a given country, the level of innovative activity by national researchers. In low-income countries the ratio of patents filed by nonresidents to those filed by residents is 690 to 1, while in high-income countries the ratio is, on average, only 3.3 to 1 (World Bank 2000d: table 5.12).

Figure 1.1, which compares the economic evolution of Ghana and the Republic of Korea between 1958 and 1990, illustrates the significant difference a knowledge-based development strategy made for two countries with similar gross domestic product (GDP) per capita in 1958. The figure, based on the standard Solow method of accounting for economic growth, represents a stylized attempt to estimate the relative contribution of two types of factors: tangible factors such as the accumulation of physical capital and additional years of schooling in the labor force, and other factors linked to the use of knowledge, such as the quality of education, the strength of institutions, the ease of communicating and disseminating technical information, and management and organizational skills (Solow 2001). In this model, technical progress raises the potential output from a given set of inputs. Empirical measures are then applied to assess the extent to which growth is attributable to increased inputs (more labor and capital) or to the use of inputs in a more productive way. The latter measure, commonly referred to as total factor productivity (TFP), is generally considered to be closely linked to the way in which knowledge is used in production. Because TFP is a measure of output per unit of input, raising it leads to higher standards of living. Tertiary education is one of the most influential of the set of complex factors that determine TFP for a given economy. Other factors, too, have to be taken into account; among these are divergent economic policies and political climates—both of which have strongly influenced industrial growth paths, labor markets, and conditions for retaining and utilizing skills in the two countries (Box 1.1).

In the Solow model, the difference in economic growth between Ghana and Korea is a telling example of a more general pattern. Easterly and Levine (2000) have reviewed and analyzed findings from several studies of cross-country growth, similar to the comparison here between Ghana and Korea. They arrive at the conclusion that TFP—which measures factors other than physical and human capital—explains the bulk of the differences in economic growth. They accordingly recommend that policymakers shift their focus from capital accumulation as such to policies that promote TFP growth.

Developing and transition countries must achieve greater economic productivity if they want to be able to compete effectively in the global economy. *World Development Report 1998/1999* observes that "the need for developing countries to increase their capacity to use knowledge

Figure 1.1 Knowledge as a Factor in Income Differences
between Countries: Ghana and the Republic of Korea, 1956–90

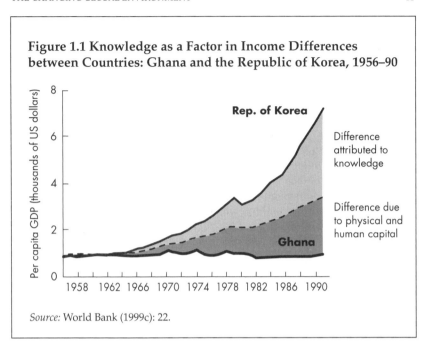

Source: World Bank (1999c): 22.

cannot be overstated" (World Bank 1999c: 16). Lagging countries will miss out on opportunities to improve their economies through, for example, more efficient agricultural production and distribution systems—which would increase yields and lower the proportion of food wasted due to poor distribution—or by making exports more competitive through better metrology, standards, and quality testing.

One of the greatest and most urgent challenges facing the poorest countries may be to produce an adequate supply of affordable, nutritious food for their growing populations without causing further environmental degradation. The utilization of modern biotechnology techniques such as genetically modified crops and modern genomics can play a critical role in increasing yields, enhancing nutritional value (protein, calories, micronutrients, and vitamin supplements), improving plant characteristics (e.g., resistance to drought, pests, salinity, and herbicides), and decreasing postharvest loss. But the development of genetically modified crops poses serious issues of possible environmental and human health risks that require careful risk management and biosafety procedures. To make informed decisions on how to address these challenges, countries need to call on highly qualified specialists—who will not be available unless investments in advanced human capital are made.

Countries without a minimum scientific and technological capacity will also lag in realizing social and human benefits such as rising life

Box 1.1 Tertiary Education Strategies in Ghana and the Republic of Korea Contrasted

Divergent evolutionary paths in tertiary education policies and practices may have contributed to the growing difference in total factor productivity (TFP) between Ghana and the Republic of Korea. The following is a very general description of tertiary education policies in the two countries.

The development of tertiary education in Korea took place in four distinct phases: (1) in the 1950s, the expansion of public institutions, with cost sharing equivalent to 30 percent of expenditures; (2) in the 1960s, encouragement of private institutions, with limited public funding for capital costs and scholarships; (3) in the 1970s and 1980s, the expansion of engineering and technical education to meet manpower requirements; and (4) in the 1990s, a focus on quality, R&D capacity, accountability, deregulation, and performance-based funding.

In Ghana enrollment in public tertiary education has grown slowly over the years. In the late 1980s the government formulated a reform program that included measures to improve the financial sustainability of the system, increase quality and relevance, and promote expansion of enrollments, but many of the proposed reforms were reversed by subsequent administrations.

The enrollment of students in science and technology disciplines has remained relatively constant in both countries and is approximately equivalent, at about 50 percent of the student population. But in other important respects, the outcomes of the two strategies are strikingly different:

• The enrollment ratio in tertiary education for the eligible age cohort in Korea skyrocketed from 5 to 80 percent between 1960 and 2000. In the same period, Ghana's enrollment ratio stagnated at less than 2 percent.

• Private tertiary institutions have proliferated in Korea, enrolling 85 percent of the total student population in 2000. In Ghana private institutions have emerged only recently and account for no more than 6 percent of total enrollment.

• Public expenditure per student has risen steeply in Korea, from US$2,700 in 1990 to US$4,500 in 2000. In Ghana it fell by nearly one third, from US$1,200 in 1990 to US$850 in 2000.

• The Korean government has actively promoted university-industry partnerships since the late 1980s. Linkages between tertiary education and industry have been relatively uncommon in Ghana.

Source: World Bank data.

expectancy, lower infant mortality, and improved health, nutrition, and sanitation. Such countries will be increasingly vulnerable to emerging threats.

For example, poverty exacerbates the problems of dealing with the HIV/AIDS epidemic, in that the resulting lack of capacity hampers the emergence of more effective coping strategies. Low-income countries with high infection rates can afford neither to develop their own solutions nor to buy existing remedies from the industrial world. Gains in life expectancy that were achieved over the past 40 years are in some cases being reversed. Only a few countries, including Brazil, Senegal, and Uganda, have shown initial success in fighting the AIDS epidemic. Their positive results have been founded on (a) effective outreach health programs targeting poor people; (b) firm political decisions to suspend intellectual property rights in the context of the health emergency and to encourage production of generic drugs; and (c) in the case of Brazil, the existence of a local pharmaceutical industry with the technical and human capital capacity to manufacture the needed drugs.

Low-income countries, which are, on average, disproportionately vulnerable to the effects of climate change and natural disasters, stand to benefit most from better use of emerging technological know-how in areas such as meteorology and remote sensing. New knowledge and technology make possible greatly improved forecasting and early-warning techniques that can dramatically reduce the effects of land and environmental degradation and of natural disasters. The catastrophic floods in Mozambique in December 2000 furnish a negative example: six months beforehand, British meteorologists had issued warnings about the danger, but there was no in-country capacity to analyze the scientific data, draw concrete conclusions, and recommend preventive measures that could have saved thousands of lives.

The Information and Communication Revolution

One specific dimension of scientific and technological progress that is already having a strong effect on the tertiary education sector is the information and communication revolution. The advent of printing in the 15th century brought about the first radical transformation in modern times in the way knowledge is kept and shared. Today, technological innovations in informatics and telecommunications are once more revolutionizing capacity to store, transmit, access, and use information. Rapid progress in electronics, telecommunications, and satellite technologies, permitting high-capacity data transmission at very low cost, has brought about the quasi neutralization of physical distance as a barrier to communication and as a factor in economic competitiveness. In

1985 the cost of sending 45 million bits of information per second over one kilometer of optical fiber was close to 100 dollars; in 1997 it was possible to send 45,000 million bits per second at a cost of just 0.05 cents (Bond 1997). Alternative energy sources such as solar energy and crank technology eliminate some of the electric power constraints in remote locations. Generally speaking, the convergence of increased computing power and reduced communication costs means that there are few logistical barriers to information exchange and communication among people, institutions, and countries, at least for those with access to the Internet and in places where telecommunication policies encourage affordable access.

The accelerated pace of technological development has made access to knowledge a crucial requirement for participation in the global economy. The impact of new information and communication technologies (ICT) has significantly changed the speed of production, use, and distribution of knowledge, as evidenced by the increased publication of scientific papers and the number of patent applications. A country's capacity to take advantage of the knowledge economy therefore depends on how quickly it can adjust its capacity to generate and share knowledge. A recent study by the International Labour Office (ILO) found that the new technologies can have a positive impact on countries, whatever their level of economic development. Brazil, China, Costa Rica, India, Malaysia, and Romania have successfully created—with the help of relatively effective education systems—information technology (IT) niches that allow them to compete in the global market (ILO 2001).

Although this transformation offers many potential benefits to developing and transition countries, increasing reliance on digital information and advanced communication technologies carries, at the same time, the real danger of a growing digital gap among and within nations. Disparities in per capita income and standards of living could translate into the marginalization of entire societies or segments of society. The digital divide has several dimensions. On a global scale, it divides industrial and developing countries according to their ability to use, adapt, produce, and diffuse knowledge. In Korea the number of households connected to the Internet in 2000 doubled, raising the total to 3 million homes, whereas in Japan only 450,000 homes are connected. The technological gap between high-income and low-income countries is reflected in the number of personal computers per 1,000 inhabitants— less than 1 in Burkina Faso, compared with 27 in South Africa, 38 in Chile, 172 in Singapore, and 348 in Switzerland. Sub-Saharan African countries together have 1 Internet user per 5,000 population; in Europe and North America the proportion is 1 user for every 6 inhabitants (International Communications Union data). Figure 1.2 illustrates this global inequality.

Among developing countries, the digital divide sets apart the technologically more advanced countries from the less advanced ones. Whereas a few African countries with small populations still lack even one Internet host, in Singapore 98 percent of households use the Internet. Within a given region, some countries have a stronger information and communication infrastructure than others. In Sub-Saharan Africa the number of Internet hosts per 1,000 population ranges from 0.01 in Burkina Faso to 3.82 in South Africa (International Telecommunications Union data).

Within countries, technological change often means that groups which were already disadvantaged or excluded—low-income families, rural populations, women, minorities, and the elderly—fall farther behind. In the United Kingdom, for example, only 4 percent of households in the poorest income quintile are connected to the Internet, compared with 43 percent in the top quintile, and the gap is increasing every year. In the United States the proportion of Afro-American families that are connected is half that for white families (OECD 2001: 149). The 2001 ILO report reveals a "digital gender gap" in many parts of the world, including OECD countries. Although some economies have near parity in Internet use (examples are Taiwan, China, with 45 percent female users, and Korea, with 43 percent), the situation is more often far from balanced.[3] In Latin America 38 percent of Internet users are women, but in the European Union (EU), Japan, and the Middle East, the shares are 25, 18, and 4 percent, respectively (ILO 2001: 16). In Senegal 12 percent of Internet users are women, but only a tiny 0.1 percent of the population is on the Internet. In South Africa, where 3 percent of the population is on the Internet, 19 percent of the users are women (International Telecommunications Union data).

Appropriate, well-functioning information and communications technologies are of vital importance to tertiary education because they have the potential to (a) streamline and reduce administrative tasks and, in general, make possible greater efficiency and effectiveness in the management of tertiary education systems and institutions; (b) expand access and improve the quality of instruction and learning on all levels; and (c) vastly broaden access to information and data– cross-campus, or across the globe. The appearance and the rapid evolution of ICT have created at least two major challenges for education: to achieve the appropriate integration of ICT into overall education systems and institutions, and to ensure that the new technologies become agents of expanded access and equity and increase educational opportunities for all, not just for the wealthy or the technologically privileged. Indeed, early policy research in the United States, one of the first widespread adopters of new ICT, found strong evidence that uneven access to the technologies was worsening existing equity gaps in education. Explicit attention needs to be given to equity considerations so that the new technologies, which "shatter geographical barriers [may do so without] erecting new ones and worsening the digital divide" (Gladieux and Swail 1999: 17).

Figure 1.2 Distribution of Internet Hosts and of World Population, by Region, 1999

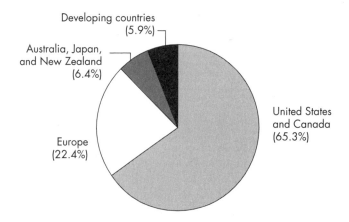

Distribution of Internet hosts

Developing countries
(5.9%)

Australia, Japan,
and New Zealand
(6.4%)

Europe
(22.4%)

United States
and Canada
(65.3%)

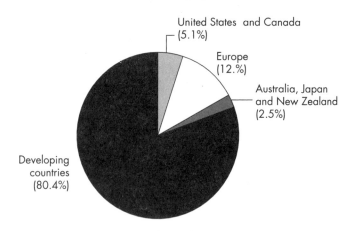

Distribution of world population

United States and Canada
(5.1%)

Europe
(12.%)

Australia, Japan
and New Zealand
(2.5%)

Developing
countries
(80.4%)

Source: Data from the International Telecommunications Union and the United Nations Population Fund.

The Global Labor Market

Globalization, declining communication and transportation costs, and the opening of political borders combine to facilitate increased movements of skilled people. This dynamic is de facto leading to a global market for advanced human capital in which individuals with tertiary education are the most likely to participate (Carrington and Detragiache 1999). In this 21st century marketplace, the richer countries strive to attract and retain the world's best-trained minds in many ways. Among the more powerful "pull" factors are effective policies that stimulate R&D activities and increase direct investment, offer attractive postgraduate training and research opportunities, and recruit younger graduates and professionals (Glanz 2001). OECD countries are increasing their investments in R&D not only in the S&T sector but also in other knowledge-based sectors, thus creating job opportunities for well-trained people. For example, in early 2001 the Australian government announced a 100 percent increase in the funding of the Australian Research Council and a tax write-off equivalent to 175 percent of the value of R&D spending by firms.[4]

Roughly 25 percent of the science and engineering students in U.S. graduate schools come from other countries. This amounts to somewhere between 50,000 and 100,000 students from abroad who are introduced into the U.S. market for advanced human capital. Most of these students received their basic education and first degrees in their home countries—meaning that the cost of their initial training was probably assumed by the countries of origin rather than by the country of employment (NSF 2000: app. table 4-22). Advanced countries are opening recruitment offices in countries where, because of lack of opportunity and political instability, graduates are available. Australia, Canada, EU members, and others all compete for their share of well-trained people in the global marketplace. France and Germany have freed up the issuance of visas to attract foreign professionals in technology-related areas, and in October 2000 the United States introduced an amendment to its immigration laws that made available 600,000 new visas for scientists and engineers.[5]

The global labor market for advanced human capital is an expanding reality that brings the circulation of skills and the related problem of "brain drain" to the forefront of national concern, particularly in developing countries (see Table 1.2). Whether it results from push or pull factors, brain drain can have a debilitating effect on national governing structures, management capacities, productive sectors, and tertiary institutions. It is estimated, for example, that at least 40 percent of the graduates of the highly regarded Indian Institutes of Technology seek employment abroad. The countries of Sub-Saharan Africa have an average tertiary enrollment rate of only 4 percent, compared with 81 percent in the United States, yet it is estimated that about 30,000 Africans holding Ph.D.s live outside Africa and that 130,000 Africans are currently studying overseas. One of Venezuela's most prestigious private universities, Metropolitan University, lost 50 percent of its graduates in academic year 2000 to multinational corporations abroad. In Bulgaria the Union of Scientists estimates that 65 percent of all university graduates (close to 300,000 persons) left the country during the past decade. Universities in developing and transition countries are struggling to recruit professors with advanced degrees, and the lack of adequately trained staff is leading to declining quality of instruction.

The rising international mobility of skilled human resources can have positive as well as negative effects on countries at all levels of development. Developing countries, however, tend to suffer largely adverse consequences, as they may lose the very technical and professional specialists who would be capable of contributing to poverty-alleviating improvements in the living conditions of the local population. Despite its potentially far-reaching consequences, brain drain has rarely been an explicit public policy concern. The reasons for this benign neglect include respect for universally accepted human rights such as freedom of movement and choice of employment (embodied in the Universal Declaration of Human Rights, Articles 13 and 23), as well as the complex and shifting interplay of "pull" and "push" factors motivating individuals to enter or leave a country. Nevertheless, it is clear that whatever its causes, the interna-

Table 1.2 Emigrants with Tertiary Education Qualifications, Selected Countries and Regions, 1990

Country or region of origin	Number of emigrants living in United States	Number of emigrants with tertiary education in the United States	Emigrants with tertiary education as share of total emigrants (percent)
Mexico	2,700,000	351,000	13
Philippines	730,000		50
China	400,000	200,000	50
India	300,000+	225,000+	75
Korea, Rep.	300,000+	159,000+	53
Sub-Saharan Africa	128,000	95,000	75
Jamaica			42
Trinidad and Tobago			46
South America			About 50

Note: Includes only immigrants to OECD countries; actual totals are probably higher.
Source: Carrington and Detragiache (1999).

tional mobility of skilled and scarce human resources will continue to present long-term risks for tertiary education investments in many nations.

Political and Social Change

Rapid changes are occurring worldwide, not only in economics, science, and technology but also in political and social dynamics. The dissolution of the former Soviet Union, the African political renaissance, the consolidation of civilian rule in Latin America, and other events have altered the global political landscape of the planet. The outcomes include a transition to democracy in many parts of the world, a greater concern with issues of political development in areas such as governance and accountability, increased awareness of human rights, and the rise of civil society organizations as legitimate stakeholder voices in increasingly pluralistic environments. The proportion of the world's countries practicing some form of democratic governance rose from 40 percent in 1988 to 61 percent in 1998 (World Bank 2000e: 43). Tertiary education institutions themselves have been profoundly influenced by the changes around them, which are heightening their importance as pillars of social cohesion, forums of public discourse, and contributors to open debate.

Persistence of Conflict

Notwithstanding these encouraging steps forward, the political situation in many countries remains insecure. Threats from regional and ethnic conflict, increased poverty, growing economic inequality, rising levels of crime and corruption, and the expanding AIDS epidemic combine to put severe pressures on political and social institutions of all kinds, including tertiary education institutions, thereby limiting their effectiveness. Internal and ethnic strife, once suppressed by Cold War pressures or postcolonial influences, have proliferated over the past 10 years. These conflicts, which have been felt most acutely in Africa, Eastern Europe, and the countries of the former Soviet Union, have resulted in an estimated 5 million deaths and the displacement of 50 million refugees (World Bank 2000e: 36). Although some analysts claim that the number of major armed conflicts is on the decline throughout the world, a recent study conducted by a group monitoring the political stability of national governments declared 33 countries to be at high risk of instability and 47 more, including China, India, and Russia, to be at moderate risk (Smith 2001). In 1996 a third of the countries of Sub-Saharan Africa experienced armed conflict, causing enormous human suffering, material devastation, human resource depletion, and damage to the social and cultural

fabric of the nations concerned (World Bank 2001a). And since the terror-
ist attacks in the United States on September 11, 2001, the overall level of
instability may be higher than was once believed.

Income Inequality

Throughout the world, income inequality both within and across nations
has grown as people have benefited differentially from the rise of the
global economy. In 1973 the income difference between the richest and
poorest countries was 44 to 1, but by 1992 the gap had widened markedly,
to a ratio of 72 to 1 (World Bank 2001e: 6). Throughout this period, the
gulf between the economic well-being of industrial nations and that of
the developing world grew as the share of world exports contributed by
the least-developed countries declined from 0.6 percent in 1980 to 0.4
percent in 1998 (UNDP 2000: 82). Today, with 1.2 billion people living on
less than one dollar a day, it is estimated that the benefits of globalization
have remained out of reach for nearly half of the developing world's
inhabitants (World Bank 1997: 12).

Within nations, too, income inequality is on the rise. For example, in
Brazil, Guatemala, and Jamaica the income of the richest 20 percent is
more than 25 times that of the poorest 20 percent (UNDP 2000: 34). In less
than 10 years, inequality in Eastern Europe and the former Soviet Union,
as measured by the Gini coefficient, increased from an average 25–28
(showing greater equality than the OECD average) to 35–38 (greater
inequality than the OECD average). In some countries, such as Bulgaria,
Russia, and Ukraine, the increase in inequality has been even more dramatic, outpacing the yearly speed of Gini increase in the United Kingdom and the United States in the 1980s by three to four times (Milanovic
1998). In many countries social disparities and poverty have translated
into a steep increase in crime and lawlessness. Equitable access to tertiary education opportunities is important for easing inequalities and
related social problems.

The HIV/AIDS Crisis

The spread of the AIDS virus is contributing to economic and political
instability. According to estimates by the Joint United Nations Programme on HIV/AIDS (UNAIDS) for 2001, 40 million people worldwide
are living with HIV/AIDS. In 2000 alone, there were an estimated 5 million newly infected individuals and 3 million deaths.

Africa is commonly described as a continent in peril. Of the nearly 34
million people infected with HIV worldwide at the end of 1999, 23 million resided in Sub-Saharan Africa. Since the beginning of the AIDS epidemic in the early 1980s, more than 17 million Africans have died, 3.7

million of them children. It is estimated that 8.8 percent of African adults are infected with the HIV/AIDS virus, and the incredibly high rate of premature adult death is expected to result in 40 million children becoming orphaned within the next decade.

In the seven Sub-Saharan African countries with the highest infection rates—Botswana, Lesotho, Namibia, South Africa, Swaziland, Zambia, and Zimbabwe—between 20 and 36 percent of the adult population lives with HIV.[7] The rise of HIV over the last decade has caused life expectancy to slip by more than 10 years in some of these countries. The epidemic has serious implications for economic and human development. For example, by 2010, South Africa is expected to be 20 percent poorer than it would have been had the AIDS virus never existed.

The threat of an AIDS epidemic is also very real in all Asian and Eastern European nations, where the world's fastest rising infection rates, combined with the high cost of antiretroviral drugs and inadequate access to health care services, have placed effective AIDS treatment out of reach for most citizens. Recently, the Chinese government acknowledged that by 2010 the incidence of AIDS in China will reach levels similar to those for Sub-Saharan African countries.

These trends combine to exert severe pressures on political and social institutions of all kinds. It is estimated that some countries of Africa are losing one-quarter of their health care personnel to HIV/AIDS. One-third of the nurses in Natal Province, South Africa, have died from AIDS in the past three years (ACU 2001). Meanwhile, professors, teachers, administrators, and students are dying or are leaving their academic institutions because of illness or to care for someone who is sick with AIDS. In Zambia the loss of teaching staff in primary and secondary schools is staggering, equaling about half the number of teachers trained each year. Tertiary education institutions are also losing large numbers of their teaching staff members, administrative personnel, and students.

These statistics do not begin to measure the losses experienced in other sectors of the economy and in the government, all of which depend on skilled professionals, technically trained adults, and strategic thinkers and planners. In order to maintain education, health, judicial, and other essential public service sectors, replenishment of these losses is imperative. This need is even more important in the poorest countries, where the numbers of highly educated persons were already often barely sufficient to provide the capacity necessary for democratic governance and a functioning civil service, let alone for enhancing development.

Outside the modern sector, agricultural productivity in many countries is declining as a result of HIV/AIDS. Thailand has seen output from rural households drop by 50 percent, and UNAIDS estimates that the most afflicted countries will lose more than 20 percent of their GDP by 2020 if current trends continue.

As noted above, tertiary education institutions face major disruptions because of HIV/AIDS. Yet this is precisely the time when tertiary education is essential as a means of making up for the losses, providing the human capital required to keep governments functioning and economies moving forward, and producing teachers and health care workers. A strong, flexible tertiary education sector can help build the capacity needed to temper the negative effects of HIV/AIDS and other threats to public health.

Conclusion

The last decade of the 20th century was characterized by momentous changes and significant new trends in the global environment. The resulting challenges present both opportunities and threats that are likely to affect not only the shape and mode of operation but also the very mission and purpose of tertiary education systems. In the next chapter, we describe the current situation of tertiary education in developing countries and examine how educational institutions are adapting, or may find it possible to adapt, to the new tasks and realities.

Notes

1. *World Development Report 1998/99* described two broad categories of knowledge into which specific forms of knowledge fall: technical knowledge (know-how), and knowledge about attributes (information and awareness that permit analysis and decisionmaking).

2. OECD (2000): 220, table 2. Knowledge-based industries include high- and medium-high-technology industries; communication services; finance, insurance, and other business services; and community, social, and personal services.

3. For reports on Internet use in Korea, "Gate4Korea.com," < http://www.india2korea. com>. On the surge in numbers of women online in the East Asia and Pacific region, see "Women a Formidable Force on the Web," Nielsen//Netratings, <http://www.nielsen-netratings.com/pr/pr_010628_au.pdf>.

4. The prime minister declared that "in an extremely competitive world of highly mobile capital and labor, it is all the more important that Australia has the right incentives and opportunities to translate Australian ideas into income and jobs at home for Australians" (reported in Maslen 2001).

5. U.S. Public Law 106-313, *American Competitiveness in the Twenty-first Century Act of 2000.*

6. Vorozhtsov (1999).

7. "UNAIDS AIDS Epidemic Update, December 2001," available at <www.unaids.org/ epidemic_update/report_dec01/index.html>.

2

Contribution of Tertiary Education to Economic and Social Development

In questions of mind, there is no medium term: either we look for the best or we live with the worst.

John Gardner

Tertiary education institutions have a critical role in supporting knowledge-driven economic growth strategies and the construction of democratic, socially cohesive societies. Tertiary education assists the improvement of the institutional regime through the training of competent and responsible professionals needed for sound macroeconomic and public sector management. Its academic and research activities provide crucial support for the national innovation system. And tertiary institutions often constitute the backbone of a country's information infrastructure, in their role as repositories and conduits of information (through libraries and the like), computer network hosts, and Internet service providers. In addition, the norms, values, attitudes, and ethics that tertiary institutions impart to students are the foundation of the social capital necessary for constructing healthy civil societies and cohesive cultures—the very bedrock of good governance and democratic political systems (Harrison and Huntington 2000).

To successfully fulfill their educational, research, and informational functions in the 21st century, tertiary education institutions need to be able to respond effectively to changing education and training needs, adapt to a rapidly shifting tertiary education landscape, and adopt more flexible modes of organization and operation. This chapter looks at the challenges and at how tertiary institutions are responding to the multifaceted demands placed on them, including the need for a lifelong-learning model of education. It examines the emergence of new types of tertiary education institutions in the context of a borderless market and outlines the ways in which institutions are transforming themselves to respond to evolving educational needs, new forms of competition, and changing information and communication technologies. A detailed list of the questions and challenges associated with the new trends discussed in this chapter is presented in Appendix A.

Changing Education and Training Needs

This section examines three broad activities of tertiary education institutions that assist the construction of democratic, knowledge-driven societies:

- Supporting innovation by generating new knowledge, accessing global stores of knowledge, and adapting knowledge to local use
- Contributing to human capital formation by training a qualified and adaptable labor force, including high-level scientists, professionals, technicians, basic and secondary education teachers, and future government, civil service, and business leaders
- Providing the foundation for democracy, nation building, and social cohesion.

The discussion includes an overview of the new demands that today's world markets and emerging technologies are making on higher education and of some of the ways in which tertiary education systems are responding.

The Innovation System

Knowledge by itself does not transform economies, nor is there any guarantee of positive returns to investments in research and development or in other products of tertiary education. Numerous countries, including large ones such as Brazil, India, and some of the former Soviet republics, had invested heavily in building up capacity in science and technology without reaping significant returns. This is because scientific and technological knowledge yields its greatest benefits when it is used within a complex system of institutions and practices known as a national innovation system (NIS).

An NIS is a web made up of the following elements: (a) knowledge-producing organizations in the education and training system; (b) the appropriate macroeconomic and regulatory framework, including trade policies that affect technology diffusion; (c) innovative firms and networks of enterprises; (d) adequate communication infrastructures; and (e) other factors such as access to the global knowledge base and certain market conditions that favor innovation (World Bank 1999c). Tertiary education systems figure prominently in this framework, serving not only as the backbone for high-level skills but also as a network base for information sharing.

Unfortunately, the logic of national innovation systems favors the strong becoming stronger. Countries that want to improve their innovative capacity have to make significant efforts to acquire and maintain the critical mass of appropriate infrastructure, institutions, and human resources that function in concert to allow benefits to accrue. A few countries appear to have done this in high-technology manufacturing. By 1995, developing countries accounted for 30 percent of worldwide exports—significantly more than a few years earlier—and the value of their high-technology exports had for the first time exceeded that of their low-technology products (Lall 2000: 11).

Notwithstanding the difficulties involved in constructing an adequate NIS, there are several favorable factors that can assist countries aspiring to close the gap separating them from scientifically advanced countries. First, thanks to sound research in the social sciences, much is being learned about the process of innovation, and this growing body of evidence can be used in selecting the policies and practices that make investments in human resource development more effective (see Box 2.1). Second, much of the international science community is by nature open to cross-border collaboration, since the progress of science depends on a culture of freely shared basic knowledge.[1] This bodes well for policies that encourage research and collaboration. Third, new information and communication technologies are providing unprecedented access to existing knowledge. Finally, what countries need to accomplish in order to use scientific and technological knowledge more effectively does not involve cutting-edge research but, rather, revolves around the mundane yet essential tasks of developing effective policies and institutions in science– and technology–related sectors and producing well-trained people. Whatever the specific path a country chooses to close the knowledge gap between itself and industrial countries, improvements in the level and quality of human resources are required.

Universities are the main locus of both basic and applied research. It is important to maintain advanced training and research programs at the postgraduate level, for several reasons. According to recent studies on the determinants of national innovative capacity, "countries that have located a higher share of their research and development activity in the educational sector have been able to achieve significantly higher patenting productivity" (Stern, Porter, and Furman 2000: 25). Graduates of postgraduate programs are needed to staff public and private R&D institutes, as well as high-technology manufacturing firms. Such institutions and firms are the main mechanisms through which the results of research are infused into the local economy, transforming the technical bases of agricultural and manufacturing production. Porter, in his seminal 1990 work on competitiveness, noted that "education and training constitute perhaps the single greatest long-term leverage point available to all levels of government in upgrading industry" (Porter 1990: 628). Postgraduate programs are essential for training university professors and thus improving the quality of tertiary education, today and for future generations.

Human Capital Formation

A new development framework that can support knowledge-driven growth requires expanded and inclusive education systems which reach larger segments of the population. These systems need to impart higher-level skills to a rising proportion of the workforce; foster lifelong learning for citizens, with an emphasis on creativity and flexibility, to permit constant adaptation to the changing demands of a knowledge-based economy; and promote international recognition of the credentials granted by the country's educational institutions.

More education for more people. Knowledge-driven economies demand higher-level skills in the workforce. In OECD countries the proportion of employees with tertiary-level qualifications is increasing, as are rates of return on tertiary education. In these industrial countries, the proportion of adults with tertiary education qualifications almost doubled between 1975 and 2000, rising from 22 to 41 percent. But even this significant growth of the pool of workers with tertiary education has proved inadequate to meet the rising demand. Studies on the evolution of labor markets in Canada, the United Kingdom, and the United States document a continuously rising demand for young workers with a college education. In the United States jobs that require tertiary education have grown faster than those that require less education, and this trend is expected to accelerate. Before the recession that began in 2001, the U.S. Department of Labor had projected that during the 1998–2008 period, jobs that require some form of tertiary education qualification would grow systematically faster than the average growth rate for all jobs in the economy. It was estimated, for instance, that the number of positions requiring a master's degree would increase by 19 percent, on average, and those requiring an associate degree by 31 percent, compared with only 14 percent for all jobs (USDL 2000). For the cohort of men age 26–30, the wage premium linked to completion of tertiary education increased threefold in the United States and the United Kingdom between 1980 and 1996, while in Canada the wage premium almost doubled (Card and Lemieux 2000).

Recent analyses of rates of return on tertiary education in several Latin American countries confirm that this trend also holds in successful developing economies. In Argentina, Brazil, and Mexico, for example, rates of return on tertiary education grew significantly in the late 1980s and the 1990s, representing a clear reversal of the trends in the 1970s and the early 1980s (Pessino 1995; Barros and Ramos 1996; Lächler 1997). In Brazil the rising demand for skilled labor observed between 1982 and 1998 resulted in a 24 percent increase in the private rate of return to tertiary education, while returns to secondary and primary education declined by 8 and 30 percent, respectively (Blom, Holm-Nielsen, and Verner 2001). Similar patterns of rising returns to education with increasing years of schooling have been found in other parts of the world—for example in India, the Philippines, and South Africa.[2]

The rising demand for highly skilled labor affects not only wages but also employment opportunities. The experience of Russia provides an illustration. On the breakup of the Soviet Union in 1991, Russian workers at different educational levels were equally likely to be unemployed. By 1996, however, the situation had changed; workers with tertiary education were less likely to be laid off and, in the event of unemployment, were 25 percent more likely to find new positions (Foley 1997). In Korea rates of return to university education increased in relation to those for primary and secondary schooling over the period 1974–88 and surpassed the rates of investment at the lower levels (Ryoo, Nam, and Carnoy 1993). This finding of rising returns to university education has been buttressed by a 2001 study (Choi 2001).

Lifelong learning. The second dimension of change in education and training needs is the short "shelf life" of knowledge, skills, and occupations and, as a consequence, the growing importance of continuing education and of regular updating of individual capacities and qualifications (Wagner 1999). In OECD countries the traditional approach of studying for a discrete and finite period of time to acquire a first degree after secondary school or to complete graduate education before moving on to professional life is being progressively replaced by a lifelong-education model. Graduates will be increasingly expected to return periodically to tertiary education institutions to acquire, learn to use, and relearn the knowledge and skills needed throughout their professional lives. This phenomenon goes beyond the narrow notion of a "second chance" for out-of-school young adults who did not have the opportunity to complete much formal study. It has more to do with the updating and upgrading of learning that will be required in order to refresh and enhance individual qualifications and to keep pace with innovations in products and services. The concept of "lifelong learning for all" adopted in 1996 by the OECD ministers of education stems from a new vision of education and training policies as supporting knowledge-based development.

Lifelong-learning requirements may lead to a progressive blurring between initial and continuing studies, as well as between training for

Box 2.1 Leapfrogging in the New Global Economy: Brazil's Success in Plant Pathology

The Botany Department at the University of São Paulo is a spare, gray two-story building surrounded by uneven grass. The lights are turned off in the hallways to save electricity. Power outages have been a problem. But inside its walls lies perhaps the best hope to protect California's $2.7 billion wine industry from a devastating predator. A team of Brazilian scientists has cracked the genetic code of the bacterium *Xylella fastidiosa*, which has decimated vineyards in Southern California and is rapidly heading north.

Under a unique combined project, the U.S. Department of Agriculture, the California Department of Food and Agriculture, and the American Vineyard Foundation are funding the work. The U.S. government turned to Brazil for help because "Brazil is now the leader in this area of agriculture," said Edwin L. Civerolo of the USDA's Agricultural Research Service. "We did not have the experience or infrastructure to do the work."

Brazil's accomplishment illustrates the new rules of science in the global economy. Researchers anywhere in the world who do quality research and master the Internet can leapfrog national borders and challenge the traditional citadels of science in the United States and Europe. Brazil's achievement took money, focus and the right microbe.

The Brazilian team broke into the major leagues last year when its genetic analysis of a *Xylella* strain that attacks orange trees was published in the leading research journal *Nature*. That feat made the São Paulo scientists the first in the world to decode the genome of a plant pathogen. Since then they have carved out their niche in the global scientific community as leading experts on plant pathology.

Their funding initially came from the state of São Paulo, which sets aside 1 percent of its tax revenue every year for scientific research. The brains came from 200 researchers in 34 laboratories throughout São Paulo state led by biologists Marie-Anne Van Sluys and Mariana C. de Oliveira of the University of São Paulo and João Paulo Kitajima, a computer software specialist at the University of Campinas.

The University of São Paulo's laboratories house the latest gene-sequencing equipment and analyzers. Each machine rapidly sequences units of DNA, essentially spelling out in order all the letters of the microbe's genetic code. The results are then sent electronically to the bioinfomatics laboratory at the University of Campinas, where genes are identified and described by computer analysis. The results are sent back to the biologists to determine the genes' function and significance.

Key to Brazil's success was the decision not to follow the conventional route of most countries on a quest for scientific glory and build a special institute for genetic research. Instead, the São Paulo State Research Foun-

continued on next page

Box 2.1, *continued*

dation created a virtual genomics institute, called the Organization for Nucleotide Sequencing and Analysis, out of existing laboratories. Rather than bricks and mortar, funding went into sequencers and computers. The network has grown to 50 centers throughout Brazil. Researchers are connected by the Internet and communicate daily.

"No buildings, no walls, no turf battles," said the president of the foundation. The operating imperative was one of cooperation, rather than competition, among scientists. Andrew Simpson, of the Ludwig Institute for Cancer Research, put it this way: "It's human nature to be competitive. What we did was to turn it outward. We're competing as a group against the rest of the world."

Source: Washington Post, Dec. 29, 2001. © **2001,** *The Washington Post,* **reprinted with permission.**

---

young adults and midcareer training. Finland, one of the leading promoters of continuing education in Europe, is among the most advanced nations in conceptualizing and organizing tertiary education along these new lines. Today, Finland has more adults engaged in continuing education programs at the tertiary level (200,000) than young people enrolled in traditional degree courses (150,000).

The lifelong-learning approach stresses the primacy of the learner. Tertiary education institutions will have to organize themselves to accommodate the learning and training needs of a more diverse clientele: working students, mature students, stay-at-home students, traveling students, part-time students, day students, night students, weekend students, and so on. New patterns of demand are emerging whereby learners attend several institutions or programs in parallel or sequentially, thus taking the initiative to define their own skill profiles on the labor market.

Another important consequence of the acceleration of scientific and technological progress is the diminished emphasis on remembering countless facts and basic data and the growing importance of methodological knowledge and analytical skills—the skills needed for learning to think and to analyze information autonomously. Today, in a number of scientific disciplines, elements of factual knowledge taught in the first year of study may become obsolete before graduation. The learning process now needs to be increasingly based on the capacity to find and access knowledge and to apply it in problem solving. Learning to learn, learning to transform information into new knowledge, and learning to translate new knowledge into applications become more important than memorizing specific information. In this new paradigm, primacy is given to analytical skills; that is, to the ability to seek and find information, crystallize issues, formulate testable hypotheses, marshal and evaluate evidence, and solve problems. The new competencies that employers value in the knowledge economy have to do with oral and written communications, teamwork, peer teaching, creativity, envisioning skills, resourcefulness, and the ability to adjust to change.

Many of these competencies involve social, human, and intercultural skills that are not normally taught in science- or technology-based disciplines. This development calls for better integration of the hard sciences and the humanities. Tertiary curricula generally tend to be specialized because well-defined, measurable skills are recognized requirements in many fields. Nevertheless, it is important to enrich curricula with general subjects whenever possible.

A coherent intellectual complement to disciplinary work or professional programs can help broaden the foundation of knowledge and further dispose students toward a love of learning. Cooperative education—in which periods of institution-based learning that lay down the foundations of knowledge alternate with the acquisition of work-related skills, competencies, and practices in the workplaces of associated enterprises—has become an important element of tertiary education in many OECD countries.

International recognition of qualifications. The third dimension of change in the pattern of demand for training is the growing attractiveness of degrees and credentials with international recognition. In a global economy where local firms produce for overseas markets and compete with foreign firms in their own domestic markets, there is a rising demand for internationally recognized qualifications, especially in management-related fields. Many entrepreneurial university leaders have been quick to identify and capitalize on this trend, as evidenced by the multiplication and expansion of master of business administration (MBA)–type programs throughout the world.

A recent example of international collaboration is the initiative taken by the National University of Singapore in establishing a joint master's program in engineering with the Massachusetts Institute of Technology (MIT). Students from both campuses attend lectures conducted either at MIT or in Singapore, using video conferencing through the U.S. high-speed broadband network system (VBNS) in combination with SINGAREN, Singapore's high-speed research network.[3]

Nation Building, Democracy, and Social Cohesion

Adapting to the changing environment is not only a matter of reshaping tertiary institutions and applying new technologies. It is equally vital to ensure that students are equipped with the core values needed to live as responsible citizens in complex democratic societies. A meaningful education for the 21st century should stimulate all aspects of human intellectual potential. It should not simply emphasize access to global knowledge in science and management but should also uphold the richness of local cultures and values, supported by the time-honored and eternally valuable disciplines of the humanities and social sciences, including philosophy, literature, and the arts.

Tertiary education has many purposes beyond the acquisition of concrete skills in preparation for the world of work. It also involves developing a person's ability to reason systematically about critical questions and issues, to place facts in a broader context, to consider the moral implications of actions and choices, to communicate knowledge and questions effectively, and to nurture habits that promote lifelong-learning behaviors outside the formal academic setting. The skills of formulation, synthesis, analysis, and argumentation can be developed in a wide variety of curricula and a mix of pedagogical approaches. Indeed, it is important to have adequate learning resources and teaching capacity to cultivate student achievement in these higher-order skills. But opportunity is as important as the means of developing these characteristics: an environment that promotes freedom of thought and speech is essential for nurturing a cadre of self-motivated, responsible thinkers.

It is important at the tertiary level that intellectual exploration and argument be tempered by civility. Although individual inquiry and truth seeking can sometimes be a solitary exercise, classroom and collaborative activities help enrich social capacity and develop an inclination toward orderliness.

Through the transmission of democratic values and cultural norms, tertiary education contributes to the promotion of civic behaviors, nation building, and social cohesion. This, in turn, supports the construction and strengthening of social capital, generally understood as the benefits of membership in a social network that can provide access to resources, guarantee accountability, and serve as a safety net in time of crisis. The institutions, relationships, and norms that emerge from tertiary education are instrumental in influencing the quality of a society's interactions, which underpin economic, political, and social development. Universities and other tertiary institutions are the crossroads for social cooperation, which can foster strong networks, stimulate voluntary activity, and promote extracurricular learning and innovation.

A growing body of research supports the notion that the general quality of social infrastructure is a critical factor in the effectiveness of governments, institutions, and firms, helping to nurture and transfer knowledge that not only produces goods and services but also serves as the foundation of a just society (Ritzen 2000; Solow 2000). Social fragmentation, distrust, and corruption have measurable costs and are often difficult to remedy. Trust, information sharing, and sound governance are now understood as important economic agents that support development through effective interaction. Tightly knit networks and accountable communities that are created and nourished in tertiary institutions provide important venues for access to income and opportunity. Tertiary education promotes cooperation during education and after graduation, linking individuals across sectors of the economy and connecting them outside formal networks. This cooperation can ultimately improve government performance, engender civic engagement, and lower the incidence of inequality, social exclusion, and corruption—to the benefit of society, the state, and the market. In postconflict nations especially, enhanced social capital is essential for assisting societies in reinventing themselves with a sound moral compass.

Tertiary education can also play a crucial role in promoting social mobility. It is important to provide adequate and equitable tertiary education so that the entire citizenry can maximize its participation at all levels, creating new educational opportunities for all groups in society, in particular poor people.

Finally, scientific advances, especially in medicine and biotechnology, raise many complex issues that go beyond science to include matters related to ethics, public regulation, business practice, community life, globalization, and world governance. Countries cannot address issues such as genetically modified food, stem cell research, or cloning effectively without the leadership and civic engagement of individuals who have been formed by a strong tertiary education grounded in philosophy, ethics, and tradition.

The Changing Tertiary Education Landscape

Over the past two decades, many countries have experienced a remarkable diversification of their tertiary education sectors. The appearance of a variety of new institutions alongside the traditional universities—short-duration technical institutes and community colleges, polytechnics, distance education centers, and open universities—has created new opportunities to meet the growing social demand. In Latin America, Asia, and, more recently, Eastern Europe and Sub-Saharan Africa, this trend has been intensified by the rapid growth in the number and size of private tertiary education institutions. A second wave of institutional diversification is now discernible with the emergence of new forms of competition in tertiary education that transcend traditional conceptual, institutional, and geographic boundaries (CVCP 2000). The main new actors and institutions emerging in the "borderless" tertiary education market are discussed in sequence below. They are (a) virtual universities, (b) franchise universities, (c) corporate universities, (d) media companies, libraries, museums, and other institutions, and (e) education brokers (Salmi 2001). On the heels of these new actors come software producers, publishers, entertainment firms, and others seeking to tap the potential of an emerging international market in tertiary education (Bennell and Pearce 1998).

Virtual Universities

The elimination of the physical distance barrier as a result of the ICT revolution means that it is possible for outside institutions and providers to compete with local universities and reach students anywhere, in any country, using the Internet or satellite communication links. An estimate made in early 2000 suggested that there were already more than 3,000 specialized institutions dedicated to online training in the United States alone. Thirty-three U.S. states have a statewide virtual university; and 85 percent of all community colleges are expected to offer online distance education courses by 2002 (Olsen 2000).

The growth of virtual universities is not exclusively a U.S. phenomenon. The Virtual University of Monterrey, Mexico, offers 15 master's degree programs using teleconferencing and the Internet to reach 50,000 students in 1,450 learning centers throughout Mexico and 116 other centers all over Latin America. Tun Abdul Razak University, the first online institution in Malaysia, has started to extend its reach to neighboring Asian countries. The African Virtual University and the Francophone Virtual University are pioneering virtual education in Sub-Saharan Africa. As of 2002, there are 15 virtual universities in Korea, offering 66 B.A. degree programs that reach 14,550 students.

Franchise Universities

In many parts of the world, but predominantly in South and Southeast Asia and the formerly socialist countries of Eastern Europe, there has been a proliferation of overseas "validated courses" offered by franchise institutions operating on behalf of British, U.S., and Australian universities. One-fifth of the 80,000 foreign students enrolled in Australian universities are studying at offshore campuses, mainly in Malaysia and Singapore (Bennell and Pearce 1998). The cost of attending these franchise institutions is usually one-fourth to one-third what it would cost to enroll in the mother institution.

Corporate Universities

Corporate universities are another form of competition with which traditional universities dedicated solely to postsecondary degree programs and research will increasingly have to reckon, especially in the area of continuing education. Worldwide, there are now about 1,600 corporate universities, up from 400 only 10 years ago. Motorola University has been recognized in benchmarking exercises as one of the most successful of these. It operates with a yearly budget of US$120 million, representing almost 4 percent of the firm's annual payroll, and manages 99 learning and training sites in 21 countries (Densford 1999). Corporate universities may operate through their own network of physical campuses (examples are Disney, Toyota, and Motorola); as virtual universities (e.g., IBM and Dow Chemical); or through an alliance with existing tertiary education institutions (as do Bell Atlantic, United HealthCare, and United Technologies). A few corporate universities have been officially accredited and enjoy the authority to grant formal degrees. Experts are predicting that by 2010 there will be more corporate universities than traditional campus-based universities in the world and that an increasing proportion of them will be serving smaller companies rather than corporate giants.

Other Institutions

A diverse group of institutions—media and publishing companies, libraries and museums, and secondary schools—have also extended their reach into the world of tertiary education, taking full advantage of the new information and communication technologies. Although this new form of competition is more difficult to track, it is becoming significant at least in the United States and the United Kingdom. Examples include publishing companies that provide services linked to curriculum design and the preparation of educational materials for online delivery, and museums and libraries that offer continuing education courses.

Academic Brokers

Academic brokers are virtual, often Web-based, entrepreneurs who specialize in bringing together suppliers and consumers of educational services in many different areas. Companies such as Connect Education, Inc., and Electronic University Network build, lease, and manage campuses, produce multimedia educational software, and provide guidance to serve the training needs of corporate clients worldwide (Abeles 1998). Dozens of Web-based companies act as clearinghouses between schools and prospective students, offering information about academic and financial resources.

Need for New Quality-Assurance Mechanisms in a Global Marketplace

The emergence of borderless tertiary education heralds important changes in quality assurance needs and practices. First, it is doubtful that the philosophy, principles, and standards customarily applied in evaluating and accrediting campus-based programs can be used without major adjustments for assessing the quality and effectiveness of online courses and other modalities of distance education. Appropriate and reliable accreditation and evaluation processes are needed to assure the public that the courses, programs, and degrees offered by the new types of distance education institutions meet acceptable academic and professional standards. Less emphasis is likely to be given to traditional input dimensions such as qualifications of individual faculty and student selection criteria and more to the competencies and capabilities of graduates.

Second, very few developing nations have established accreditation and evaluation systems, nor do they have access to the necessary information on the quality of foreign programs or the institutional monitoring capacity to be able to detect fraud and protect their students from low-quality offerings. A recent survey in India showed that of 144 foreign providers advertising tertiary education programs in the newspapers, 46 were neither recognized nor accredited in their countries of origin (Powar and Bhalla 2001). The risk that students in low-income countries will fall prey to unscrupulous borderless operators is real.

Countries that cannot afford to or do not have the capacity to develop their own information systems should have the opportunity to participate in international accreditation and evaluation networks. Another option, following recent initiatives in Singapore, Hong Kong (China), and India, is to insist that foreign tertiary education institutions meet the same quality assurance requirements and guarantee the same type of degree recognition as prevail in the parent institution in the country of origin (see Appendix B).

New Modes of Organization and Operation

Tertiary education institutions in many countries are initiating sweeping transformations to align themselves better with new educational demands and competitive challenges. The main goal is to increase institutional flexibility and build up the adaptive capacity of tertiary education institutions and programs. These reforms are all-encompassing, touching on program offerings, academic structure and organization, pedagogical processes and modes of delivery, physical infrastructure, and the teaching profession.

Many changes are brought about or facilitated by the application of new technologies. These technologies can be used as pedagogical tools for transforming the learning process; as communication tools supporting new modes of information sharing; as resource tools (electronic libraries, for example); and as administrative tools to improve the efficiency and cost-effectiveness of academic management processes. ICT innovations create new challenges concerning pedagogy, academic management, governance and financing, quality assurance requirements, and intellectual property rights.

New Educational Programs and New Clients

In a lifelong-education perspective, changes at the level of program offerings have two aspects. First, the content and learning objectives of traditional programs need to be adjusted in such a way as to provide the foundation knowledge and skills necessary to equip all students with the capacity to undertake further learning and relearning over their lifetimes (Wagner 1999). Second, tertiary education institutions must expand their program options to address the learning needs of nontraditional students with a variety of motivations and aims—for example, individuals wishing to change professions, returning graduates who want to update their skills, and retired people pursuing personal growth interests. One can therefore expect a significant change in the demographic shape of tertiary institutions, with more students pursuing a second or third degree or a professional degree and a larger share of students, both young and mature, enrolled in short-term continuing education activities.

Organization and Management

As tertiary education systems move from elite to mass systems and from an emphasis on teaching to a focus on learning, students become more important actors—as primary clients, consumers, and learners. This shift requires the establishment of appropriate organizational and management mechanisms to handle these new roles and the new challenges that they represent. Tertiary education institutions need to develop, in particular, capacities to conduct beneficiary assessments, to inform and guide students concerning career choices, to accommodate the needs of students with special difficulties, and to maintain linkages with graduates as resources for student placement and fund raising.

Effective labor market feedback mechanisms, such as tracer surveys and regular consultations with employers and alumni, are indispensable for adjusting curricula to meet the changing needs of industry. There is no better linkage than when a new tertiary education institution is fully integrated into a regional development strategy. This was what happened in Finland, where the young University of Oulu has become one of the best universities in the Nordic countries despite being located in a remote area close to the Arctic Circle. The small rural community of Oulu has been transformed into a high-technology zone where winning companies (led by Nokia), science parks dedicated to applied research in electronics, medicine, and biotechnology, and the 13,000-student university function in symbiosis.

As regards organizational structure, there is a need to articulate traditional disciplines differently to respond to the emergence of new scientific and technological fields, the shift toward a problem-based mode of production of knowledge and away from the classic discipline-led approach, and the blurring of the distinction between basic and applied research. Among the most significant new areas are molecular biology and biotechnology, advanced materials science, microelectronics, information systems, robotics, intelligent systems and neuroscience, and environmental science and technology. Training and research in these fields require the integration of a number of disciplines that were previously regarded as separate and distinct. The result is the multiplication of interdisciplinary and multidisciplinary programs that cut across traditional disciplinary barriers. The new patterns of knowledge creation imply not only a reconfiguration of departments into a different institutional map but also, and more important, the reorganization of research and training around the search for solutions to complex problems rather than the analytical practices of traditional academic disciplines. This evolution is leading to the emergence of "transdisciplinarity," characterized by distinct theoretical structures and research methods (Gibbons and others 1994). Even Ph.D. programs are increasingly affected by this change, as students become less involved in the production of new knowledge and more involved in contributing to the circulation of knowledge across traditional disciplinary boundaries. The trend goes beyond hard science and touches social sciences as well. For example, in 1990 Japan's private Keio University established a separate entity, the Shonan Fujisawa Campus, to provide interdisciplinary programs in policy management, environmental information, and nursing and medical care. This program is regarded as revolutionary in the Japanese context because its graduates are well received by high-performing Japanese multinational enterprises, which traditionally preferred graduates of pure social science disciplines.[4]

Flexibility is vital if institutions are to adapt to the changing environment. Tertiary education institutions need to be able to react swiftly by establishing new programs, reconfiguring existing ones, and eliminating outdated programs without being hampered by bureaucratic regulations and processes.

To increase flexibility in the design and organization of academic programs, many tertiary education institutions throughout the world have adopted the U.S. standard of credit-based courses. This evolution has affected entire national university systems, as in Thailand, as well as networks of institutions, such as the Indian Institutes of Technology, and single institutions like the University of Niger (Regel 1992). At a historic meeting in Bologna in June 1999 ministers of higher education from 29 European countries committed themselves to the introduction of the credit approach in their university systems and the establishment of the European Credit Accumulation and Transfer System (EUROCATS). Some industrial countries, such as Denmark, are in the process of reshaping the entire tertiary education and S&T landscape. Danish officials are considering how best to encourage the formation of broad consortia by existing tertiary education institutions, national research institutes, and a wide spectrum of lifelong-learning programs. Such learning and knowledge consortia would facilitate the shared use of physical and human resources and enable students to move freely across traditional academic and institutional boundaries throughout their lives (Denmark 2001).

The organization of studies and the pattern of admission are evolving in many countries to accommodate in a more flexible way different moments of entry, exit, and reentry for various groups of students. In 1999, for the first time in the United States, a number of colleges decided to stagger the arrival of new students throughout the academic year instead of restricting them to the fall semester. In China a spring college entrance examination was held for the first time in January 2000. Many Korean universities also recruit students throughout the year; thus, students who fail the traditional July examination no longer have to wait a full year for a second chance.

Pedagogical Methods

The introduction of new pedagogical approaches supported by alternative delivery mechanisms has just begun to revolutionize teaching and learning in tertiary education. The concurrent use of multimedia, computers, and the Internet can make possible more active and interactive learning experiences through, for example, peer tutoring and self-directed learning, experiential and real-world learning, resource-based and problem-based learning, reflective practice and critical self-awareness, or any combination of these approaches. Traditional in-person teaching can be replaced by or associated with asynchronous teaching in the form of online classes that can be either scheduled or self-paced. A pioneer study (Kozma and Johnson 1991) conducted at the beginning of the 1990s analyzed several ways in which information technology could play a catalytic role in enriching the teaching and learning experience. It suggested a new pedagogical model involving active engagement of the students rather than passive reception of information, opportunities to apply new knowledge to real-life situations, representation of concepts and knowledge in multiple ways rather than with text only, learning as a collaborative activity rather than as an individual act, and an emphasis on learning processes rather than memorization of information.

Infrastructure

The adoption of pedagogical approaches and modes of delivery that rely significantly on information technology have far-reaching implications, both positive and negative, for developing countries, with respect to the design and the cost of the physical infrastructure of tertiary education institutions. The new technologies require considerable investment in equipment and in cable or wireless networks, followed by high costs for infrastructure maintenance, training, and technical support. It is estimated that the initial capital outlays represent only 25 percent of the total costs associated with the purchase, use, and maintenance of information and communication hardware and software; the recurrent costs can thus represent as much as 75 percent of the life-cycle costs of technology investments. Such important capital investments and recurrent costs present major fiscal challenges for tertiary institutions in developing countries. Realigning the programs and curricula of universities on the basis of interdisciplinary and multidisciplinary learning and research similarly entails significant modifications in the organization of the laboratory and workshop infrastructure supporting basic science and engineering programs.[5]

At the same time, the judicious use of new technologies can be a source of major savings. In the United Kingdom the cost of producing an Open University graduate is about one-third that at a regular university. Traditional libraries are evolving into multifunctional information centers as digitization of information transforms their core work. Many academic libraries are now using networked information resources such as commercially available electronic databases as a means of expanding access to relevant information for all members of the academic community. Together with other departments and institutions, libraries are also engaged in the preservation of educational materials in digital form. Some of these projects can help academic libraries in developing countries cope with the pressure of the ever-increasing costs of reference documents, especially scientific journals.[6] The Korean Education and Research Information Service (KERIS), a government-funded organization established in 1999, supports the purchase and sharing of quality international academic databases and online academic journals to help tertiary institutions and research institutes conserve financial resources.[7]

Reliance on CD-ROMs and networked databases can partially replace expensive journal and book collections and alleviate the shortage of storage space that many libraries face. In Canada 64 universities recently pooled their resources to establish nationwide site licenses for online scholarly journals. This project should give access to a larger pool of digital information to smaller universities that may not have the financial capacity to maintain a large stock of journals (Paskey 2001). Under any circumstances, however, whether to subscribe to particular networked information resources has to be determined on the basis of the pros and cons, including the cost implications, of using digitized resources or printed resources.[8]

Modern technology is not a panacea. To create a more active and interactive learning environment, faculty must have a clear vision as to the purpose of the new technologies and the most effective way of integrating them into program design and delivery—what experts call "instructional integration." Then they must educate themselves in the use of the new pedagogical channels and supports.

A recent report from the University of Illinois on the use of Internet classes in undergraduate education sounds a few notes of caution (Mendels 2000). Quality online education is best achieved with relatively small class sizes, not to exceed 30 students. It does not seem desirable to teach an entire undergraduate degree program exclusively through online classes if students are expected to learn to think critically and interact socially in preparation for professional life. Combining online and regular classroom courses gives students more opportunity for human interaction and development of the social aspects of learning through direct communication, debate, discussion, and consensus building. These pedagogical desiderata also apply to the design and delivery of distance education programs, which need to match learning objectives with the appropriate technological support.

The Teaching Profession

The teaching profession is itself evolving as a result of transformations in academic and pedagogical approaches. With a proper integration of technology in the curriculum, teachers can move away from their customary role as one-way instructors toward becoming facilitators of learning. The introduction of multimedia and computer-based teaching is leading toward the unbundling of professors' traditional functions: course design, selection of textbooks and readings, course delivery, and assessment of resources. The need for tertiary education institutions to be able to respond rapidly to changing labor market signals and to adjust swiftly to technological change may also imply more flexible arrangements for the deployment of academic staff and the evaluation of its performance. These adjustments may include moving away from civil service regulations and abandoning tenure-track appointments. Under a more radical scenario, the multiplication of online programs and courses could induce tertiary education institutions to contract independent professors not affiliated with a specific college or university to prepare tailor-made courses.

Conclusion: Demise or Renewal of Traditional Tertiary Institutions?

Momentous changes in the global environment are stretching the traditional time and space boundaries of tertiary education, in OECD countries and in developing and transition countries. The time dimension is altered by the requirement for lifelong learning, and space barriers are falling before the new information and communication technologies. These challenges can be seen as serious threats or as tremendous opportunities for tertiary education everywhere. The hegemony of classical tertiary institutions, especially universities, has been definitively challenged, and institutional differentiation is bound to accelerate, resulting in a greater variety of organizational configurations and patterns, including the emergence of a myriad of alliances, linkages, and partnerships within tertiary institutions, across institutions, and even extending beyond the tertiary education sector.

Under any scenario, traditional universities will continue to play a major role in both industrial and developing countries, especially in advanced training and research, but they will undoubtedly have to undergo significant transformations prompted by the application of new education technologies and the pressure of market forces. The impact of these changes is multifaceted and complex, as reflected in Table 2.1.

Table 2.1 Evolving Tertiary Education Systems

Desired outcomes	Changing education and training needs	Changing tertiary education landscape	Changing modes of operation and organization
Advanced human capital	Demand for higher skills	Appearance of new providers	More interactive pedagogy with emphasis on learning
New knowledge	Methodological and analytical skills	Development of borderless education	Continuing education programs
Adaptation of global knowledge for resolution of local problems	Demand for internationally recognized degrees and qualifications		Increased reliance on ICT for pedagogical, information, and management purposes
			Multi- and transdisciplinarity
Democratic values, attitudes, and cultural norms			Humanistic dimension of education and training
			Adaptability and flexibility

In the next chapter, we look at the current realities of tertiary education systems in developing and transition economies. In particular, we explore the continuing problems of access, equity, quality assurance, and governance faced by these institutions.

Notes

1. Although this remains true in a large number of areas of basic research, a growing number of scientific fields—notably, biotechnology—that produce commercially applicable knowledge are rapidly becoming more "closed," and scientists are less willing to cooperate freely for the sake of building capacity. The World Bank is studying the magnitude and consequences of this change.

2. For India, Duraisamy (2000); for the Philippines, Schady (2002); for South Africa, Lam (1999).

3. Radm Teo Chee Hean, minister for education, Singapore, keynote lecture to the 30th International Management Symposium, University of St. Gallen, Switzerland, May 26, 2000, available at <http://www1.moe.edu.sg/speeches/2000/sp26052000c.htm>.

4. See "Keio University Shonan-Fujisawa Campus," <http://www.sfc.keio.ac.jp/english/welcome/glance.html>.

5. Two examples from the United States will illustrate. The Georgia Institute of Technology has developed an interdisciplinary "mechatronics" laboratory that cost-effectively serves the needs of students in electrical, mechanical, industrial, computer, and other engineering departments. The Pennsylvania State University, the University of Puerto Rico–Mayaguez, the University of Washington, and Sandia National Laboratories have formed a unique partnership to establish "learning factory" facilities that allow teams of students from industrial, mechanical, electrical, and chemical engineering and business administration programs in the partner schools to work together on interdisciplinary projects (Lamancusa, Jorgensen, and Zayas-Castro 1997).

6. Cornell University in the United States, for example, has created the "Essential Electronic Agricultural Library," a collection of CD-ROMs that stores texts from 140 scientific journals in the field of agriculture from 1993 on (see <http://teeal.cornell.edu/#TEEAL>). The CD-ROMs are shared with libraries in 115 developing countries at the low cost of US\$22,500 for the years 1993 to 1999 and US\$5,000 for updates that become available one year after the original year of publication. Many of the developing county libraries obtained the CD-ROMs with assistance from donors. The cost of buying all the journals included in the CD-ROM database is estimated at US\$375,000 (reported in McCollum 1999).

7. See Korean Education & Research Information Service, <http://www.keris.or.kr>.

8. Academic librarians have some reservations about using networked information resources: (a) publishers do not always ensure updating of digital resources as computers are upgraded, which could result in libraries not being able to use the previous version with their new equipment, and (b) subscription to networked information resources means that libraries purchase access to resources without having any control over publishers' decisions to drop certain resources from the database or to stop archiving them.

3
Confronting the Old Challenges: The Continuing Crisis of Tertiary Education in Developing and Transition Countries

Problems of quality and lack of resources are compounded by the new realities faced by higher education, as higher education institutions battle to cope with ever-increasing student numbers. Responding to this demand without further diluting quality is an especially daunting challenge. . . Expansion, public and private, has been unbridled, unplanned, and often chaotic. The results— deterioration in average quality, continued interregional, intercountry, and intracountry inequities, and increased for-profit provision of higher education—could all have serious consequences.

Report of the Task Force on Higher Education and Society
(World Bank and UNESCO 2000)

Tertiary education can play a catalytic role in helping developing and transition countries rise to the challenges of the knowledge economy and fulfill the roles and functions outlined in Chapter 2. But this is conditional on these countries' ability to overcome the serious problems that have plagued tertiary education systems and have pushed some systems into a situation of severe crisis.

Presenting a panoramic assessment of the main issues facing tertiary education systems worldwide is a daunting, if not impossible, task. Unlike primary schools, which share many similarities across countries, tertiary education systems come in all sizes and configurations. Still, notwithstanding the many contrasts among tertiary education systems as to size, degree of diversification, participation of private institutions, financing patterns and unit costs, and modes of governance, there is a set of common challenges that can be looked at in a global perspective. To a large extent, these problems are generated by the process of shifting from elite to expanded, mass tertiary education under severe resource constraints and with the burden of a legacy of persistent inequalities in access and outcomes, inadequate educational quality, low relevance to economic needs, and rigid governance and management structures. OECD countries have faced similar challenges in the recent past and have addressed them through a variety of approaches and with varying degrees of success.

The Need to Expand Tertiary Education

Despite the rapid growth of tertiary enrollments in most developing and transition countries over the past decades, the enrollment gap between these economies and OECD countries has not diminished. In fact, the opposite has occurred, as is illustrated by Figure 3.1. In 1980 the tertiary enrollment rate in the United States was 55 percent, whereas the average

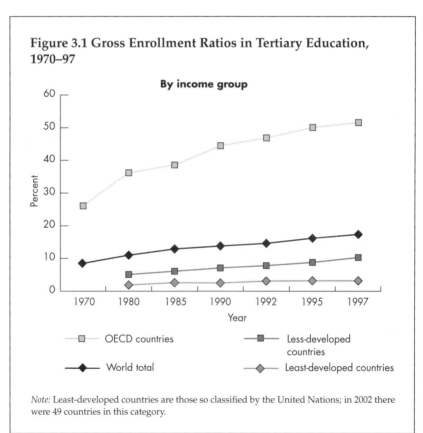

Figure 3.1 Gross Enrollment Ratios in Tertiary Education, 1970–97

Note: Least-developed countries are those so classified by the United Nations; in 2002 there were 49 countries in this category.

for developing countries was 5 percent.[1] In 1995 the rates were 81 for the United States and 9 percent for developing countries.

Enrollment rates have even decreased slightly in Eastern Europe and Central Asia, from 36 percent in 1990 to 34 percent in 1997. The regional average masks very different trends. Rapid growth has occurred in Bulgaria, the Czech Republic, Hungary, Poland, and Slovenia, where enrollment rates are now in the 20–30 percent range, but the levels are stagnant or decreasing in such Central Asian countries as Tajikistan (9 percent) and Uzbekistan (5 percent).

Of the other regions of the world, Latin America and the Middle East have the highest averages (1997 data), with 18 and 15 percent, respectively, and South Asia and Africa the lowest (7 and 4 percent, respectively). The East Asian average of 11 percent conceals wide differences, from less than 2 percent in Cambodia to almost 30 percent in the Philippines and 51 percent in Korea, which is on a par with the OECD average. The need to invest in expanding coverage at the tertiary level is

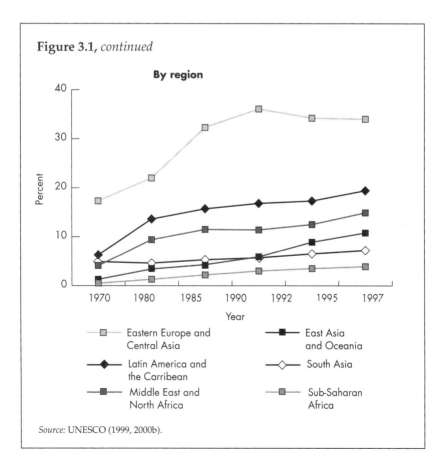

Figure 3.1, *continued*

Source: UNESCO (1999, 2000b).

nowhere more visible than in the large countries of Asia, such as China (5 percent in 1997), India (6 percent), and Pakistan (3 percent), and of Latin America, where Brazil and Mexico have enrollment rates of less than 15 percent.

Although population growth is more rapid in the developing world than in OECD countries, transition rates from secondary to tertiary education have been higher in the latter, for several reasons. Among these are significant increases in secondary school completion rates, students' perception of educational attainment as a means of achieving higher incomes, and the need for highly skilled labor in a rapidly changing global economy.

In the developing world secondary-level enrollment rates have grown most rapidly in East Asia (from 47 to 66 percent between 1990 and 1997), followed by Latin America (from 51 to 62 percent) and the Middle East (from 52 to 57 percent). In Sub-Saharan Africa, by contrast, the growth of secondary school enrollments has slowed as a result of a decline in primary-level enrollment and the dramatic demographic impact of HIV/AIDS. Eastern Europe and Central Asia is the only region in which secondary enrollment rates have actually decreased (from 92 to 87 percent), mainly because of a flight from vocational training courses.

One reason why tertiary enrollment levels are still relatively low in many parts of the developing world is the lack of institutional differentiation to accommodate diverse and growing demands. In Latin America, for instance, although some countries have a significant nonuniversity tertiary sector (79 percent of total tertiary enrollment in Cuba, 43 percent in Peru, 38 percent in Brazil, and 35 percent in Chile), in others—among them, El Salvador, Guatemala, Honduras, Nicaragua, and Panama—the nonuniversity sector accounts for less than 5 percent. Most Sub-Saharan African countries, too, have a small nonuniversity sector, with the exceptions of Kenya and South Africa (54 percent), Ghana (35 percent), and Nigeria (31 percent).

There is strong evidence that nonuniversity institutions such as junior colleges produce graduates with qualifications that correspond to labor market needs. In Taiwan (China) more than 90 percent of exports are produced by junior college graduates in small and medium-size enterprises (SMEs), which employ 78 percent of the working population and have played a pivotal role in overall economic development.[2] The lack of institutional differentiation in many parts of the world is a major concern, not only because nonuniversity institutions can absorb a significant share of the demand for tertiary education but also because they are in general better able to respond rapidly to changing labor market needs, as is illustrated by the positive contribution of two-year junior colleges in Korea.

Within the context of the growing enrollment gap, an equally worrisome issue is the slow expansion of postgraduate education in many parts of the world. In the Latin America and Caribbean region, students enrolled in postgraduate programs represented, on average, only 2.4 percent of overall tertiary enrollment in 1997, compared with 12.6 percent in the United States. Whereas OECD countries produce, on average, one new Ph.D. graduate per year per 5,000 population, the ratio is 1 graduate per 70,000 population in Brazil, 1 per 140,000 in Chile, and 1 per 700,000 in Colombia. More than two-thirds of all Latin American postgraduate students are concentrated in just two countries, Brazil and Mexico.

In Thailand postgraduate studies represent 3 percent of overall enrollment, compared with 8 percent in Korea. The relative underdevelopment of graduate education in several Asian countries is traceable to a tradition of sending students overseas.

In Africa the growth of postgraduate education has been very slow except in South Africa. A recent study of eight East African countries (Ethiopia, Kenya, Malawi, Mozambique, Rwanda, Tanzania, Uganda, and Zimbabwe) showed that their total annual production of master's graduates in economics, which was 20 in 1990, increased only to 94 in 2000. During the same period the number of Ph.D.-level graduates, especially in the basic sciences, was very low, and the few degrees that were granted were based on dissertations, with little or no course work (Obwana and Norman 2000). In Nigeria, where 20 percent of Africa's population lives, only 15 scientists and engineers per million persons are engaged in research and development; the number per million population is 150 in India, 350 in China, and 3,700 in the United States.

In several Eastern European and Central Asian countries brain drain is a major obstacle to the development of postgraduate studies. In Bulgaria, for instance, the number of doctoral students has dropped from 5,000 to 3,400 since 1996. This circumstance seriously constrains the building up of those elements of national innovation systems that are so essential for increasing national productivity—research capacity, university-trained researchers and professionals, graduates with advanced technical and managerial skills, and dynamic university-industry linkages.

In many countries the fiscal constraints experienced in recent years have undermined financial capacity to undertake further expansion of the public tertiary education system while maintaining satisfactory quality. In the past 10 to 15 years expenditures for tertiary education as a percentage of the total public education budget have declined significantly in several countries, including Bangladesh (from 13 to 8 percent), China (from 20 to 16 percent), Ghana (from 15 to 12 percent), Guinea (from 29 to 17 percent), Nepal (from 35 to 19 percent), Oman (from 15 to 7 percent), and the Philippines (from 22 to 18 percent). In Ecuador, Mexico, and Peru per-student expenditures fell by 30, 20, and 30 percent, respectively, between 1980 and 1990.

The demand for high-quality tertiary education can be seen in the large numbers of students from developing countries who choose to study abroad, particularly in the United States. During the 2000–2001 academic year, there were 547,867 foreign students in the United States, making up approximately 3.8 percent of total enrollment in U.S. colleges and universities and bringing almost US$11.04 billion into the U.S. economy. In 2000–2001 the top 10 places of origin of foreign students in the United States were (in descending order) China, India, Japan, Korea, Taiwan (China), Canada, Indonesia, Thailand, Turkey, and Mexico.[3] The United States remains the leading destination for international students, but the United Kingdom, Australia, France, and Germany are also key destinations for students from developing countries.

In several countries public sector tertiary enrollments have failed to grow or, where they have grown, resources have been pinched. In Sri Lanka enrollments in public tertiary institutions have stagnated at 2 percent since 1990 for lack of government funding. In Africa expenditures per student have declined in real terms in 10 of the 15 countries for which data are available. The HIV/AIDS epidemic has exacerbated the problem of dwindling resources and reduced funding. Universities have been forced to spend much more as a result of the epidemic, both in direct costs—for medical services, testing and treatment, premature payment of terminal benefits, funeral expenses, and replacement, recruitment, and training of staff and in the form of indirect costs stemming from increased absenteeism, generous sick leave provisions, and general loss of productivity.

The fiscal constraints become even more acute in times of economic and financial crisis, sometimes leading to significant decreases in tertiary enrollment. In East Asia, for example, typical responses to the 1997–98 financial crisis in Indonesia, Korea, and Thailand were for low-income students to drop out without completing their studies and for middle- and high-income students to shift from private to public tertiary institutions (Varghese 2001). Similar patterns have been observed in some South American countries, notably Bolivia and Colombia. The Colombian National Association of Universities has calculated that the country's private universities have lost close to 20 percent of their students since 1999. In Central and Eastern Europe the lingering economic crisis and the introduction of market principles of economic organization in the early 1990s resulted in a sharp (between 30 and 80 percent) decline in public funding for colleges, universities, and scientific academies. Following the collapse of the Soviet Union, investment in research and development in Russia declined drastically, from more than 2 percent in 1990 to barely 1 percent at the end of the decade; the comparable OECD average is 2.2 percent (Cervantes and Malkin 2001).

The problem of insufficient, and sometimes declining, funding is often compounded by the inefficient use of available resources. In many Central and Eastern European countries, for instance, per-student public expenditures are no more than 10 to 25 percent of the OECD average, but in relation to per capita GDP they are significantly higher than in OECD countries, implying a high degree of inefficiency in resource utilization. In the formerly socialist countries the tertiary education sector continues to be fragmented despite attempts (notably in Estonia and Hungary) to encourage mergers. There are too many small institutions operating at high unit costs and offering similar programs.

Management inefficiencies drain scarce resources away from the fundamental objectives of increasing access, quality, and relevance. Examples of such inefficiencies include underutilized facilities, duplicative program offerings, low student-staff ratios, high dropout and repetition rates, uneconomical procurement procedures, and allocation of a large share of the budget to noneducational expenditures. Many public tertiary institutions are overburdened by students, yet facilities often go underused. Because of civil service regulations or agreements with trade unions, many university facilities are closed evenings and weekends

Low student-staff ratios and high repetition and dropout rates drive up the cost per graduate. In China and Brazil, for example, student-teacher ratios are very low in the public universities—between 5:1 and 9:1 in Chinese universities and 9:1 in the Brazilian federal universities, compared with a range of 15:1 to 20:1 in European universities. In four Nigerian universities the graduation rate is 10 percent or less (Hartnett 2000: 5). In many parts of the world high repetition and dropout rates are among the most important causes of low internal efficiency in public universities. Low internal efficiency is especially prevalent in countries with open access, as is the case in most francophone African countries and in a few Latin American countries (Argentina, the Dominican Republic, Guatemala, and Uruguay). The problem is sometimes compounded by the longer than usual duration of first degrees. In Bolivia, for instance, the first degree is supposed to be earned within five years, but students actually take nine years to graduate, on average. Guatemala's public universities spend 22 student-years to produce a graduate of a 6-year undergraduate program. In Indonesia the average duration for degree completion in four-year undergraduate programs is seven years.

In many countries a large share of the public tertiary education budget is devoted to noneducational expenditures in support of student scholarships and subsidized student services such as housing, food, transportation, medical services, and loans. Student support represents only 6 percent of recurrent expenditures in Asia, but 14 percent in OECD countries, around 15 percent in Eastern Europe and Central Asia, about

20 percent in North Africa and the Middle East and in Latin America, and close to 50 percent in francophone Sub-Saharan Africa. In Sri Lanka all students receive a maintenance grant regardless of socioeconomic considerations.

Another source of inefficiency in some public institutions is the high proportion of overhead expenditures and of salary expenditures for nonteaching staff. In China nonteaching staff in universities are more numerous than teachers. In Nigeria only 2.7 percent of university budgets goes for teaching support, as against 35 percent for administration (Hartnett 2000: 15). Finally, a number of countries offer very generous salary benefits to staff, and these benefits account for the bulk of expenditures, leaving only limited resources for nonsalary expenditures for educational purposes (educational materials, library resources, laboratory supplies, maintenance, and so on). In Venezuela salaries of active professors and pensions for retired faculty members represent 69 percent of the budget of public universities; in Brazil these items amount to 90 percent of the total budget.

Persisting Inequalities

Along with rapid enrollment growth, noteworthy progress has been made in many countries in access to tertiary education for traditionally less–privileged groups, including students from rural areas and women. Yet tertiary education, especially in the university sector, generally remains elitist, with most students coming from wealthier segments of society. Although most countries and institutions do not systematically collect data on the socioeconomic origin of students, where statistics and household survey data are available the pattern is clear. In Latin America the share of students from the lowest third of the income distribution enrolled in tertiary education is only 6 percent in Peru, 11 percent in Chile, and 18 percent in Uruguay (García Guadilla 1998). In francophone Sub-Saharan Africa the children of white-collar employees account for 40 percent of tertiary enrollment even though this group of professionals represents only 6 percent of the total labor force (World Bank 1994: 23).

One of the main determinants of inequity is family income, but, depending on the country, other factors may contribute to unequal access and outcomes. Among these are caste, ethnicity, language, regional origin, gender, and physical disability. In India special efforts have been made to reduce barriers linked to caste, but the representation of students from scheduled castes and tribes in Indian tertiary institutions is still low. In Venezuela the widespread but not much publicized custom of preferential admission for children of university professors and employees is an example of positive discrimination in favor of the children of the already privileged intellectual elite.

Language can contribute to social inequity in countries where tertiary education is conducted in a language different from that of primary and secondary education. In Sri Lanka and Tanzania, for example, English is the language of tertiary instruction, and in the countries of North Africa French is used in most scientific disciplines. Language can also be an obstacle in multicultural societies such as Guatemala, where 90 percent of the population does not speak Spanish, the language of instruction, at home.

Except in Latin America, gender inequity persists in most regions of the developing world, as illustrated in Table 3.1.

Gender differences in tertiary enrollments are particularly marked in the Arab world, in some countries of Sub-Saharan Africa, and in South Asia. In the Republic of Yemen, for instance, the female enrollment ratio in tertiary education is only 1 percent of the eligible age cohort, as against 7 percent for men. In Bangladesh female students represent 24 percent of the student population in public universities; gender disparities are even stronger in the country's private universities, where only 17 percent of all students (and less than 1 percent of all teachers) are female. In some countries where male and female enrollment ratios were once relatively equal, as was the case in Russia in the early 1990s, gender inequalities increased slightly. There are gender disparities among countries within the same region. Over the past two decades only a few countries (Argentina, Chile, Jordan, Kuwait, Panama, Uruguay, and Venezuela) have managed to move toward a higher female-to-male ratio while expanding overall tertiary enrollment.

Women are clearly underrepresented in the teaching profession in many countries. Worldwide, female teacher representation is approximately 30 to 50 percent lower at the tertiary than at the secondary level. Women are also less likely to have access to management positions than men. In Indonesia in 1996 women occupied only 2 percent of rector's positions in tertiary education and 9 percent of dean's positions, even though their share of tertiary-level enrollment was 35 percent and they accounted for 24 percent of academic positions at public universities (Koswara 1996). In Bangladesh the proportion of female instructors at the tertiary level is estimated at a mere 4 percent of the teaching staff. The proportions of female teaching staff at tertiary institutions in East Asia are also low: China, 20 percent (1980), Indonesia, 18 percent (1985), Japan, 22 percent (1996), Korea, 24 percent (1996), Malaysia, 22 percent (1985), and Singapore, 31 percent (1995) (World Bank 2001b). In the United States only 29 percent of the women teaching in the fields of science, engineering, and technology are tenured full-time professors, as against 58 percent of the male faculty members in the same fields. In Ger-

Table 3.1 Gender Disparity in Enrollment and Teacher Deployment, Selected Countries, 1997

Region and country	Combined primary- and secondary-level gross enrollment ratio (percent)[a]		Tertiary-level students per 1,000 population		Proportion of women in tertiary education (percent)	Share of female teachers (percent)	
	Female	Male	Female	Male		Secondary	Tertiary
Africa							
Botswana	93	90	5.5	6.4	47	43	28
Madagascar	51	51	1.6	1.9	45	—	29
South Africa	40	47	14.6	15.9	48	64	37
Asia							
Cambodia	68	86	0.3	1.7	16	27	17
China	95	98	3.3	6.1	—	36	—
India	62	81	4.8	7.9	36	—	—
Indonesia	79	85	8.1	15.2	35	37	—
Kuwait	68	69	25.9	19.3	62	54	—
Yemen, Rep.	34	90	1.1	7.3	13	—	—
Latin America							
Brazil	—	—	11.7	10.1	53	—	38
Colombia	89	87	18.2	17.1	52	48	28
Guyana	87	85	8.9	10.2	48	62	31
Industrial countries							
Austria	102	104	28.2	31.3	48	55	26
New Zealand	108	105	49.9	40.1	56	57	40
United States	99	100	58.4	48.2	56	56	39

—Not available.

a. Proportion of the population age 6–17 attending primary or secondary school.

Source: United Nations (2000).

many only 6 percent of full professors are women. In Brazil women make up 20–29 percent of researchers in the natural sciences; in health sciences women are at parity with men, at about 53 percent.

Caution must be exercised when looking at improved female enrollment rates. Such statistics often conceal the concentrated presence of women in degree programs preparing for low-income professions. In fact, "gender streaming" can be observed in all regions, even in Latin America, where women are overrepresented in the humanities and in vocational and commercial/secretarial schools and underrepresented in science and engineering departments (Subbarao and others 1994). In Japan women make up only 6.8 percent of the Ph.D. students in physics and 7.1 percent of those in engineering. In many countries, moreover, sexual harassment poses a major additional obstacle to the advancement of female education, even though, for obvious reasons, there is little evidence on this topic in the research literature.

Lodging can be a barrier for women. Tertiary education institutions are typically located in urban areas, limiting access for rural students and even more so for female students, since families may be less inclined to permit daughters than sons to live outside the home in mixed-gender environments in urban areas. Many countries have addressed this constraint by providing boarding facilities segregated by gender, with adequate space to accommodate ever greater numbers of women. Tunisia addressed gender equity issues by building smaller campuses in locations around the country and in remote areas to provide higher education within commuting distance, obviating the need for students to live away from their families.

But access is not the only determinant of equity at the tertiary level. Recent household survey data from Argentina illustrate that even open-access tertiary education systems can be deceptive from an equity standpoint. Despite the appearance of democratic access for all secondary education graduates, academic outcomes are strongly influenced by socioeconomic origin. Only a fifth of the students from the poorest two quintiles who enter as first-year students under Argentina's open-access policy actually graduate from public universities. By contrast, there are relatively few failures among students from the richest quintile (Kisilevsky 1999).

In most countries where public tertiary education is free, public expenditures at that level represent regressive social spending in that the proportion of university students from upper- and middle-income families is higher than their share in the overall population. In Rwanda, for example, 15 percent of the overall public budget for education goes to just 0.2 percent of the students at the tertiary level. In Indonesia and Jordan students from the richest quintile receive, respectively, 50 and 39 percent of total public expenditures on tertiary education (Van de Walle 1992; World

Bank 1999b). Clearly, this is as socially inequitable as it is inefficient. In many nations the regressive character of spending on tertiary education is amplified by substantial subsidies for noneducational expenditures.

These regressive patterns are particularly widespread in countries with a significant proportion of private secondary schools. The children of high- and middle-income families who can afford the cost of high-quality private secondary schools are usually better prepared to pass the public university entrance examination giving them access to free higher education. In Venezuela 95 percent of the students attending the prestigious Simon Bolivar University come from private secondary schools. In several Asian countries such as Bangladesh, Sri Lanka, and Thailand, children from poorer families have limited access to high-quality primary and secondary education in the public sector, which reduces their chances of scoring well on the competitive university entrance examinations.

Countries that have introduced or raised user fees at the tertiary level are at risk of experiencing an increase in access disparities in the absence of effective and well-targeted financial aid mechanisms. In Scotland the concurrent establishment of tuition fees and elimination of maintenance grants in 1998 resulted in a noticeable decline in enrollment among low-income students. Countries where fees are imposed only on certain groups of students can also see an adverse equity effect. For example, in a number of former socialist economies, including Croatia, Lithuania, Poland, Russia, and Vietnam, more academically qualified students receive their education free of charge in public universities. Students who do not gain admission through the regular examination process can be admitted outside the official quota for government-sponsored places if they are able to pay tuition fees. The same pattern can be observed in East African countries such as Kenya, Tanzania, and Uganda. In those countries—as is true almost anywhere else in the world—there is usually a strong correlation between academic achievement and socioeconomic background. In Nepal, where the engineering school at the main public university has been a pioneer in introducing cost sharing, a degree of preferential access has been given to students who can afford the fees, raising the risk of compromising the rigor of academic selection.

Another type of informal fee is private tutoring, which is undertaken to prepare students for the competitive entrance examination and can become a quasi-official requirement. In Russia private classes cost between US$10 and US$40 an hour, the equivalent of a week's salary for an average worker. Private tutoring, which favors students from richer families, is also widespread in South and Southeast Asia and in East and southern Africa.

In their efforts to achieve equality in tertiary education and correct the legacy of past institutionalized or societal discrimination against specific subgroups, some countries make use of preferential treatment of minorities and disadvantaged groups ("affirmative action"). Affirmative action schemes can be mandated by law, encouraged in public discourse, or practiced by public sector employers and educational institutions. They cover a wide spectrum of measures that can include, but are not limited to, preferential treatment in university or college admissions, earmarked financial aid, remedial courses, talent searches, and special outreach programs. Affirmative action measures are often most visible in the admissions process and in competition for entry.

Affirmative action is a controversial and complex social intervention with uncertain outcomes. Remarkably little research has been conducted on the effectiveness of these practices or on their precise impact on students, institutions, and society. Some U.S. studies suggest that affirmative action does not work particularly well as a mechanism for equalizing opportunities. Bowen and Bok (1998), however, cite a longitudinal study of academic and employment patterns of U.S. black graduates which suggests that a positive equity effect for black students is associated with certain race-sensitive admissions practices in elite universities in the United States. In India, despite special provisions for free tertiary education and reservation of places for students from scheduled castes and tribes, the actual percentage of enrolled students from these groups is still low because of the proportionally small number of minority students who complete primary and secondary education. In some countries, such as the Philippines, studies have shown that even with supplemental remedial assistance to targeted groups, formal affirmative action programs have not been successful.

After the end of apartheid, universities in South Africa began experimenting with alternative admissions testing programs that sought to identify deserving black applicants who had not been given an "adequate opportunity . . . to demonstrate their ability to succeed" (Nzimande and Sikhosana 1996). The scheme was introduced in conjunction with financial aid, support facilities, and remedial programs to assist students admitted in this way. In 1995 the University of Cape Town admitted 400 out of 1,453 black students under the program. Although the long-term equity effect of the initiative has yet to be fully assessed, it has succeeded in altering the overall racial composition of entrants. The University of Cape Town is noteworthy for its comprehensive approach toward assisting disadvantaged students, which includes a full array of support services in addition to preferential admission.

Various university systems in other countries of Africa have sought to increase female enrollments through affirmative action. In Ghana, Kenya, and Uganda women university candidates have been given bonus points on their admissions examination scores so that more of them pass the cutoff point. Between 1990 and 1999 female participation increased from 27 to 34 percent in Uganda and from 21 to 27 percent in Ghana. In Tanzania, rather than provide women with a score bonus, an intensive six-week remedial course in science and math has been offered to women who did not pass the matriculation examination. Those who complete the course are given a second chance to take the exam, and university authorities report a high pass rate in the second round. The University of Dar es Salaam recently conducted a performance assessment of female students who had entered the university in this way and found that most of them were performing well; in fact, several were at the top of their classes.

The limited base of research findings, however, does seem to indicate that many affirmative action interventions at the tertiary level come too late to assist the vast majority of disadvantaged students, who have already suffered institutionalized discrimination in access to primary and secondary education. At the tertiary level, therefore, focusing on financial aid such as scholarships, grants, and student loans seems to be a much more effective form of equity intervention for capable aspirants from minority or underprivileged populations. In addition, stronger equity efforts must clearly be made much earlier in a student's educational career, particularly at the primary and secondary levels, so that all students have an equal opportunity to compete for entry into tertiary education.

Problems of Quality and Relevance

Although there are exceptions, the quality and relevance of research, teaching, and learning have tended to decline in public tertiary education institutions in developing countries. Many universities operate with overcrowded and deteriorating physical facilities, limited and obsolete library resources, insufficient equipment and instructional materials, outdated curricula, unqualified teaching staff, poorly prepared secondary students, and an absence of academic rigor and systematic evaluation of performance. Similar conditions can be found in many of the new private universities and other tertiary institutions that have emerged in many countries, especially in those that lack a formal system for licensing or accrediting new institutions. In the formerly socialist countries of Eastern Europe and Central Asia, drastic reductions in public funding are jeopardizing the quality and sustainability of existing programs and even the survival of entire institutions. In many countries the poor quality of teacher training programs has detrimental effects on the quality of learning in primary and secondary education. Weak secondary education and scientific literacy, in turn, do not arm high school graduates with the necessary skills for successful tertiary-level studies.

Most universities in developing nations function at the periphery of the international scientific community, unable to participate in the production and adaptation of knowledge necessary to confront their countries' most important economic and social problems. Although few countries have exhaustive data to document the depth of the problem systematically, in countries where information is available the situation is alarming. For example, in 1995 a task force on higher education in the Philippines concluded, after reviewing information on critical education inputs and the results of professional examinations for the 1,316 existing tertiary education institutions, that only 9 universities and 2 colleges in the country were comparable in quality to international institutions. In India highly regarded programs such as those of the Indian Institutes of Technology exist side by side with scientific and technical programs of poor quality and relevance. Even Russia, once a world leader in advanced science and technology fields such as theoretical physics, nuclear technology, and space technologies, has seen a collapse of its R&D sector. As reported in a recent OECD publication, in Russia "financial crises, decaying equipment, unemployment and higher wages in other sectors drove large numbers of researchers . . . away from science and technology" (Cervantes and Malkin 2001).

In both public and private institutions the lack of full-time qualified teachers is an important contributor to poor quality. In Latin America, for example, the share of professors with doctoral degrees teaching in public universities is less than 6 percent, and the share with a master's degree is less than 26 percent. More than 60 percent of the teachers in the public sector work part-time; in the private universities the proportion is as high as 86 percent (García Guadilla 1998). In the Philippines only 7 percent of the professors teaching in tertiary education institutions hold Ph.D.s; 26 percent have master's degrees. Expansion and diversification of tertiary education systems has often led to internal brain drain because low-paid professors at public institutions seek second and third jobs in extramural positions such as teaching at better-paying private institutes and colleges.

As colleges, universities, and scientific academies in transition countries struggle to adapt to the new realities of a market economy, they are hampered by a fragmented institutional structure, characterized by a large number of small, specialized institutions and a few big universities that have a near-monopoly on teaching at high academic levels. The small institutions are not able to diversify their programs and compete effectively, and the large, most prestigious universities are often too protected by regulations and have no incentives to engage in innovation. Hungary is unique in Eastern Europe; there, a centrally initiated merger plan has reduced the number of public institutions from more than 70 to fewer than 20.

In spite of the global trend toward market expansion of tertiary education, governmental and institutional responses are not always favorable to the new tendencies. For example when countries expand tertiary education haphazardly to meet increasing social demand, there is a high risk of graduate unemployment. (To mention just two countries in different regions, in Nigeria graduate unemployment is 22 percent, and in Sri Lanka it is 35 percent.) In many countries the mismatch between the profile of graduates and labor market demands is most apparent among graduates in the social sciences and humanities. The Republic of Yemen, for instance, has an oversupply of liberal arts graduates, and their skills do not meet the needs of the economy. On the faculty side, this can lead to an oversupply of teachers of nonscientific subjects. Tertiary education institutions often lack adequate labor market information to guide prospective students, parents, and employers.

In many countries of Africa the toll of HIV/AIDS is changing tertiary education institutions in tragic ways. At the University of Nairobi, an estimated 20 to 30 percent of the 20,000 students are HIV positive (Bollag 2001; Kelly 2001), and in South Africa infection rates for undergraduate students have reportedly reached 33 percent (ACU 2001). Not only have students been directly affected by the pandemic, whether suffering from the disease themselves or caring for someone at home; so too have the faculty and administration. In some instances HIV/AIDS has robbed colleges and universities of their instructors and other personnel, crippling the institutions and further reducing the countries' development opportunities, let alone their capacity to produce local leaders, civil servants, and trained intellectuals. Zambia's Copperbelt University is said to have lost approximately 20 staff members in 2001, and Kenyatta University in Nairobi estimates that it lost 1 staff member or student per month during the same period.

Problems of quality and relevance are not confined to traditional universities. Even in countries that have diversified the structure of tertiary education, relevance can become a serious issue in the absence of close linkages between tertiary education institutions and the labor market. Jordan, for instance, has actively encouraged the development of public and private community colleges. Nevertheless, the status, quality, and relevance of these institutions have become so problematic that the country experienced a decline in community college enrollment from 41,000 in 1990–91 to 23,000 in 1995–96.

Lack of access to the global knowledge pool and the international academic environment is a growing issue. In many countries poor command of foreign languages among staff and students complicates access to textbooks and the Internet, especially at the graduate level. In countries such as Malaysia and Sri Lanka that had opted for the use of the national language in tertiary education, officials are now considering reversing this policy to improve the quality of tertiary education, especially in the basic and applied sciences.

Many countries that experienced a doubling or tripling of tertiary enrollments and increased participation rates for young people in recent decades have seen the negative effects of rapid expansion on quality. Issues of quality assurance and quality enhancement have become a major focus of attention (El-Khawas, DePietro-Jurand, and Holm-Nielsen 1998). Many governments, whatever the size and stage of development of their tertiary education sectors, have decided that traditional academic controls are inadequate for dealing with today's challenges and that more explicit quality assurance systems are needed.

Countries differ in their approaches to quality promotion. Some have taken steps to strengthen quality by introducing new reporting requirements or other mechanisms of management control. In Argentina the authorities have introduced quality assurance mechanisms that depend on an enhanced information and evaluation system and new rules for funding public universities. About 20 transition and developing countries have developed accreditation systems, while others have established evaluation committees or agencies that carry out external reviews. In many cases independent bodies have been established. While the most common setup is a single national agency, in some countries, such as Colombia and Mexico, separate agencies are responsible for different institutions, regions, purposes, and types of academic program. Such variation in the approaches to quality assurance bodies reflects political and cultural preferences within each country, differences in government leadership, and the varying stages of development of tertiary education sectors.

The scope of responsibilities given to quality assurance systems has varied widely. Scotland and England, for example, have procedures for monitoring teaching effectiveness, while Hong Kong (China) is focusing on high-quality management processes. Some countries, such as Chile, have established systems for licensing new institutions and certifying educational credentials. Others have directed their efforts toward rewarding research productivity, either of individual scholars (as in Mexico) or of entire academic departments (as in the United Kingdom). There is also wide variation in the extent to which quality assurance agencies have managed to address issues related to student transfer and to study abroad. Countries and agencies also differ in their concerns arising from the expansion of new modes of educational delivery, including video-based education, interactive transmission to remote sites, and, most recently, Internet-based learning.

Change-Resistant Governance Structures and Rigid Management Practices

In many countries the governance structure and management traditions of public tertiary institutions are characterized by weak leadership and a total lack of regulatory and management flexibility that inhibits any type of effective reform or innovation. Academic freedom is frequently and mistakenly equated with managerial independence. Thus, in the name of academic freedom, institutions (and their individual constituents, faculty, administrators, and students) are generally not accountable for their use of public resources or for the quality of their outputs. Poor management practices also help to explain some of the inefficiencies mentioned earlier in this chapter.

The ownership of tertiary institutions has often shifted away from those who should be the main clients (students, employers, and society at large) to control by the teaching staff. The raison d'être for some institutions has become to provide staff employment and benefits rather than to serve as educational establishments focused primarily on the needs of the students and the labor market. Such systems are rigorously guarded by cadres of academic leaders represented in academic councils that operate within a framework of institutional autonomy and are accountable almost exclusively to administrative staff and academics. This deviation of purpose could almost be described as a form of privatization of public institutions to the benefit of specific internal stakeholder groups.

Academic leaders such as rectors, deans, and department heads are rarely trained in the management of large, complex institutions. In most public universities in Latin America and Eastern Europe reform-oriented rectors stand little chance of getting elected because they are perceived as threats to established practices. In some countries the election of rectors takes place after a lengthy and costly campaign plagued with all the problems that can affect elections in the larger world—threats, violence, bribes, and clientelism. In many tertiary systems, when there is a change in leadership the entire management team is replaced, sacrificing institutional continuity.

Often, the management and support systems do not provide guidance in the form of monitoring and evaluation of the institutions' performance. Few institutions have a governance structure allowing for participation by representatives of local employers and civil society. Universities in countries as diverse as Bangladesh, Bolivia, and Russia have no boards of trustees that would constitute an explicit channel for external accountability. Reliance on performance indicators as management and planning tools is not a common practice in most developing countries.

At the national level a stalemate often exists between academically powerful rectors' conferences (or councils) and governments over line-item budgets that are seldom linked to institutional performance or national strategies, reflecting, instead, the needs of regional constituencies. This leads to a political rather than a professional system of management and governance. The consequence is a governance system that lacks flexibility and innovative capacity (since programs are developed to serve the needs of existing staff rather than the country's development goals) and that lacks programmatic accountability because academic autonomy is not paired with financial and legal responsibility. In Nigeria the introduction in 2000 of substantially increased institutional autonomy for universities, following the country's return to democratic government, is designed to combat such rigidities and encourage local management initiatives.

The unhappy situation of deficient governance is often compounded by cumbersome administrative rules and bureaucratic procedures. In many countries the ministry of education determines staffing policy, budgetary allocations, and the number of students admitted, and universities have little say about the number of positions, the level of salaries, or promotions. Brazil's Law of Isonomy establishes uniform salaries for all federal jobs, including those in the federal universities. In many countries lengthy procedures at the level of the ministries of finance and education often cause delays in the transfer of funds to tertiary education institutions. Some Bangladeshi public universities, for example, have been forced to borrow from commercial banks in order to meet monthly salary payments, adding to their institutional deficits. In some of the former socialist republics that face fiscal difficulties, payment of salaries is chronically delayed. These inefficiencies affect the purchase of laboratory equipment; by the time equipment arrives, it may already be obsolete, and some institutions receive their equipment after the courses have ended.

Many countries and institutions have rigid administrative procedures that govern changes in academic structures, programs, and modes of operation. Only when confronted in the mid-1990s with competition from emerging private universities did Uruguay's venerable University of the Republic—which had exercised a monopoly over higher education in the country for 150 years—start a strategic planning process and consider establishing postgraduate programs for the first time. In Venezuela the Instituto de Estudios Superiores de Administración (IESA), a dynamic private business administration institute, had to wait several years to receive official approval from its Council of Rectors for a new MBA program designed and delivered jointly with the top-rated Harvard Business School.

Recently, Nicaragua's Council of Rectors, concerned to protect the country's public universities from foreign competition, denied the University of Mobile (located in the U.S. state of Alabama) a license to operate in Nicaragua. CODECS, Romania's first distance education institution, created in the early 1990s, had trouble gaining recognition of its degrees by the national higher education authorities. It opted instead for an alliance with the U.K. Open University, whose degrees are recognized by the same Romanian authorities. At an April 2000 meeting of the U.S.-based International Association of Management Education, leaders of business schools expressed alarm at the slow and bureaucratic response of their institutions to technological advances and labor market changes.[4]

By contrast, the recent institutional management reforms at Makerere University in Uganda and at the University of Dar es-Salaam in Tanzania (described in Box 4.1 in the next chapter) have yielded positive results and are recognized as among the few recent success stories in African tertiary education. Confronted with an acute financing and quality crisis, the leaders of the two universities brought about remarkable changes by introducing new management structures and implementing alternative financing strategies without government interference. But innovations of this type are not encouraged everywhere. In Bangladesh and Sri Lanka, for example, entrepreneurial spirit is punished de facto in that institutional income generated through tuition fees and other remunerated activities cannot be used by the institution but must be transferred to the finance ministry. Such practices discourage innovation and creative fiscal activity.

Eastern Europe and Central Asia suffer from many similar constraints, but with a different historical context and dynamic. Following the collapse of the state socialist regimes, universities and other tertiary education institutions reclaimed their autonomy from state control. In some cases, protection from government intervention has been guaranteed in the newly revised constitutions. This autonomy, however, has rarely been accompanied by corresponding financial authority or improvements in the institutions' management and strategic planning capabilities. Even university and college leaders have tried to resist the newly gained autonomy for fear that public funding will be reduced. Furthermore, line-item budgeting and limited control over revenues and savings do not provide incentives for adopting medium-term development strategies.

A particular problem of rigidity inherited from the Soviet system is the institutional separation of research and teaching, the former being administered and conducted principally in scientific academies. In countries with this type of binary system, academic doctoral training is assigned to universities, and technical and applied (including teacher training) programs are carried out in colleges, with very limited or no possibilities of partnership or transfer. The separation between education and research and the lack of articulation between different forms of institutions within national systems can seriously compromise the quality and competitiveness of tertiary education.

In some countries students can often muster sufficient political power to block entire systems from functioning over prolonged periods of time. One example occurred in 1999 in Mexico, when the 270,000-student National Autonomous University of Mexico (Universidad Nacional Autónoma de México, UNAM), the country's largest university, was forced to close down for almost an entire year because of a student strike over a proposed increase in tuition fees (see Box 4.3 in the next chapter). Other countries have seen an alarming increase in campus violence that is sometimes politically motivated, as in Colombia, or even the result of criminal activities, as in Bangladesh. In some African countries, particularly in West Africa (Ghana, Nigeria, and Senegal), strong academic staff unions have regularly gone on strike for a year or more to win higher salaries. Such disruptions can severely damage the functioning of the institutions.

Another element of distortion is cheating, which seems to have become more widespread in many settings throughout the world. For example, according to the rector of the Georgian Institute of Foreign Affairs, "corruption has become practically a total form of existence [in the former republics of the Soviet Union]" (MacWilliams 2001). Recent allegations of corruption in Chinese college admissions have tainted the process of student selection (Xueqin 2001). Kenyan authorities in February 2002 claimed to have broken up a ring within the Ministry of Education that had been producing and selling bogus university diplomas, polytechnic certificates, exam results, academic transcripts, and even counterfeit identification documents such as passports.

Finally, student democracy sometimes works against the academic interests of the very students it is intended to protect. In some systems extended campaigning and election periods for student or rector offices can detract from teaching and learning and lead to inefficiencies rather than to better opportunities and improved education for students. One example of the potential negative effects of student democracy can be seen in Nepal, where classes are regularly suspended for at least a month during student elections. Although the growth in the number of private institutions can often be explained by increased demand for tertiary education, in many instances it is a symptom of disenchantment with public universities, which are perceived to be less attractive because of political agitation and resulting poor academic quality.

The next chapter looks at the new challenges facing tertiary education, in particular the growing importance of the marketplace, shifts in the magnitude and character of state support and intervention, and the altered educational landscape produced by globalization and the ICT revolution. It pays particular attention to the proper responsibilities of the state as it moves away from direct provision and funding of tertiary education and toward an enabling and guiding role.

Notes

1. The tertiary enrollment rate measures the proportion of the population in the 18–24 age group that is actually enrolled in a tertiary education institution.

2. See Small and Medium Enterprise Administration, "The Current Status of Labor Utilization in Taiwan's SMEs," <http://www.moeasmea.gov.tw/english/2001whitepaper/C-03.htm>.

3. See NAFSA: Association of International Educators, "Data on International Education," <http://www.nafsa.org/content/PublicPolicy/DataonInternationalEducation/FactSheet.htm>.

4. For example, at Haas School of Business (University of California, Berkeley), it took five years to approve a new master's degree in financial engineering, by which time many competitors had already started to offer similar programs (reported in Mangan 2000).

4

The Changing Nexus:
Tertiary Education Institutions,
the Marketplace, and the State

There is no favorable wind for those who do not know where they are going.

Seneca

This chapter examines the evolving relationship between the marketplace, the state, and tertiary education institutions. The context of these relations has evolved strikingly in recent years, which have seen three major developments: growing system differentiation, changing governance patterns, and diminished direct involvement of governments in the funding and provision of tertiary education. This chapter first describes the key dimensions of the rise of market forces in tertiary education throughout the world and the main implications of this phenomenon. It then articulates the rationale for continuing public intervention in the sector and, in conclusion, outlines the nature of an appropriate enabling framework for the further development of tertiary education.

The Rise of Market Forces in Tertiary Education

As OECD countries enroll increasingly large numbers of students, achieve higher levels of participation in tertiary education, and move toward the goal of lifelong education for all, they are experiencing significant transformations in the structure, governance, and financing of their tertiary systems. This section looks at these changes in OECD countries and then turns to how governments and tertiary education institutions in developing and transition countries are dealing with similar conditions in the shape of financial pressures, expanding demand, and the introduction of private institutions.

The Response in OECD Countries

A major driver for change in OECD countries has been widespread concern about the rising costs of expanded tertiary education systems. Although public funding remains the main source of support for tertiary education in OECD countries, it is being channeled in new ways and supplemented increasingly by nonpublic resources. Of the eight OECD countries for which data are available, private expenditures for tertiary education have grown faster than public expenditures in seven. (France is the exception.) In Canada, Italy, the Netherlands, and Switzerland public expenditures have actually decreased in real terms (OECD 2001).

The changes in the balance of private and public funding bring market forces to bear more directly on tertiary institutions. New financing strategies, for instance, have been put in place to generate business income from institutional assets, to mobilize additional resources from students and their families, and to encourage donations from third-party contributors. Some countries have introduced or raised tuition fees, usually in combination with a student loan scheme (OECD 1998a).[1] Following the example of Japan and the United States, a few countries have encouraged the creation of private institutions. In Portugal private universities have expanded in less than a decade to represent 30 percent of tertiary education institutions, and they enroll close to 40 percent of the total student population.

Another important lever of transformation in OECD countries has been the willingness of governments to make provision of tertiary education more demand driven. Specifically, these countries are encouraging institutions to be more responsive to the new education and training needs of the economy, the shifting demands of employers, and the changing aspirations of students. With these objectives in mind, a number of countries have replaced or supplemented the traditional budget transfer mechanisms with resource allocation formulas pegged to the value of inputs and outputs. This formula-funding approach to budgetary allocation is designed to foster greater institutional autonomy by giving more management discretion to tertiary education institutions in the internal distribution and utilization of their resources. For instance, in Australia, Denmark, New Zealand, and Sweden, where funding is based on actual enrollments, tertiary education institutions have been given more autonomy in allocating resources across faculties, departments, and programs. Formula funding also provides financial incentives for improved institutional performance in relation to national policy goals.

The Rise of Private Institutions in Developing and Transition Countries

Similar trends have been observed in many developing and transition countries. In many regions one legacy of national independence was a state monopoly on tertiary education—a situation that lasted for the better part of three decades. Today, this prevailing "culture of privilege" at public expense is increasingly under pressure to change. The sources of the pressure include the spread of economic liberalism, growing political pluralism, and a rising public demand for tertiary education—a result of demographic growth and of increased access at lower educational levels that has outstripped governments' capacity to pay for provision of education at higher levels. Government funding for tertiary education has declined in relative (and sometimes even absolute) terms, forcing countries and institutions to consider alternative sources of funding and modes of provision. In particular, the growth of private institutions in response to rising demand has been much more rapid in developing countries than in most OECD countries. In many parts of the globe the growing presence of private institutions has drastically altered the traditional pattern of dominant state financing and provision. In Sub-Saharan African countries the number of private sector institutions grew from an estimated 30 in 1990 to more than 85 in 1999.

Much of this expansion has occurred in countries where economic liberalism is now fairly well established, including Kenya (21 institutions), Tanzania (14), Ghana (12), Uganda (11), and Mozambique (5). In Sudan, with eight institutions, and the Democratic Republic of Congo, with six, private provision appears to be a response to a breakdown of government capacity to maintain an effective tertiary system. In contrast to the apparent trend in anglophone countries, private initiatives in the provision of tertiary education have been nearly absent in the French-speaking nations of Africa, with the notable exception of Côte d'Ivoire, where private institutions enroll 30 percent of the student population.

Even though most private universities in Sub-Saharan Africa are quite small, with enrollments ranging from 300 to 1,000 students, this emerging sector is introducing healthy competition, innovation, and managerial efficiency. The resulting diversification of tertiary education may encourage the growth of systems that are more closely attuned to labor market demand and development needs.

In the Middle East and North Africa the growth of private tertiary education has been more recent and less dramatic. In only a handful of countries are shares of enrollments in private institutions significant. Among these countries is the Islamic Republic of Iran, where private tertiary education appeared for the first time in 1983 and where private institutions now enroll more than 30 percent of the total student population. In Jordan private tertiary education is a fairly recent phenomenon (since 1991), but growth in enrollment has been rapid; in 1999 private institutions accounted for 35 percent of total tertiary enrollment.

Most other nations in the region still depend on the state to provide and finance the bulk of tertiary education. But even countries that had an exclusively or predominantly public sector, such as the Arab Republic of Egypt, Morocco, Tunisia, and the Republic of Yemen, have opened up in the past decade. These countries are proceeding cautiously in setting up an institutional framework that will allow for the expanded development of the private tertiary education sector. The Tunisian and Moroccan governments conducted internal discussions for several years before submitting legislation on private higher education to their respective parliaments. In Egypt at the beginning of the 1990s the government revoked the automatic guarantee of a public sector job for university graduates, and it has allowed the operation of private tertiary education institutions. Recently, the heads of state of Oman and the Syrian Arab Republic announced that private providers, including foreign ones, may enter the tertiary education market. The relative reluctance to embrace private tertiary education in the region might be explained by strong opposition from existing public institutions but also by the technical complexity of the issues—notably, quality control, fiscal equity, and relations between public and private institutions—and by fears of foreign influence if the private sector is allowed to expand without appropriate safeguards.

The shift in the balance between the state and the market has been more marked in the former socialist countries of Eastern Europe and Central Asia, where economies have been moving from central planning to liberalization. There were no private tertiary institutions in the region at the beginning of the 1990s, but today close to 350 private institutions operate there, enrolling a quarter-million students. In the Czech Republic, Hungary, Poland, and Romania private sector enrollments expanded from 12,000 students in 1990 to 320,000 in 1997. The average proportion of students in private institutions is 22 percent for the four countries, similar to that in the United States. In Romania 54 private tertiary education institutions, 15 of which are about to receive full accreditation, compete with 57 public institutions.

The emergence of the private sector is even more significant in the former Soviet republics. In Armenia the rapidly growing private sector already amounts to 36 percent of total enrollment. There are more than 100 private institutions in the Kyrgyz Republic and Ukraine, and there are over 300 in Russia, representing one-quarter of all tertiary institutions in that country. Perhaps the most extraordinary example is that of Kazakhstan, where, only two years after private higher education was legalized, 65 private institutions were in operation. Kazakhstan's president recently announced a plan to privatize the entire tertiary education sector over the next five years.

In several countries of South and East Asia private institutions have absorbed most of the demand for tertiary education. In the Philippines and Korea, for instance, the private sector represents 80 and 75 percent of total enrollment, respectively. Until a few years ago, India and Indonesia did not have large private sectors in tertiary education, but today, in both countries, more than half of all students attend private institutions. Even in Bangladesh, where until 1992 private universities were not allowed to operate, enrollments in private tertiary education institutions already account for 15 percent of the country's student population and are growing fast.

A recent study of tertiary education in Latin America and the Caribbean found that the rapid expansion of enrollment and the increased institutional diversification in the region have not been directed by the state but, rather, have come about in response to rising social demand and changing labor markets (IDB 1999). Many countries in the region have experienced an impressive growth of private tertiary education institutions during the past 15 years. In the Dominican Republic and El Salvador the share of student enrollment in the private tertiary education sector rose from about 25 percent in 1970 to about 70 percent in 1996 (García Guadilla 1998). For the region as a whole, enrollment in private institutions represents more than 40 percent of the total student population, the next highest proportion in the world after East Asia.

Financing

The scope of state intervention has diminished in financing as well as provision. Although most cost-sharing efforts take the form of payment of tuition fees by students attending private institutions, public institutions have moved increasingly toward cost sharing, with students being charged fees in one form or another. Such cost sharing can represent between 10 and 30 percent of total costs, depending on the country and the institution. In Russia, for example, an estimated 27 percent of the students paid some fees in 1999, up from 9 percent in 1995. The Czech Republic has shifted a third of the previously highly subsidized costs of meals and accommodations to students and their families.

In Latin America and the Caribbean, fees have been introduced in public universities in Chile (beginning in the early 1980s), some Mexican universities (mid-1990s), and the University of the West Indies (late 1980s). Mongolia and China have introduced fees on a national scale. In an increasing number of countries, including Pakistan and Vietnam, although there are no charges for students who pass the university entrance examination, students who do not achieve high scores yet still want to enroll can do so on a fee-paying basis. In Nepal the Institute of Engineering at the country's flagship tertiary institution, Tribhuvan University, has been a pioneer in imposing substantial cost sharing, coupled with a scholarship scheme for academically qualified students from low-income families. In Nigeria, where university education is provided tuition free, other forms of cost sharing and cost recovery have enabled the proportion of university budgets derived from fee income to grow from 3.6 percent in 1991 to 8.7 percent in 1999 (Hartnett 2000: 13).

Increased Autonomy in Financing and Institutional Policies

Throughout the developing world, many governments have tried to encourage greater autonomy at the institutional level, allowing universities and other tertiary education institutions more freedom to manage their resources and develop proactive income-generation policies. Box 4.1 describes the reforms at the University of Dar es Salaam in Tanzania. Japan's Ministry of Education recently made a significant move to combat institutional rigidity when it granted national universities corporate status and legal personality, with the assurance that their independence would be respected. The aim was to give the universities more flexibility in managing the resources provided through government grants, thus introducing market mechanisms and accountability and obviating the need for them to seek government approval for management actions.[2] The 1998 decision by Chinese authorities to transfer responsibility for university financing to the provinces and the larger municipalities led to significant changes in management practices and increased reliance on resource mobilization efforts. In Indonesia the four leading public universities were granted a new autonomous status at the end of 2000. In Brazil the federal government recently made efforts in that direction, but the initiative met with considerable opposition from the Congress, and the necessary legislation has not yet been passed. In May 2000 Morocco adopted a comprehensive higher education reform law with the aim of promoting university autonomy as a stimulus for improved quality and a better focus on the development needs of the country.

Caveats Regarding Market Forces

In many parts of the world increased competition from private institutions has brought about greater diversity and choice for students and has served as a powerful incentive for public universities to innovate and modernize. Although the influence of market forces is often beneficial, it can have adverse consequences if there is unbridled competition without adequate regulatory and compensatory mechanisms.

Box 4.1 A Successful Management Reform at the University of Dar es Salaam

In 2000 the University of Dar es Salaam introduced an institutional transformation program designed to bring about an overall institutional overhaul under a 15-year corporate strategic plan. Financial reforms included the separation of educational (university) and sponsorship (government) roles; the introduction of a financial information system for recording accounting and procurement activities; the divestiture of noncore services to private entities; the intensification of income-generation activities through a newly established Income Generation Unit; and a shift from block grants to directly paid student sponsorship by the government.

The parallel reform of the administrative structure involved strengthening the university's core roles and shifting noncore services to other entities; changing the composition of the council, senate, and college management boards; decentralizing decisionmaking; articulating more clearly the lines of accountability and responsibility; introducing departmental boards; and institutionalizing a culture of strategic planning. As part of the institutional transformation, core teaching and research functions are to be supported by automating all library activities, strengthening the computing center, conducting an academic audit, and installing a registration and student tracking system.

Among the factors that contributed to the success of the reform were careful planning, leadership commitment, regular reviews by the council, government support, donor assistance, and lessons from reforms in other countries.

Source: Mkude (2001).

To begin with, from an equity perspective, increased institutional choice for students is meaningful only for those who can afford to pay tuition at private institutions or for those with access to financial aid. The absence of scholarship and loan programs can lead to a paradoxical situation in which students from high-income families are overrepresented in the tuition-free public universities and students from low-income families are overrepresented in private, fee-paying universities, as is the case in Bolivia and Venezuela. In Bolivia the proportion of students from the lowest two quintiles who enrolled in private universities grew from 2 percent in 1990 to 14 percent in 1997. In several formerly socialist countries in Eastern Europe, including Russia, the introduction of tuition fees without accompanying student financial aid mechanisms has had a negative effect on equity. Students with limited financial resources are also more vulnerable in time of economic crisis, as evidenced by the sharp (20 percent) drop in tertiary education enrollments in Thailand as a consequence of the 1998–99 financial crisis.

When funding disparities among institutions are too large, it becomes increasingly difficult to maintain competition on equal terms, even in high-income countries. In the United States, for example, rising costs in tertiary education institutions, combined with reduced government budgetary support, have led to growing disparities in financial resources between public and private universities. Of the top 20 U.S. universities (*U.S. News and World Report* rankings for 2001), only two, the University of California at Berkeley and the University of Michigan, are public universities. A major factor in this evolution, as revealed by a recent survey (Smallwood 2001), is the mounting salary gap between private and public universities, making it difficult for the latter to attract the best professors and researchers. One coping strategy for public universities has been to rely increasingly on nonregular or adjunct teaching staff for undergraduate courses, thereby creating a second tier of teachers with precarious employment status and substandard remuneration.

In a global labor market for faculty, higher salaries in the universities of one country may have a negative impact on tertiary education institutions in other parts of the world and thus contribute to the brain drain described in Chapter 1. Not even top universities in Europe are immune to this threat, as is illustrated by recent complaints by British university leaders that they are no longer able to offer competitive salaries to attract eminent specialists into the academic profession (Adam 2001).

Differing Forms of Private Institutions: For-Profit and Nonprofit

Not all private institutions operate under the same regulations. While many private tertiary institutions are profit-making corporations subject to pure market mechanisms and corporate tax laws, many others are nonprofit institutions operating in countries where the laws permit the registration of corporations with special status. Nonprofit institutions differ from for-profit institutions in that they operate under a special financial requirement (a "nondistribution constraint") forbidding them to distribute surplus revenue or profits to shareholders or individuals. Any such funds must be retained within the institution for capital investment, future operating expenses, or endowments. Nonprofit tertiary education institutions often enjoy tax exemptions on surplus income and other revenue, depending on the particular country's laws. Some theorists believe that nonprofits combine market benefits with a certain social sensitivity and that the lack of a profit motive encourages them to offer fields of study that are valuable to society (the arts, the humanities, and the social sciences) but that may not be commercially lucrative. It is also suggested that the regulatory status of nonprofits may help protect underfunded disciplines, such as expensive programs in medicine and engineering, by encouraging cross-subsidy through the recycling of financial surpluses to the more costly programs. In several Latin American countries, including Colombia and Peru, private universities are able to charge higher fees for prestige professional programs in law and accounting while subsidizing more costly disciplines such as engineering.

Nonprofits may stimulate greater private philanthropy in education by signaling to donors that investments will not be used for the private gain of trustees or owners. Tax codes can encourage private largesse by exempting philanthropic donations from taxation.

Some studies show that consumers and governments are more likely to trust nonprofit corporations over for-profit enterprises in the delivery of public goods such as education and health care. Many countries permit private for-profit and private nonprofit tertiary institutions to operate side by side, with the understanding that both types of institution have benefits and drawbacks and that a mix of institutional forms helps diversify the tertiary system. It is important for countries to focus their energies on effective quality assurance mechanisms, to be applied equally to all tertiary institutions regardless of their form—whether public or private, for-profit or nonprofit.

Rationale for State Intervention

Public goods, quasi public goods, and externalities are fairly common in the real world. They are common enough that it is necessary to take proposals for government intervention in the economy on a case-by-case basis. Government action can never be ruled in or ruled out on principle. Only with attention to detail and prudent judgment based on the facts of the case can we hope to approach an optimal allocation of resources. That means the government will always have a full agenda for reform—and in some cases, as in deregulation, that will mean undoing the actions of government in an earlier generation. This is not evidence of failure but of an alert, active government aware of changing circumstances.

Paul Krugman (1996)

As was noted earlier, the traditionally predominant role of the state in the financing and provision of tertiary education was rooted in political and economic circumstances that have now radically changed. Developing countries are rapidly moving from small, elite systems toward expanded tertiary education systems. This massification process has often outstripped government ability to finance it, leading to erosion of educational quality. Even in transition economies, where universities and research institutes had traditionally been strong, the process of modernizing tertiary education systems has been hampered by diminished fiscal resources and competing claims from other sectors. This has severely affected the countries' ability to support tertiary education to the same extent and in the same manner as before. Again, rapid loss of educational quality at the tertiary level has been an inevitable consequence.

Although governments cannot keep up with all the fiscal demands of offering ever higher quality tertiary education, they have at least three strong reasons for supporting the sector:

• Investments in tertiary education generate external benefits essential for economic and social development. These benefits, including long-term returns from basic research and technology development and the social gains accruing from the construction of more cohesive societies, transcend the private benefits captured by individuals.

• Capital markets are characterized by imperfections and information asymmetries that constrain the ability of individuals to borrow adequately for education. These imperfections have adverse equity and efficiency consequences, undermining the participation of academically qualified but economically disadvantaged groups in tertiary education.

• Tertiary education plays a key role in support of basic and secondary education, buttressing the economic externalities produced by the lower levels of education.

Externalities

Despite the methodological difficulties involved in measuring externalities, it can be shown that tertiary education produces an array of important economic and social benefits (see Table 4.1, on page 81). Public economic benefits reflect the overall contribution of tertiary education institutions and graduates to economic growth beyond the income and employment gains accruing to individuals. As discussed in Chapter 2, in economies that rely increasingly on the generation and application of knowledge, greater productivity is achieved through the development and diffusion of technological innovations, most of which are the products of basic and applied research undertaken in universities. Progress in the agriculture, health, and environment sectors, in particular, is heavily dependent on the application of such innovations. Productivity is also boosted by higher skill levels in the labor force and by qualitative improvements that enable workers to use new technology. Increased workforce flexibility, resulting from the acquisition of general skills that facilitate adaptation, is increasingly seen as a crucial factor in economic development in the context of knowledge economies. Sustainable transformation and growth throughout the economy are not possible without the contributions of an innovative tertiary education system, which helps build the absorptive capacity needed if private sector investment and donor resources are to have a lasting productive impact.

In addition to its overall contribution to economic growth, tertiary education has broad economic, fiscal, and labor market effects:

- The existence of universities and nonuniversity training institutions is important to regional development, through both direct linkages and spillover effects. The successful experiences of technology-intensive poles such as Silicon Valley in California, Bangalore in India's Karnataka State, Shanghai in China, and Campinas in São Paulo State, Brazil, attest to the strongly positive effects that the clustering of advanced human capital alongside leading technology firms can have. East Asia has several examples of technology-intensive poles, including the Daeduck Research Complex in Korea, Tsukuba Science Town in Japan, and the Hsinchu Science-Based Industrial Park in Taiwan (China) (Shin 2001). A similar pattern has been observed in human capital–intensive countries such as Singapore and Finland.
- Econometric studies undertaken by the U.S. Bureau of Labor Statistics have shown that the overall growth in consumption in the United States over the past 40 years is correlated with the general increase in educational levels, even after controlling for income (IHEP 1998: 14).
- There are indications from several OECD countries, including the United States and Canada, that increased participation in tertiary education is correlated with reduced dependence on government financial support for medical and social welfare services (housing, unemployment, food stamps, and so on).
- The population with tertiary education is more likely to contribute to an expanded tax base.

Turning to public social benefits, tertiary education promotes nation building through its contributions to increased social cohesion, trust in social institutions, democratic participation and open debate, and appreciation of diversity in gender, ethnicity, religion, and social class. Pluralistic and democratic societies need the kinds of research and analysis that are fostered through social science and humanities programs. Tertiary education may contribute to reduced crime rates and corruption and to an increased community service orientation, as manifested in philanthropic donations, support for NGOs, and charity work. There are also strong social benefits from tertiary education associated with improved health behaviors and outcomes (Wolfe and Zuvekas 1997).

When looking at the public benefits of tertiary education, it is important to highlight the existence of joint-product effects linked to the complementarities between undergraduate and postgraduate education and between tertiary education and lower levels of education. Although many undergraduate and professional education programs can be conducted in separate institutions—especially low-cost training in fields like business and law that are primarily private goods and are easily offered by private sector providers able to charge full cost—high-cost activities such as basic research and various types of specialized graduate training are more efficiently organized in combination with undergraduate training (Birdsall 1996). The high degree of cross-subsidization across disciplines, programs, and levels of study makes it difficult to look at the public-good components of tertiary education institutions in isolation from other activities. In addition, economies of scale can justify public support of expensive programs, such as those in basic sciences, that are almost natural monopolies.

Capital Market Imperfections

Although more than 60 countries have student loan programs, access to affordable loans frequently remains restricted to a minority of students. The loans are not necessarily available to the students with limited resources who are in greatest need of financial aid. Except for rich economies such as Australia, Canada, New Zealand, Sweden, the United Kingdom, and the United States, few countries have national programs that reach a large proportion of students (Salmi 2000). Even where there is national coverage, top universities may remain out of reach for a significant proportion of low-income students, as indicated by a recent survey of student aid programs in the United States. That report, prepared by the Lumina Foundation, a research organization specializing in student aid issues, concludes that despite the wide range of funding options available to students, most private colleges and universities and a majority of top public institutions are not accessible for low-income students without "extraordinary financial sacrifice" (Lumina Foundation 2002). Colombia's ICETEX, the first modern student loan institution, established in 1950, has never managed to reach more than 12 percent of the student population. It has been struggling for financial survival in recent years, with coverage falling to less than 6 percent in 2001.

Where they do exist, student loans are not always available for the whole range of academic programs and disciplines. Under the innovative student loan scheme recently set up by the Mexican federation of private universities, for instance, loan eligibility is restricted to degree programs with a high market value such as engineering, business management, and law. They are not available for important disciplines in the arts and social sciences that are associated with less favorable labor market outcomes but have a potentially high social value.

Support of Primary and Secondary Education

Tertiary education institutions play a key role in support of basic and secondary education, and there is a need for more effective links among all levels of education. In fact, it is doubtful that any developing country could make significant progress toward achieving the United Nations Millennium Development Goals for education—universal enrollment in primary education and elimination of gender disparities in primary and secondary education—without a strong tertiary education system. Preservice and in-service training of teachers and school principals, from preschool to the upper secondary level, is primarily the responsibility of tertiary education institutions. Education specialists with tertiary education qualifications and university personnel participate in curriculum reform and design, in policy research and evaluation for all levels of the education system, and in setting questions for secondary school leaving examinations. In some countries, including Japan, Korea, Mexico, Nepal, and the United States, universities are even directly involved in the management of primary and secondary schools. U.S. President George W. Bush's 2002 education plan provides funding to encourage the formation of partnerships between lower-level schools and colleges and universities to improve mathematics and science instruction. In Uganda a transformed Makerere University was asked by the government in 2001 to assist in the training of local officials to improve decentralized service delivery in the social sectors. In the field of health, medical education, especially the training of medical doctors, epidemiologists, public health specialists, and hospital managers, is essential for meeting the basic Millennium Development Goals. (See Box 4.2 for an account of an initiative to improve basic health provision in Uganda.)

The linkages between tertiary education and the lower levels of schooling are multifaceted. Many dimensions of inequity at the tertiary level are conditioned by the access and opportunities available to various groups in primary and secondary education. The quality of tertiary education institutions and programs is strongly determined by the quality of secondary school graduates. Conversely, the terms of access to tertiary education institutions can influence the content and methods of teaching and learning at the high school level in a powerful way. Under conditions of severe competition for entrance into elite colleges and universities, admission criteria can significantly alter the behavior of both students and teachers in secondary schools. In most countries the content of previous examination papers, rather than the official curriculum, tends to dictate what is taught and how it is taught—and, more important, what is learned and how it is learned. Because in many countries (for example, Korea and Singapore) "elite" universities tend to select students primarily on the basis of test scores, schools and students often

Box 4.2 Leveraging Traditional Systems and Modern Knowledge to Achieve Uganda's Goals for Health

Uganda is one of the least urbanized countries in Africa; more than 80 percent of its 20 million inhabitants live in rural areas. The fertility rate is high (6.9), but only about 38 percent of all births are attended by trained health workers who have completed specialized tertiary education. The remaining 62 percent of births are attended by practically experienced but untrained traditional birth attendants (TBAs) and by relatives. The lack of trained health care workers at the tertiary level is a significant problem in a country where the maternal mortality rate (MMR) is very high, an estimated 506 maternal deaths per 100,000 births.

Uganda's Ministry of Health has chosen to address this problem partly through improvement of communications between trained health care professionals and TBAs. This initiative is being supported through the Rural Extended Services and Care for Ultimate Emergency Relief (RESCUER) project, launched in March 1996 as a pilot program. RESCUER has three components—communication, transportation, and health services delivery—that depend explicitly on highly trained health care specialists.

Uganda's rural areas are beset by classic communication problems: lack of telephone wiring, of electric current, and of enough trained health care professionals to staff all localities. Solar-powered VHF radio was identified as the means of communication that offered the broadest coverage and could link to sufficient numbers of rural community health care providers. The use of radio communications made possible an increase in the number of deliveries attended by trained personnel, and the provision of transportation services led to a rise in referrals to health units. Together, these brought about a 50 percent reduction in MMR within three years in the communities surveyed.

The RESCUER program is an elegant merger of traditional practice with modern knowledge and technology that has improved maternal health and has generated social capital by networking midwives who had been working in isolation. Interviews with the TBAs showed that the radio technology, combined with the advice of trained health care professionals, resulted in empowerment, enhanced image and local credibility of TBAs, improved patient compliance with directives, alleviation of TBAs' isolation, a reduction in delivery complications, and less panic in complicated deliveries, as well as higher TBA incomes because of the increased numbers of patients served.

Source: Musoke (2002).

focus their time and efforts on the acquisition of the narrow skills needed to pass college admission tests. This happens at the expense of generic competencies such as creative thinking, problem solving, and interpersonal and communication skills, which are increasingly valuable in an age of rapidly changing technologies.

The role of tertiary education in support of the overall education system is bound to become even more important as countries move from the universalization of basic education to the progressive massification of secondary education and become stricter in demanding mandatory tertiary education qualifications for primary and secondary school teachers. In Brazil, for instance, under federal legislation passed in 1997, by 2007 all teachers will be required to be tertiary education graduates. A teacher certification system is being developed to enforce this requirement, following the example of OECD countries such as Australia and the United States.

Although the mechanisms through which tertiary education contributes to social and economic development are not fully understood and precise measures of these contributions are not available, a preliminary effort can be made to map the interactions, as Table 4.1 illustrates.

Table 4.1 Potential Benefits from Tertiary Education

Benefits	Private	Public
Economic	Higher salaries	Greater productivity
	Employment	National and regional development
	Higher savings	Reduced reliance on government financial support
	Improved working conditions	Increased consumption
	Personal and professional mobility	Increased potential for transformation from low-skill industrial to knowledge-based economy
Social	Improved quality of life for self and children	Nation building and development of leadership
	Better decisionmaking	Democratic participation; increased consensus; perception that the society is based on fairness and opportunity for all citizens
	Improved personal status	Social mobility
	Increased educational opportunities	Greater social cohesion and reduced crime rates
	Healthier lifestyle and higher life expectancy	Improved health
		Improved basic and secondary education

Source: Adapted from IHEP (1998): 20.

Determining the Appropriate Level of Support

The existence of these important public economic and social benefits indicates that the costs of insufficient investment in tertiary education can be very high. These costs can include a reduced ability of a country to compete effectively in the global and regional economies; growth in economic and social disparities; declines in the quality of life, in health status, and in life expectancy; rising public expenditures on social welfare programs; and a deterioration of social cohesion.

At the same time, the need to consider the education system as a whole demands a comprehensive approach to resource allocation. While there is no magic number defining the "correct" proportion of resources to be devoted to tertiary education, certain guidelines can be applied to ensure a balanced distribution of budgetary resources and a sequencing of investment across the three subsectors of the education system that is appropriate to a given country's level of educational development, pattern of economic growth, and fiscal situation. Looking at the experience of OECD countries that have emphasized the role of education in supporting economic growth and social cohesion, it would seem that an appropriate range for the overall level of investment in education as a share of GDP would be between 4 and 6 percent. Expenditures on tertiary education would then generally represent between 15 and 20 percent of public education expenditures. Developing countries that devote more than 20 percent of their education budget to tertiary education (as do Bolivia, Egypt, Jordan, Swaziland, Togo, and Venezuela), and especially those countries that have not achieved universal primary education coverage (Mauritania and Niger, for example), are likely to have a distorted allocation that favors an elitist university system and does not adequately support basic and secondary education. Countries such as Senegal that spend more than 20 percent of their tertiary education budget on noneducational expenditures such as student subsidies are underinvesting in nonsalary pedagogical inputs that are crucial for quality learning.

An examination of the patterns of public spending on tertiary education in East Asia shows dramatic variation. Except for Hong Kong (China) and Singapore, the economies of the region appear to spend, on average, relatively less on tertiary education than on primary and secondary education. In the mid-1990s (1994 or 1995) public expenditure on tertiary education as a share of total government expenditure on education was 15.6 in China, 37.1 percent in Hong Kong (China), 11.4 percent in Indonesia, 12.1 percent in Japan, 8 percent in Korea, 16.8 percent in Malaysia and in the Philippines, 34.8 percent in Singapore, and 19.4 percent in Thailand (World Bank 2001b).

The Evolving Role of the State: Guidance through an Enabling Framework and Appropriate Incentives

There is no prescription for how a country creates such a culture [of knowledge] . . . But government does have a role—a role in education, in encouraging the kind of creativity and risk taking that the scientific entrepreneurship requires, in creating the institutions that facilitate ideas being brought into fruition, and a regulatory and tax environment that rewards this kind of activity.

Joseph E. Stiglitz, Nobel Prize lecture, 2001

Developing countries and transition economies face both the new challenge of supporting knowledge-driven development and the old challenge of promoting quality, efficiency, and equity in tertiary education. Given the severe fiscal and budgetary constraints affecting governments' capacity to sustain past levels of direct provision and financing of tertiary education, as well as the rise of market forces at both national and international levels, the purpose, scope, and modalities of public intervention are changing in significant ways. Instead of relying on the traditional state control model to impose reforms, countries are choosing increasingly to bring about change by guiding and encouraging tertiary education institutions, whether public or private, in a noncontrolling, flexible manner. This can be achieved in three complementary ways:

- By establishing a coherent policy framework
- By creating an enabling regulatory environment
- By offering appropriate financial incentives.

Figure 4.1 illustrates how the regulatory framework and the types of incentives used by the state interact with market forces and civil society to beget better performance and greater responsiveness among tertiary education institutions. Starting from the observation made in *World Development Report 1997* that changes in government rules and constraints are not sufficient to bring about reforms in an effective manner, the proposed analytical framework stresses the significance of three categories of mechanisms that together bear on the behavior and results of tertiary education institutions: state regulations and financial incentives; participation and partnerships with industry, civil society, and professional associations; and competition among tertiary education providers (public and private, university and nonuniversity, campus-based and virtual, and so on).

In the past the dominant role of the government in the financing and provision of tertiary education in most countries translated into a relatively simple relationship between the state and tertiary education institutions. Depending on country conditions, this relationship was characterized either by a high degree of centralized control or by a great deal of institutional autonomy. Today, the growing competition for resources and customers in the context of a global education market is producing a much more complex interplay of forces that requires proper consideration in order to understand how the transformation of tertiary education systems and institutions takes place and what levers the state and society can use to promote change.

Establishing a Coherent Policy Framework

The first step for countries and tertiary education institutions willing to take advantage of the new opportunities presented by the knowledge economy and the ICT revolution is to question the relevance of their existing structures and procedures. They cannot afford to remain pas-

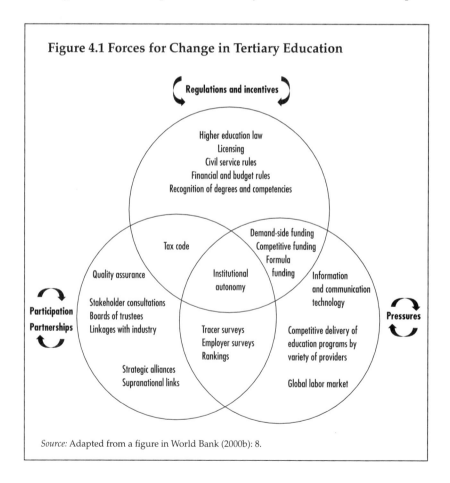

Figure 4.1 Forces for Change in Tertiary Education

Regulations and incentives

Higher education law
Licensing
Civil service rules
Financial and budget rules
Recognition of degrees and competencies

Tax code

Demand-side funding
Competitive funding
Formula
funding

Quality assurance

Institutional
autonomy

Information
and communication
technology

Participation

Stakeholder consultations
Boards of trustees
Linkages with industry

Pressures

Partnerships

Tracer surveys
Employer surveys
Rankings

Competitive delivery of
education programs by
variety of providers

Strategic alliances
Supranational links

Global labor market

Source: Adapted from a figure in World Bank (2000b): 8.

sive but must be proactive in fostering innovations and launching meaningful reforms within a coherent policy framework. Although no rigid blueprint exists that is valid for all countries and institutions, a common prerequisite may be the formulation of a clear vision for the long-term development of a comprehensive, diversified, and well-articulated tertiary education system. This implies at least three dimensions: (a) outlining how the tertiary education system can most effectively contribute to national growth in the context of a globally articulated knowledge-based economy; (b) agreeing on the roles of different types of institutions within that system; and (c) determining the conditions under which the new technologies can be harnessed to improve the effectiveness and expansion of the learning experience. Many initiatives have been undertaken to develop such a vision at the national level, in both industrial and developing countries. The more recent examples come from the United Kingdom (the Dearing Report, 1997); New Zealand (the Tertiary Education Green Paper, 1998, and the Report of the Special Task Force, 2001); France (Plan for the University of the Third Millennium, 2000); Spain (the Bricall Report, 2000); South Africa (Report of the Council on Higher Education, 2000); Australia (An Agenda for the Knowledge Economy, 2001); and India (India as Knowledge Superpower: Strategy for Transformation, 2001).

The design of a tertiary education development strategy needs to reflect a comprehensive approach that integrates all the elements constituting a diversified tertiary system into a coherent, long-term vision of the mission of tertiary education as a whole and of the respective roles of each type of institution. One of the key decisions each country needs to make relates to the optimal size and shape of its tertiary education system and the choice of an appropriate strategy for raising enrollment, given the prevailing constraints on public resources. As a way of achieving quantitative expansion without sacrificing quality, countries should seek to differentiate further the provision of higher learning by encouraging a variety of institutions—public and private, large and small, universities and nonuniversity institutions, short- and medium-duration programs, liberal arts and technological institutions, research-based and scholarship institutions, campus-based and distance education programs, and so forth.

Tertiary institutions, which were once focused on training civil servants, must recognize that they are no longer producing graduates simply for public sector and civil service jobs. An increasing proportion of tertiary graduates seek work in the private sector and, in particular, the service sector. This is certainly the case in South Asia and in the Middle East and North Africa, where in the past most graduates could expect to be employed in public sector positions. But although opportunities in the private sector are increasing, private sector employment is less predictable and less secure than public employment. Tertiary education institutions and entire tertiary systems must become increasingly agile in responding to changes in the labor market. A diverse system that includes a strong set of private providers and autonomous public providers of tertiary education affords the necessary flexibility.

Increased differentiation does not necessarily imply increased segmentation of institutions and students. On the contrary, within a lifelong-learning perspective with the emphasis on responsiveness to new training demands and a more diversified clientele, student mobility can be encouraged by removing barriers to articulation among the segments of the tertiary education system, among institutions within each segment, and among disciplines and programs within institutions. The promotion of open systems can be achieved through recognition of relevant prior professional and academic experience, degree equivalencies, credit transfer, tuition exchange schemes, access to national scholarships and student loans, and creation of comprehensive qualifications frameworks like those being established in Ireland and New Zealand.[3] Multiple pathways linking secondary education, both general and vocational, to tertiary education are also needed; examples include remedial courses (such as those offered in community colleges) and bridge courses on fundamental subjects, particularly in mathematics and science. It should be noted that removal of the barriers between sectors and segments of the tertiary education system often encounters resistance because, among other reasons, increased mobility can sometimes result in a reduced share of public funding for the more privileged university sector.

Last, but not least, important for the development of a country's tertiary education vision and the necessary policy framework is consideration of the political economy of reform. Translating a vision into successful reforms and innovations depends on the ability of decision-makers to build consensus among the diverse constituents of the tertiary education community, allowing for a high degree of tolerance for controversies and disagreements (see Box 4.3). A potentially effective approach for addressing the political sensitivity of the proposed reforms is to initiate a wide consultation process concerning the need for and content of the envisaged changes. This effort involves a blend of rational analysis, political maneuvering, and psychological interplay to bring all the concerned stakeholders on board. Involving potential opponents in the policy discussion process carries risks. In Hungary, for instance, lack of success in building a consensus on the vision for tertiary education developed in the mid-1990s has resulted in poor implementation of the proposed reforms. In South Africa implementation of the tertiary education reform announced in February 2001—the culmination of four years of national consultations involving wide political debates based on the initial work of expert committees—has been stalled by the political resistance of some constituencies. Yet ignoring the opposition altogether is a recipe for failure.

Creating an Enabling Regulatory Environment

The second important responsibility of government is to create a regulatory environment that encourages rather than stifles innovations in public institutions and initiatives by the private sector to expand access to good-quality tertiary education. Key dimensions of sector regulation include the legislative framework governing the establishment of new institutions, especially private and virtual universities; quality assurance mechanisms for all types of institutions; the administrative and financial rules and controls to which public institutions are required to conform; and legislation on intellectual property rights.

In countries with limited public resources for sustaining the expansion of tertiary education, private provision can expand educational opportunity at little or no direct public cost. Governments can encour-

---

Box 4.3 Consensus Building and Cost Sharing in Northern Mexico

The Mexican constitution provides for free public education at all levels, and cost sharing has always been fiercely resisted by the professors and students of the country's largest public university, the National Autonomous University of Mexico (UNAM). In 1999 the university was closed for almost a year by a strike supported by the majority of its 270,000 students after the rector suggested a US$100 increase in tuition fees, from US$8 a year.

In northern Mexico, by contrast, the rector of the University of Sonora was successful in introducing cost sharing after initiating, in 1993, a consensus-building process to explain to the staff and students the need for supplementary resources to maintain the quality of teaching and learning. After some initial resistance, including a widely publicized 2,000-kilometer march by protesters from Hermosillo to Mexico City, the students accepted the principle of a yearly payment to generate supplementary resources. A participatory process was to determine the allocation of these resources to equity and quality-improvement initiatives. Since 1994, the students have been paying an annual contribution of about US$300 for this purpose. A joint student-faculty committee administers the funds, which are used to provide scholarships for low-income students, renovate classrooms, upgrade computer labs, and purchase scientific textbooks and journals. A poster is prepared every year to disseminate information on the use of the money collected at the beginning of the academic year.

age the growth of good-quality private tertiary education institutions as a means of increasing the diversity of program offerings and broadening participation. For this to happen, it is important to remove cumbersome administrative requirements that constitute entry barriers in countries with little tradition of private tertiary education. In Spain, for instance, private universities must comply with stringent rules regarding, among other things, the number of academic programs offered, the student-teacher ratio, the proportion of full-time professors, and their academic qualifications. By contrast, in Chile the only requirement for a new university to start operating is approval of its curriculum plans and programs by an examining public university. Any direct concern with quality assurance should be deferred to accreditation bodies, not embedded in the laws that give tertiary institutions legal personality. Countries should aim for straightforward licensing procedures that outline minimum safety and educational requirements, complemented by effective quality assurance mechanisms that focus on the outputs of the new institutions.

Conscious that independent assessment is the best way to help set and maintain high standards in increasingly differentiated tertiary systems, a growing number of countries have established evaluation or accreditation bodies to promote higher-quality teaching and learning. Depending on the context, systematic modes of quality control and enhancement can take different forms. The most common approach has been a national evaluation or independent accreditation agency with authority over both public and private tertiary education institutions. In Africa Nigeria has conducted periodic accreditation assessments for 25 years, Ghana established a National Accreditation Board in 1993, and South Africa is currently engaged in a major exercise to reform its qualifications framework and adapt it to the requirements of the 21st century. In Latin America accreditation agencies have recently been created in Argentina, Chile, Colombia, and El Salvador. In the Middle East Jordan has pioneered the establishment of a national evaluation body. In Asia Indonesia was one of the first countries to create a quality assurance system, and even poorer countries with less developed tertiary education systems are following suit, as exemplified by Cambodia's current efforts to set up an accreditation committee. In Eastern and Central Europe, Hungary, Romania, Poland, and Slovenia have taken the lead in quality assurance efforts.

Notwithstanding the diversity of organizational setups among countries, corresponding to their specific needs and institutional frameworks, there are emerging areas of consensus on what constitutes an appropriate system of quality assurance aimed at discouraging ineffective educational practices and reinforcing positive ones. The core elements of quality assurance include reliance on semiautonomous agencies; agreement on explicit standards and expectations; an initial self-study by the academic department, faculty, or institution concerned to complement an external review conducted by visiting peers; preparation of written recommendations; public reporting of the results; and recognition that the evaluation process in itself is at least as important as the results (El-Khawas, DePietro-Jurand, and Holm-Nielsen 1998).

Self-evaluation can promote a sense of institutional responsibility by allowing teachers and administrators, with student inputs, to identify areas of strengths and weaknesses and propose corrective actions in the form of a plan for institutional self-improvement. This process can be enhanced by independent assessments carried out by a professional association or a government oversight agency. Quality assurance mechanisms should preferably apply to both public and private tertiary education institutions, to create a level playing field.

Areas of debate surrounding quality assurance processes remain. Among them are whether accreditation should apply to specific courses or programs or whether entire institutions should be evaluated; whether accreditation should be voluntary or mandatory; whether performance indicators should be closely linked to financial rewards; and whether the same evaluation modalities should be used for different segments of the tertiary education system and different delivery modes (in-person teaching, distance education, and online programs). Clearly, with the increased focus on lifelong learning and multiple learning paths and the expansion of nontraditional educational modalities, there is an irreversible trend toward evaluation approaches that emphasize learning outcomes and acquired competencies of students over the input and process aspects of education. International experience also shows that, rather than impose rigid, punitive evaluation mechanisms, it is more effective to put in place flexible systems under which only licensing is compulsory, in order to guarantee minimum academic and public safety requirements, while accreditation and evaluation are designed as voluntary activities that can be encouraged through public information, financial incentives, and nonmonetary rewards. Table 4.2 summarizes the status of quality assurance systems, highlighting a pattern of unequal development across regions.

After quality assurance, institutional autonomy is a key element in the successful transformation of public tertiary education institutions. Autonomous institutions are more responsive to incentives for quality improvement, resource diversification, and efficient use of available resources. Tertiary education institutions must be in a position to exercise meaningful control over the principal factors affecting the quality and costs of their own programs. Autonomy includes among its many characteristics the ability of each institution to set its own admission requirements, determine the size of its student body, assess tuition and

Table 4.2 Quality Assurance Systems Worldwide

Region	National evaluation or accreditation system present
Eastern Europe and Central Asia	Bulgaria, Czech Rep., Estonia, Hungary, Latvia, Lithuania, Mongolia, Poland, Romania, Russia, Slovak Rep., Slovenia
East Asia and Pacific	Australia, Hong Kong (China), Indonesia, Japan, Rep. of Korea, Malaysia, New Zealand, Philippines, Singapore
Latin America and the Caribbean	Argentina, Belize, Bolivia, Brazil, Chile, Colombia , Costa Rica, El Salvador, Mexico, Nicaragua
Middle East and North Africa	Israel, Jordan
South Asia	India
Sub-Saharan Africa	Côte d'Ivoire, Ghana, Kenya, Mauritius, Namibia, Nigeria, South Africa
Western Europe and North America	Austria, Belgium, Canada, Denmark, Finland, France, Germany, Iceland, Ireland, Italy, Netherlands, Portugal, United Kingdom, United States

Source: World Bank data.

fees, and establish eligibility criteria for financial assistance to needy students. Institutions must also be free to determine their own employment conditions, such as hiring and staff remuneration, so that they can be responsive to new and rapidly changing labor market demands. Finally, institutions must have independent fiscal control, including the ability to reallocate resources internally according to self-determined criteria. Many countries deny institutions such control because of popular, but rigid, line-item budget systems. Independent fiscal control is necessary so that institutions can strengthen weak academic units, cross-subsidize programs, and fund new initiatives quickly and flexibly in response to evolving needs.

The mushrooming of virtual institutions, online education programs, and Internet-based courses raises challenging issues of intellectual property rights and academic freedom with respect to the ownership and control of educational materials developed exclusively for online or multimedia dissemination. The lack of clarity in the definition of ownership rights and in the rules for use of new educational materials can pit academics against their home institutions or against the institution contracting them to prepare course materials for online dissemination or broadcasting. Recent controversies in the United States have involved the ownership of online courses, which has become a problematic issue debated in negotiations on the renewal of faculty collective bargaining agreements.[4] Many tertiary education institutions insist on retaining sole ownership of all online and Web courses created by their professors. Some universities, however, such as the University of North Texas, not only recognize ownership of online courses by their creators but also encourage professors to develop such courses through monetary incentives, including royalties, licensing fees, and a share of tuition fees paid by distance education students (Young 2001). The University of Vermont has even considered splitting the ownership of online courses into a content part, belonging to the professor, and an instructional design part, controlled by the university staff (Carnevale 2001). MIT's decision in 2000 to make all of its course content and materials available free of charge online is likely to influence the debate at other institutions. In many developing countries and transition economies there may be a need for the active involvement of the state in defining clear rules and mechanisms for the recognition and protection of the respective intellectual property rights of tertiary education institutions and professors.

Distance education and open universities hold out the promise of increasing coverage and facilitating access to tertiary education. As with any emerging institution, whether for-profit or nonprofit, there must be not only a realistic business plan but also an appropriate regulatory framework and institutional acceptance to improve the chances of success. (See Box 4.4, on the failure of a U.S. distance education institution.)

Because of the rapidly growing utilization of ITC in tertiary education, the level of development of the national telecommunication infrastructure and its pricing structure have a significant impact on the ability of tertiary education institutions to harness the potential of the technologies. Where the telecommunication sector has not been deregulated—for example, in the Caribbean area and in many countries of Sub-Saharan Africa—prices can be very high, and the quality of services often remains below international standards.

Offering Appropriate Financial Incentives

Government funding is likely to remain the dominant source of financing for tertiary education institutions in most countries. Financial incentives can be applied creatively to steer tertiary education institutions more effectively toward compliance with quality, efficiency, and equity goals.

To create incentives for fiscal efficiency, many OECD members and some developing countries such as Ethiopia and South Africa have abandoned the traditional approach of "negotiated" budgets, which are generally based on historical trends and political influence. These countries now favor alternative mechanisms that link funding to performance in

---

Box 4.4 The Failure of the United States Open University

The United States Open University (USOU), which began operation in
2000 on the model of the U.K. Open University, failed to achieve fiscal
solvency. It was forced to close at the end of academic year 2002 for two
critical reasons: lack of accreditation, and failure to qualify for student
financial aid from public sources.

The USOU had a business plan that was perhaps overoptimistic, pre-
dicting wide acceptance of its program through name recognition and
affiliation with the well-known U.K. Open University and with established traditional American universities such as the University of Mary-
land and Indiana State University. Accreditation was anticipated by May
2002 but that prospect did not generate enough public confidence in the
program to attract sufficient numbers of students. The delay in accreditation may have been critical as a signal to students of the program's quality and the value of USOU credentials. Moreover, the ineligibility of
USOU students for financial aid prevented needy students from paying
tuition through public subsidy, an important element in the financing of
U.S. higher education.

Source: Chronicle of Higher Education, February 10, 2002.

---

one way or another. A more transparent and objective way to distribute
funds for recurrent expenditures uses a formula linking the amount of
resources spent on inputs such as the number of students or professors
to some indicator of institutional performance such as the number of
graduates. Some U.S. states, including Arkansas, Kentucky, South Car-
olina, and Tennessee, have experimented with an approach based on the
benchmarking of their tertiary education institutions against reference
universities and colleges in other states. In Ontario, Canada, the funding
of community colleges is linked to the outcome of key performance indicators that measure the degree of satisfaction of students, graduates, and
employers with the quality and relevance of the colleges' programs and
services.

It is important to note that no single ideal formula exists that is valid
for all countries under all circumstances. Rather, each country, province,
or state must choose an allocation mechanism consistent with the goals
and priorities of its tertiary education development strategy and must be
prepared to make changes over time as these goals and priorities evolve.
In Poland, for instance, when a funding formula was introduced at the
beginning of the 1990s to bolster quality in public universities, one of the
main parameters in the funding equation was the number of full-time
professors holding a doctorate. The government was successful in promoting an active training and recruitment policy for all universities, and

academic qualifications rose significantly. But in recent years university leaders have observed that the funding formula does not take into account part-time professionals who are needed to teach classes in key science and technology–related subjects. It is now recognized that the funding formula must be modified accordingly.[5]

Governments can also encourage tertiary education institutions to be more responsive to the needs of society and industry by providing incentives for them to mobilize additional resources through increased cost sharing, the sale of goods and services, and donations. The long list of income-generation activities observed in various parts of the world (see Appendix C) attests to the dynamism and ingenuity of leaders of tertiary education institutions. A critical feature of any policy designed to encourage funding diversification is to allow incremental resources to remain available for use within the institutions that generate them. Regulations that seek to capture resources obtained by the efforts of individual public institutions for use by a central authority, or policies that reduce government budget allocations to offset the incremental resources raised by the institutions, are self-defeating because they eliminate the institutions' incentive to generate additional income. Positive government incentives for income generation can take the form of, for example, matching funds linked to income generated from outside sources in some ratio, or even of a multiplier coefficient with a funding formula, as practiced in Singapore and in the U.S. state of Kentucky. Favorable tax incentives are also essential to stimulate philanthropic and charitable giving to tertiary education institutions. (In 2001 record donations of US$360 million and US$400 million, respectively, were received by the Rensselaer Polytechnic Institute from an anonymous donor and by Stanford University from the Hewlett Foundation.) Among developing countries, India has one of the most generous tax concession schemes; 100 percent of individual and corporate donations to universities is exempt from taxation.

To encourage creative investment in tertiary education institutions, some countries have established competitive funds to promote quality improvements. Under such systems, institutions are typically invited to formulate project proposals that are reviewed and selected by committees of peers according to transparent procedures and criteria. The eligibility criteria vary from country to country and depend on the specific policy changes sought. In Argentina and Indonesia, for instance, proposals can be submitted by entire universities or by individual faculties or departments. In Chile both public and private institutions are allowed to compete. In Egypt a fund was set up specifically to stimulate reforms within faculties of engineering. The system of performance contracts in France is a variation on the competitive fund mechanism. A four-year contract is prepared and signed by both the state and the institution; the latter commits itself to a plan of action to achieve quality improvements in return for extrabudgetary financial resources.

One of the added benefits of competitive funding mechanisms is that they encourage tertiary education institutions to undertake strategic planning activities that help them formulate proposals based on a solid identification of needs and a rigorous action plan. Tertiary institutions operate in an increasingly challenging environment in which they compete for students, teaching staff, funding, and markets for their outputs (graduates and research findings). By linking institutional behavior to internal strengths and weaknesses, institutions can use systematic assessment to help define their missions, market niches, and development objectives and to formulate concrete plans for achieving their objectives. It is important to stress that strategic planning is not a one-time exercise. The more successful organizations in the business and academic worlds are those that are relentless in challenging and reinventing themselves in the pursuit of better and more effective ways of responding to the needs of their clients and stakeholders.

Another critical domain of government intervention is student financial aid. As more countries and institutions introduce cost-sharing measures—often in the form of higher tuition fees and reduced subsidies on noninstructional expenditures for such items as food, dormitories, and transportation—the state must play a crucial role in ensuring that no academically qualified student is prevented from studying by lack of financial resources. The statement by the director general of UNESCO on the need for students from well-off families to contribute more toward the cost of their education, made at the October 1998 World Conference on Higher Education, and the February 2001 declaration by the Association of African Universities on the importance of cost sharing, reflect a growing recognition that the cost of tertiary education must be shared in a more equitable way.[6] But increased cost sharing in public universities and further expansion of private tertiary education cannot be implemented equitably without the parallel development of scholarship and loan programs that can guarantee the necessary financial support to deserving low-income students unable to absorb the costs of tertiary education—both the direct costs and the indirect costs in the shape of forgone earnings.

The availability of financial aid for low-income, minority, and other disadvantaged students is a determining factor in equity. Many countries have scholarship programs for the neediest students enrolled in public tertiary education institutions, and some governments offer grants to deserving students wishing to enroll in private institutions. Chile, for instance, operates a system of financial awards for the 28,000 top students selected on the basis of their scores in the national aptitude tests given at the end of secondary school. These awards can be used for study at either a public or a private university. Mexico and Bangladesh mandate that private universities offer scholarships to at least 5 percent of their students. But public funds for scholarships are limited, and only a small proportion of low-income students is ever likely to benefit. It appears that large-scale assistance affecting a broader segment of financially disadvantaged students can only be made available through student loan programs.

An international review of student loan schemes conducted by the World Bank (Albrecht and Ziderman 1991) found mixed results in both industrial and developing countries.[7] Because of heavily subsidized interest rates, high default rates, and substantial administrative costs, the proportion of loans repaid has not been significant in most cases, seriously compromising the long-term financial sustainability of the programs. Experience suggests that in order to design and administer an efficient and financially viable student loan scheme, the following basic conditions must be met: an appropriate marketing strategy; transparent eligibility criteria to ensure that any subsidy element is targeted to the most deserving students (academically and on social criteria); close supervision of the academic performance of the beneficiaries; carefully designed interest rate and subsidy policies to protect the long-term financial viability of the scheme; efficient collection mechanisms to minimize default; and efficient and stable management (adapted from Woodhall 1997).

In the case of private sector financing for student loan programs, positive regulatory conditions must be in place if commercial banks are to be willing to offer credits to individual students. Three key determinants of the availability of private student loans are (a) physical and logistical access based on geographic location and the capacity of the banking system; (b) the existence of good management information systems in the private banks; and (c) the availability of affordable credit. When these conditions can be satisfied, the development of private student loan schemes is possible.

Even those loan programs in developing countries that have functioned reasonably well, such as ICEES in northern Mexico, CONAPE in Costa Rica, and FUNDAPEC in the Dominican Republic, are relatively small in scale, covering no more than 10 percent of the student population. It is unclear whether efficient administration could be maintained if the programs were substantially expanded. To build up effective and sustainable large-scale programs, two options might be considered: a mixed-loan system of private funding with government guarantees, and an income-contingent loan system.

Under the first approach, following the models prevailing in Canada and the United States, student loans are administered and financed by commercial banks, with a government guarantee in case of default and an interest subsidy to keep the loans affordable. The system being piloted in Poland since 1998 operates along these lines.

A growing number of countries—among them, Australia, Ghana, New Zealand, South Africa, and Sweden—have opted for the second approach of income-contingent loan systems (sometimes referred to as a graduate tax), in which loan repayments are a fixed proportion of a graduate's annual income. Although experience to date is limited, these systems can in theory achieve a better balance between effective cost recovery and risk to the borrower than mixed-loan programs. Administration is generally simpler and cheaper because loan recovery is handled through existing collection mechanisms such as the income tax administration or the social security system. Income-contingent loans are also more equitable and satisfy more fully the ability-to-pay principle, since repayments are in direct proportion to a graduate's income. Although income-contingent loans have considerable promise, their feasibility depends heavily on the existence of a reliable income tax or social security system with access to accurate income information and the administrative capacity to handle loan collection efficiently and effectively.

The development of borderless education represents a new challenge for student financial aid agencies. Eligibility rules and loan features must be adjusted to accommodate the financial needs of the growing number of students who are enrolled on a part-time basis, who pursue distance programs offered by a foreign institution, or who have registered for short-duration continuing education courses instead of traditional degree programs.

Finally, it should be noted that beyond their primary social purpose of providing financial aid to needy students, loan programs can also have a positive impact on the quality of tertiary education. First, the eligibility criteria for the types of universities and colleges in which beneficiaries may enroll tend to favor good-quality institutions over less reputable ones. In Mexico, for instance, the Association of Private Universities, which created a student loan agency in 1998, requires that its members be evaluated by a U.S. accreditation agency, providing a minimum quality standard. Second, student loan beneficiaries tend to achieve better academic results than their peers who do not receive a loan. Recent data released by the Student Loan Institute of Sonora show an 85 percent pass rate for beneficiaries versus 53 percent for the overall student population.

Having reviewed tertiary education and its relationship with the state, we turn, in the next chapter, to what the World Bank Group should be doing to help developing and transition countries transform their tertiary education systems and close the enrollment, equity, and quality gaps between them and the industrial countries.

Notes

1. Examples are Australia, Austria (in its newly established technical institutes modeled after the German *Fachhochschulen*), Italy, New Zealand, Portugal, Spain, and the United Kingdom.

2. Yamada Reiko (2001). See also Japan, Ministry of Education, Culture, Sports, Science and Technology, "The Education Reform Plan for the 21st Century," <http://www.mext.go.jp/english/topics/21plan/010301.htm>.

3. The National Qualifications Framework (NQF) is a key part of New Zealand's skill development strategy, a new coordinated approach to education and training that aims to raise skill levels in the country. The NQF offers a variety of entry points and pathways for people to gain new skills and qualifications at any age and at any stage in their careers; the objective is lifelong learning, from senior secondary school onward. The NQF gives all citizens the opportunity to receive national recognition for their skills and qualifications. Skills learned on the job can be recognized without the individual's having to attend a formal training course. The NQF offers greater flexibility for the learner and removes many traditional barriers to learning. Unit standards and qualifications span general, vocational, and industry-based education and training, and each is registered at an appropriate level on the NQF. There are eight levels: levels 1–3 correspond to approximately the same standard as senior secondary education and basic trades training; levels 4–6 approximate advanced trades, technical, and business qualifications; and levels 7–8 are comparable to advanced graduate and postgraduate qualifications. See New Zealand Qualifications Authority, "Framework Explained," <http://www.nzqa.govt.nz/services/frameworkexplained.html>.

4. In November 1999 a Harvard School of Law professor was reprimanded by Harvard administrators for selling videotaped lectures to the Concord University School of Law, an online degree-granting institution. An Arizona professor who developed a televised writing course for Pima Community College a few years ago has become a celebrity on local television but has had no success in getting the college to acknowledge his copyrights for the broadcast, year after year, of the videotapes he prepared (reported in Carnevale and Young 1999: A45).

5. At the Technology University of Warsaw, the impossibility of offering adequate remuneration to qualified computer science specialists from the private sector is now seen as a major obstacle to maintaining the relevance of some advanced programs (interview with the rector of the Technology University of Warsaw, Jerzy Woźnicki, February 1999).

6. "African Universities must continue to engage their governments, communities and other stakeholders in a dialogue aimed at arriving at appropriate understandings on the issue of the diversification of sources of funding, including cost-sharing initiatives" (para. 4; Association of African Universities, "Declaration on the African University in the Third Millennium," <http://www.aau.org/releases/declaration.htm>, Nairobi, February 9, 2001.

7. More than half the countries reviewed in this study were in Latin America and the Caribbean.

5
World Bank Support for Tertiary Education

It is impossible to have a complete education system without an appropriate and strong higher education system. . . . I am not for a moment suggesting that primary education and secondary education are not at the very essence of development . . . [but that is] not enough. You have to have centers of excellence and learning and training if you are going to advance the issue of poverty and development in developing countries. . . . the key . . . is higher education, not just on the technological side, but to create people with enough wisdom to be able to use it.

James D. Wolfensohn,
Launch of the Report of the
Task Force on Higher Education and Society,
March 1, 2000

In continued pursuit of its mandate to help developing and transition countries reduce poverty and improve living standards through sustainable growth and investment in people, the World Bank has renewed and deepened its commitment to enhancing the contribution of tertiary education to economic and social development worldwide. Through effective partnerships with other multilateral institutions, national governments, NGOs, and the private sector, the World Bank aspires to apply its financial resources and extensive knowledge base toward increased efforts in the tertiary education and science and technology sectors, which will help create the foundations for democratic, knowledge-based economies and societies. This chapter reviews the Bank's experience in supporting tertiary education reforms in developing and transition countries in recent years and offers a framework for continued support of tertiary education development.

Assessment of Recent World Bank Experience in Tertiary Education, 1995–2001

Since 1963, when it began to lend for the education sector, the World Bank has had a prominent role in assisting countries in their efforts to expand tertiary education and improve the quality of institutions and programs. Between 1992 and 1998, lending for tertiary education averaged US$481 million a year. The Bank is currently implementing tertiary education projects, or projects with tertiary education components, in 28 countries. (See Appendix D for a listing by country; see Appendix E for a synopsis of the World Bank's analytical work on tertiary education, Appendix F for graphical presentations of breakdowns of lending, and Appendix G for project descriptions and lessons from projects.) The general types of intervention, with some examples of specific objectives, are as follows:

• Vision development, strategic planning, and consensus building at both the national and institutional levels
• Finance reforms (e.g., allocation of recurrent budget; competitive funding; cost sharing; student loans; scholarships)
• Governance and management reforms (creation of policy bodies; mergers and federations; adoption of academic credit systems; management information systems)
• Quality improvement (strengthening of existing programs; evaluation and accreditation systems; innovations in program content and delivery; innovations in academic organization; information and communication infrastructure)
• Institutional diversification (establishment or strengthening of polytechnic or technical institutes)
• Science and technology development (strategy development; capacity for monitoring and evaluation; reform of resource allocation mechanisms; competitive funding; promotion of research in priority areas; joint public–private sector technology development; capacity for metrology, standards, and quality testing; intellectual property rights).

In the 1970s and 1980s much of the support provided by World Bank tertiary education projects was piecemeal, with a narrow focus on the establishment of new programs or on discrete measures for improving the quality of existing teaching and research activities. These projects occasionally created well-equipped academic oases—which tended to become unsustainable over time—but the Bank was rarely able to offer the long-term comprehensive support for tertiary education that is required for successful reform efforts and effective institution building.

An internal review of implementation experience with tertiary education projects undertaken in 1992 and an assessment of recent and ongoing interventions in the subsector have offered insights into more productive ways of supporting tertiary education reforms and innovations. The most salient lessons about the relative effectiveness of different approaches toward supporting tertiary education reform and development can be grouped according to three general themes:

- Comprehensiveness of the intervention strategy and sustained long-term engagement in the reform effort
- Political-economy aspects of reform
- The role of positive incentives in promoting change.[1]

The Need for a Systemwide, Sustained Approach

Comprehensiveness and sustained long-term engagement are important predictors of outcome. Policy measures and investments that are integrated into a broad reform program based on a global vision and strategy for change are most likely to bear fruit. For example, the implementation of an ongoing project in Argentina has been successful because it has accompanied a well-articulated reform program sanctioned by a new higher education law. The reform program promotes the introduction of internal and external evaluation mechanisms, including a national accreditation system, increased autonomy for the public universities in human and financial resource management, support for quality improvements throughout the university system, institutional strengthening of the Ministry of Higher Education and the public universities, and a new funding formula.

Even in the technical aspects of quality improvement, there is a need for a comprehensive approach reflecting the interrelatedness of academic programs and tertiary education institutions. The various institutional components of the tertiary education subsector, both public and private, constitute a system. How they relate to each other and to the tertiary education system as a whole needs to be considered. High-quality instruction in engineering, medicine, agriculture, and the applied social sciences, for example, requires sound training in the natural sciences, mathematics, and even the humanities (the importance of which for economic development is perceived as less obvious, making the field less attractive as regards donor support). Advanced scientific training and research require strong undergraduate programs and a large, diversified tertiary education system so that undergraduate and postgraduate programs do not compete for scarce staff and financial resources. Centers of excellence cannot be maintained if they must bear the burden of accommodating most of the increasing social demand for tertiary education as well.

Reforms of the financing of public tertiary education, especially the introduction of tuition and other fees, are difficult to implement successfully unless educational opportunity is expanded through equity measures. Financing reforms also require significant devolution of government control in matters affecting institutional costs, as well as incentives for institutions to engage in cost-saving and income-generating activities. Student loan schemes may work well technically yet fail to promote improved efficiency and cost-effectiveness in tertiary education.

The case of Venezuela provides a negative example. There, the World Bank supported the reform of the public student loan agency, FUNDAYACUCHO, with a project designed to increase coverage, improve the financial sustainability of the agency, and enhance its management efficiency. Although the operation was a great success from the viewpoint of disbursements, its real impact was limited because the project was not part of a comprehensive reform of tertiary education financing. A similar operation in Jamaica has had a more positive effect because the reform of the Student Loan Bureau has supported parallel efforts to improve the system's financial situation through increased cost sharing at the University of the West Indies and the University of Technology.

The preference for comprehensiveness does not mean that all aspects of a reform can or should be packed into a single operation. This is where sequencing plays a crucial role in the implementation of a systemwide approach. Sequencing provides the tools to respond and adjust to evolving challenges and to secure long-term involvement through a series of complementary operations. To ensure structural change in a viable and sustainable manner, sufficient time is needed.

The World Bank has been most successful in countries such as China, Indonesia, Korea, and Tunisia, where, through a series of project investments, it was able to develop a sectorwide strategy for intervention. A long-term approach has greatly enhanced the prospects for genuine reforms that are sustainable over time.

In China, for example, project loans have involved different tiers of tertiary education in ways that have strengthened the subsector as a whole. The World Bank began by supporting, within the framework of China's Fourth Modernization Plan of 1980, the country's elite national universities—institutions whose research and training programs had been disrupted by the Cultural Revolution. World Bank funding facilitated construction or rehabilitation of university laboratories and libraries, updating of instructional and research programs with the assistance of foreign scientific experts, and upgrading of the professional qualifications of academic staff through training abroad. Follow-on projects addressed the needs of the provincial universities and other types of tertiary education institutions. Later, the focus shifted toward supporting national resource allocation policies and mechanisms and then toward strengthening premier institutions engaged in advanced scientific training and research.

In Indonesia and Korea, too, the World Bank has financed multiple projects throughout the tertiary education subsector in the context of an integrated government strategy for quantitative expansion. These projects focused on promoting improvements in quality, especially in the private sector; fostering regional development; and strengthening national research and training capabilities in the public sector through enhanced linkages to the private sector. Sustained cooperation with the Indonesian government has led to a paradigm shift in the way the country's tertiary education system is governed and financed. Similarly, two successive and complementary sectorwide projects in Tunisia have contributed to substantial improvements in the tertiary education system.

Political Economy

Until the beginning of the 1990s, very little attention was paid to the political-economy aspects of tertiary education reforms. The Bank worked under the assumption that to introduce change successfully, it was sufficient to design a technically sound reform program and reach agreement with top government officials. When it came to actual implementation, however, political reality often proved stronger than the technocratic vision. For example, a number of education adjustment loans to Sub-Saharan African countries in the late 1980s and early 1990s included tertiary education reform measures aimed at containing expenditures, enrollment growth, and subsidies. The implementation experience of these operations has not been encouraging. The proposed reform programs, which often included too many conditions that never materialized, have been opposed by various interest groups and have even touched off student rioting.

Launching and implementing tertiary education reforms and innovations has been more successful when decisionmakers have used social communication campaigns effectively and have managed to build consensus among the various constituents of the tertiary education community. Mozambique provides an example. Under the auspices of a national task force, a strategic plan for higher education was debated in the newspapers and on television and radio. Extensive consultations in each province, involving students, civil society, academic staff, researchers, and employers, introduced stakeholders to the proposed plan. Undertaking a broad national consultation exercise does not always work. But to not even attempt a consultation exercise is a guarantee of failure.

Policy dialogue, stakeholder consultation, and consensus building are not discrete activities that are only useful at the beginning of a reform.

Rather, there is a need to maintain and renew attention to the politics of tertiary education reform as country conditions evolve. Failure to do so can expose the project to diminishing commitment or even reversal of policies as a result of elections, change of government, or replacement of key leaders. In Hungary and Senegal the Bank was instrumental in supporting extensive vision development and national consultation efforts, and a loan accompanied the reform. But in neither country was the momentum of consultation fully sustained, and some of the reform measures were abandoned or even reversed after political changes occurred and new actors with a different agenda arrived. The cases of these countries illustrate another important lesson in political economy: it is difficult to promote all the changes simultaneously when introducing deep reforms. Their experiences also underscore the importance of follow-up strategies for continued vision sharing with new authorities, agents, and stakeholders to ensure the sustainability of reforms.

Reliance on Incentives

The extent to which projects rely on positive incentives rather than mandatory edicts to stimulate change has a great influence on outcomes, as institutions and actors tend to respond more readily to constructive stimuli. The World Bank has had favorable experience with a number of policy instruments, including the introduction of competitive funds, accreditation mechanisms, and management information systems.

COMPETITIVE FUNDS. Well-designed competitive funds can greatly stimulate the performance of tertiary education institutions and can be powerful vehicles for transformation and innovation. Argentina's Quality Improvement Fund (FOMEC) has encouraged universities to engage in strategic planning for the strengthening of existing programs and the creation of new interdisciplinary graduate programs. Within universities, faculties that had never worked together started cooperating in the design and implementation of joint projects. In Indonesia a series of World Bank projects that began in 1993 has succeeded in stimulating ownership within the entire academic community of new paradigms in tertiary education. In Egypt the Engineering Education Fund was instrumental in introducing the notion of competitive bidding and peer evaluation in the allocation of public investment resources. The fund promoted in an effective manner the transformation of traditional engineering degrees into more applied programs with close linkages to industry.

A fundamental prerequisite for the effective operation of competitive funds—and one of their significant benefits—is the practice of transparency and fair play through the establishment of clear criteria and procedures and the creation of an independent monitoring committee. In countries with a relatively small or isolated academic community, it is desirable to draw from a regional or international pool of peer reviewers to reduce the danger of complacency and subjective evaluation among a limited group of national colleagues. Use of a transnational pool is a long-standing practice in the Netherlands, for example. The new competitive fund in Jordan has detailed guidelines that are described in an operations manual, and it relies on international peer reviewers for projects of national interest. In Chile a second wave of tertiary education reforms is being supported by a competitive fund for diversification (development of the nonuniversity sector) and quality improvement of all tertiary institutions. Brazil, Mexico, and Venezuela are encouraging the formation of advanced human capital in science and technology through competitive funding mechanisms. In all these cases, international peer review experts figure prominently.

In some cases there may be a compelling argument for opening several financing windows with different criteria or for setting up compensatory mechanisms to create a level playing field between strong and weak institutions. In Indonesia three different windows were designed to serve universities according to their actual institutional capacity. In the latest tertiary education project in China, as described in more detail in the section "Facilitating Policy Dialogue and Knowledge Sharing," below, the top universities are required to form a partnership with a university in a poor province as a condition for competing. In Egypt the competitive fund in the Engineering Education Reform project had a special window for technical assistance to help less experienced engineering schools prepare well-formulated proposals. Also in Egypt, proposals that included a partnership agreement between a stronger university and a weaker one received additional points for evaluation purposes. In Chile a special window was recently opened to provide preparation funds for universities requiring assistance in strategic planning and subproject formulation.

ACCREDITATION MECHANISMS. Quality assurance systems are necessary instruments in the diversification of tertiary education systems, and the World Bank has supported the formation of national quality assurance systems in a number of countries. In some instances the Bank has helped establish specific and limited accreditation programs, but the general strategy has been to move toward comprehensive systems that cover the entire tertiary education landscape and that are consistent with international practice regarding standard setting, evaluation, and accreditation. In Indonesia, for example, the World Bank supported the introduction of accreditation mechanisms in a project to improve teacher training standards in public institutions. The project started with a pilot program to define a set of standards for evaluating all teacher training institutions and to establish a baseline for institutional development. Small planning grants were made available to enable the five institutions that participated in the pilot to conduct a self-study, which was then externally evaluated and validated. The pilot study proved useful in generating acceptance for accreditation as a mechanism for improving the quality and relevance of teacher training. The Bank has also supported the establishment of Indonesia's National Accreditation Board for Higher Education.

Sometimes sets of policy interventions can be mutually reinforcing. In Argentina, Chile, Indonesia, and Romania, for instance, only programs evaluated by the national quality assurance system are eligible to compete for innovation and quality enhancement grants. Brazil has a long-standing and successful tradition of supporting its graduate programs in this way.

MANAGEMENT INFORMATION SYSTEMS. Many tertiary education projects supported by the World Bank have facilitated the introduction or development of management information systems (MISs) at the national and institutional levels, on the assumption that neither the state nor individual institutions can formulate and implement reforms without effective monitoring and management tools. In Argentina a Bank-financed project helped put in place intranet and Internet links among all the public universities and between the universities and the outside world. Software for all dimensions of academic management was developed and combined into an integrated MIS that provides information at the level of each individual institution and consolidates this information into a program run by the national tertiary education authorities for monitoring and planning purposes. Many universities were at first cautious, but they ended up enthusiastically embracing these innovations because the adaptations helped them invest in modern information and communication technologies and provided them with useful management tools.

DIFFICULTIES WITH POLITICALLY SENSITIVE REFORMS. The Bank has been less successful in supporting the implementation of politically sensitive reforms such as moving from negotiated budgets to formula funding, reducing subsidies, and introducing tuition fees. In several countries—for example, Argentina and Tunisia—the government has been unable to fulfill its commitment, made at the time of project preparation, to implement a transparent funding formula. In Senegal the authorities recently retracted their undertaking to streamline the scholarship program in such a way as to ensure that only socially and academically deserving students would be eligible. In Hungary the government reversed its decision to charge tuition fees for repeating students.

Directions for Future Bank Support

Immense progress has been achieved in education in the last 50 years. Immense challenges still remain. The main success has been in access, but too many people—especially girls and women—are still excluded, at all levels of education. Too many more are enrolled but learning little. The result is that far too many people in developing countries do not have the foundation skills required to survive—let alone the advanced skills needed to thrive—in our complex, competitive world. The challenges are to improve the quality of teaching and the relevance of learning, and to offer everyone—including the hardest to reach—a good education. The long-term measure of success for developing countries will be the degree to which a system and culture of lifelong learning have been achieved.

Education Sector Strategy (World Bank 1999a)

In the context of the holistic education strategy formulated by the World Bank in 1998, investment in tertiary education is an important pillar of development strategies that emphasize the construction of democratic, knowledge-based economies and societies. The World Bank can play a central role in building these societies by facilitating policy dialogue and knowledge sharing, supporting reforms through program and project lending, and promoting an enabling framework for the global public goods crucial for the development of tertiary education.

Facilitating Policy Dialogue and Knowledge Sharing

In many countries the relationship between the government and the university sector, and between public and private tertiary education institutions, is often tense if not outright conflictive. Attempts at tertiary education reform are usually fraught with controversy. Proposals that are likely to affect established practices and vested interests always meet with fierce resistance and opposition by the groups most likely to be affected by the intended redistribution of power and wealth.

Given the right circumstances, the World Bank may play a catalytic role in encouraging and facilitating policy dialogue on tertiary education reforms in client countries. The Bank can act as a bridge builder by bringing to the table stakeholders who would not normally converse and work together. In Bangladesh and Kenya, for example, the Bank supported the government in the organization of workshops involving public and private universities. In Bolivia the Bank has assisted the public universities and the government in engaging in a constructive dialogue on issues of quality enhancement and accreditation. In addition, the Bank can contribute relevant comparative knowledge about a great variety of national and institutional experiences that can enrich the debate by offering objective reference points for analyzing the local situation and assessing the range and content of policy options that may be considered. This type of policy dialogue can lead to the formulation of a long-term vision for the country's tertiary education system as a whole and for the preparation of strategic plans at the level of individual institutions.

The World Bank's comparative advantage, in relation to bilateral donors and other multilateral agencies, in supporting policy dialogue in client countries stems from two related factors. First, the Bank has firsthand access to worldwide experiences that can be assembled and shared with interested counterparts and stakeholders. Second, the comprehensive nature of the Bank's work in a given country allows it to adopt a systemwide approach linking education and other sectoral issues to the overall development framework and public finance context rather than focus on discrete, isolated interventions in support of specific institutions.

Social assessments are a tool that the World Bank can use to identify stakeholder concerns and address issues that may be controversial. The first social assessments for tertiary education projects were carried out in Indonesia, Jordan, China, and Chile. In Indonesia analysis of the social climate led the universities in the outer islands to involve young academics recently returned from graduate studies overseas in the self-evaluation exercises, which had previously been conducted only by established faculty members. The social assessment also identified a need to create more direct links with employers of university graduates. In Jordan, when the proposal to carry out a social assessment was mentioned to the seven universities preparing a new project with the Bank in 1998, most representatives were reluctant to embark on such an activity, as there was no tradition in the prevailing academic culture of systematic consultation of students and faculty. One institution, however—Al-Balqa' Applied University (BAU), which had recently been created as a federation of 20 community colleges—was enthusiastic about the concept. BAU had been mandated to overhaul the community college system, which was in a state of disrepair, and the university's officials saw the social assessment as a means of testing their proposed reforms with their stakeholders. Students, parents, faculty members, employers, and community leaders were methodically consulted, and the results of the assessment proved invaluable in ascertaining their aspirations and preparing acceptable reform instruments that carefully integrated issues of access, gender, internal perceptions, and employer expectations.

In China the counterpart agency had initially planned that the new Higher Education Reform project would include only best-performing universities—rich institutions functioning in thriving economic environments, largely on the coast. This would leave out poorer-performing institutions located in remote and economically disadvantaged areas. China is fairly unusual in that beneficiary institutions which receive credits and loans are directly responsible for repayment; universities running at a loss and needing modernization are typically bad prospects for loans and thus fall even farther behind. Stakeholders interviewed as part of the social assessment, including secondary- and tertiary-level students, parents, the academic community, minority groups (many of them located in disadvantaged areas), and village education committees, were concerned that lack of support for universities in disadvantaged areas would exacerbate the existing social and economic regional disparities. These strongly expressed stakeholder views were taken account of in the final project design through a selection criterion that required wealthy, well-performing universities to enter into official supportive partnerships with poorer universities. Funding for the disadvantaged universities' reform-oriented activities is to come from local governments, allied ministries, or the lead university.

Social marketing and communication campaigns also help engage the diverse sets of stakeholders who are involved in the tertiary education scene. In Chile a thorough stakeholder analysis led the government to accept an explicit communication strategy to support the preparation of a new project with the World Bank and to include students in the government's project preparation team.

Stakeholder interaction with other countries that face similar challenges can help overcome opposition to reform. A study tour to Uganda recently organized for Guinean officials and university leaders under a World Bank–financed project had a remarkable impact. Learning firsthand about management reforms at Makerere University encouraged the Guineans to move full speed toward institutional income-generating activities and increased university linkages with industry. World Bank policy seminars involving several neighboring countries, held recently in South Asia, Eastern Europe, Africa, and Central and South America, have had a similar eye-opening effect, inducing countries to accept more easily reforms that have already been undertaken elsewhere in the region.

Supporting Reforms through Program and Project Funding

In supporting the implementation of tertiary education reforms, the World Bank gives priority to programs and projects that can bring about positive developments and innovations in the following areas:[2]

- Increasing institutional diversification (through growth of nonuniversity and private institutions) to expand coverage on a financially viable basis and to establish a lifelong-learning framework with mul-

tiple points of entry (construction of accessible pathways from secondary to tertiary education; articulation mechanisms across tertiary education segments; recognition of relevant prior professional and academic experience; capacity building for distance learning)
- Strengthening science and technology R&D capacity (possibly in selected areas linked to a country's priorities for the development of comparative advantage)
- Improving the relevance and quality of tertiary education
- Promoting greater equity mechanisms (scholarships and student loans) intended to create and expand access and opportunities for disadvantaged students
- Establishing sustainable financing systems to encourage responsiveness and flexibility
- Strengthening management capacity through, for example, introduction of management information systems for improved accountability, administration, and governance and for more efficient utilization of existing resources
- Enhancing and expanding information technology and communications capacity to reduce the digital divide, complementing recent global initiatives of the World Bank, such as the Global Development Learning Network, the African Virtual University, the Global Development Network, and World Links, described in Appendix H.

This menu of priority areas does not apply equally to all countries at all times. The relative emphasis and mix of interventions appropriate for any given country are linked to its specific political and economic circumstances at both the macroeconomic and the tertiary education levels. The country's income level, size, and political stability and whether it is in a postconflict situation are all important factors to be taken into consideration. The depth of the World Bank's knowledge about the main challenges faced by a country's tertiary education system and about recent developments in the sector affects the Bank's capacity to provide useful support.

In setting priorities for the appropriate mix of lending and nonlending services in a given country, the Bank will be guided by the following criteria (see also Table 5.1):

- The need for and urgency of change, based on the gravity of the issues faced by the country's tertiary education system. For example, in countries experiencing rapid growth of low-quality private institutions, setting up an accreditation and evaluation system would be a high priority.
- Willingness to reform, as reflected in the government's commitment to implementing reforms and its ability to mobilize major stakehold-

Table 5.1 Priorities for Bank Involvement

Need for change	Willingness to reform	
	Low	High
High	Limited policy dialogue and lending	Full-scale policy dialogue and lending
Low	Limited policy dialogue	Full-scale policy dialogue

ers in support of the reform agenda. Having already undergone a consensus-building exercise and formulated a national vision on the future of tertiary education would be a clear sign of reform readiness.

In establishing the need for change in a given country, it is useful to distinguish between first- and second-generation reforms. First-generation reforms, which address core problems of tertiary education systems (financing, efficiency, equity, and quality assurance), are the first steps in moving from one way of doing things toward a more appropriate approach. These steps might include, for instance, changing from open-ended admissions to selective access; introducing cost sharing through fees and reduced subsidies in institutions that had charged nothing; establishing accreditation and evaluation in previously unregulated systems; transforming scholarships into student loans; creating nonuniversity institutions alongside traditional universities; adopting an academic credit system; and starting to rely on formula funding.

Second-generation reforms are undertaken by countries that have already addressed many of their basic problems but need to do some fine-tuning to take first-generation reforms one step farther or to correct unintended effects. These reforms are no less important than first-generation reforms and are also worthy of World Bank support. Examples of second-generation reforms include extending the eligibility of a student loan program to all tertiary education institutions in a diversified system, introducing flexible mechanisms of articulation and credit transfer among institutions, and establishing competency-based evaluation mechanisms for online courses. In Chile, for instance, a framework for lifelong learning is being established, and new financing mechanisms such as student loans applicable to all types of tertiary education institutions are under consideration. In Korea the government recently launched a seven-year, US$1.2 billion investment plan for tertiary education institutions, Brain Korea 21. The plan is essentially a new incentive-based financing scheme that offers institutions matching funds on a competitive and selective basis to induce them to excel in cutting-edge research training in areas such as biotechnology and information technology. Brazil, Chile, Mexico, and Venezuela are providing incentives to world-class research training through highly competitive mechanisms via the Millennium Science Initiative, also supported by the World Bank (see the description in Appendix I).

Most of the options defined in this chapter are directly relevant to middle-income countries. Important distinctions are warranted for at least three groups of World Bank clients: transition countries, low-income countries, and small states. These clients face special conditions that require a different strategic focus and a different set of priorities.

Transition Countries

Under state socialism, many countries in Eastern and Central Europe attained high rates of participation, enviable educational levels, and pathbreaking research output. The achievements of tertiary education were particularly noteworthy in mathematics, natural sciences, and engineering. The introduction of market principles of economic organization resulted in a sharp decline in public funding for colleges, universities, and scientific academies. Demand for engineers and technicians, particularly in military industries, fell sharply, and interest in fields of study relevant to a market economy (economics, management, accounting, marketing, and law) surged. Interestingly, the quickening pace of both social and technological change increased the rate at which skills became obsolete and undermined the effectiveness of the strategy of hyperspecialization that had characterized tertiary education under socialism. Demand for broad skills such as critical analysis, problem solving, and teamwork greatly increased.

Colleges, universities, and scientific academies in transition economies are struggling to adjust to these new realities. Adaptation strategies used by institutions include reallocation of resources from traditional to new areas of study, simplification of curricula and creation of modular training programs to allow greater flexibility and responsiveness to students' needs, and diversification of sources of funding. Many tertiary institutions are involved in commercial activities, including contract research, consultant services, and sale of training services to private enterprises, thus contributing to the development of tertiary education that is more responsive to economic and labor market needs. While some universities and research centers have succeeded in becoming innovative and entrepreneurial, many have failed to overcome institutional inertia.

An urgent priority among national-level public policy issues is to address the increased inequity caused by expansion of tuition-based enrollment. Barriers to reform include predominantly administrative internal governance of institutions, weak linkages with the community, shortages of resources for innovation, and insufficient consistency of public policies in the area of tertiary education.

An effective response to these issues is necessary if transition economies are to be able to provide the human resources required to advance knowledge and apply it for economic growth. The leading options for improving tertiary education include introducing more flexible and less specialized curricula, promoting shorter programs and courses, making the regulatory framework less rigid, and relying on public funding approaches that encourage institutions to respond to market demands for quality and diversity. Other important options include improving access through the provision of financial aid to students, requiring external participation in governance, and professionalizing university administration. Public investments are needed to build capacity for academic and management innovations, to expand the breadth of course offerings at individual institutions, and to create new programs in response to evolving demand-driven areas of learning.

Low-Income Countries

More than 2.3 billion people—53 percent of the total population of the developing world—live in the 79 countries with annual per capita incomes of less than US$885. These countries, half of them in Sub-Saharan Africa, are eligible for special concessional financing of their development projects through the World Bank's International Development Association (IDA). Their governments are seeking ways to provide tertiary education to over 12 million students, approximately 0.5 percent of the eligible cohort. Of this number, 70 percent are in the 42 countries where annual per capita incomes average less than US$400. This set of very poor countries will be particularly hard pressed to attain an acceptable standard of tertiary education, even given the modest estimated cost of US$1,000 per student per year for such a standard. Policymakers in the poorest countries will find it increasingly difficult to devise sustainable ways of increasing access to tertiary education. Yet expanding tertiary education is a principal means of promoting capacity building (especially in agriculture and health), poverty reduction, and increasing social equity.

Low-income countries also face many challenges in science and technology–related public policy issues: ensuring the minimum level of public understanding of science necessary for informed civic decisions; creating channels for appropriate advice on scientific issues in legislation and governance; negotiating and complying with international treaties involving scientific and technological issues; and building local capacity to harness science and technology for the resolution of key economic and social problems.

An appropriate tertiary education development direction for low-income countries should focus on three complementary priority areas:

(a) building capacity for managing and improving the basic and secondary education system, to include the training and retraining of teachers and principals; (b) expanding the production of qualified professionals and technicians through a cost-effective combination of public and private nonuniversity institutions; and (c) making targeted investments in strategic areas of advanced training and research that can yield sizable returns over the medium term.

CAPACITY BUILDING IN SUPPORT OF BASIC AND SECONDARY EDUCATION. Teacher training is essential if a country is to meet the needs for expanded coverage and improved educational quality in the entire education system and to ensure that secondary school graduates are well prepared to access the tertiary level. Universities and other training institutions have a critical role with respect to teacher preparation—not only in initial training but also through professional development programs designed as part of a continuous, lifelong-learning process. Training institutions must offer innovative ways of integrating teaching theory, classroom practice, and simple applied research and must provide continuing support to school and teacher networks regarding concrete student learning problems. The tertiary education system must also train school principals in appropriate leadership skills. To complement efforts to improve pedagogical practices and drive the necessary in-depth, sustained change in the school culture, principals should be trained in basic strategic thinking and in organizational, managerial, and instructional skills. To be fully effective, training policies for teachers and principals should be supported by appropriate remuneration and career incentives. In many low-income countries, as a result of unattractive civil service conditions and frequent turnover of personnel, institutional capacity within the ministry of education and its regional dependencies, and within key national agencies such as those in charge of curriculum development and textbook production, is very weak. Tertiary education institutions can play a critical role in offering appropriate training and advisory services.

DEVELOPMENT OF NONUNIVERSITY INSTITUTIONS. More often than not, the qualifications gap experienced in the modern sector of the economy in low-income countries reflects the unavailability of midlevel management and technical specialists rather than an insufficient supply of high-level managers, engineers, or scientists. Low-income countries should consider establishing or expanding a network of specialized two- or three-year tertiary education institutions such as technical institutes or community colleges to train technicians and applied specialists. Through curricula that are adapted to local economic needs and by building strong links with local industry, these specialized institutions can also contribute to subregional economic development. Because of the shorter duration of studies and the generally higher internal efficiency, training costs at such institutions are typically lower than those at universities. These institutions can offer access to tertiary education at a lower cost to a larger segment of the eligible population. In many parts of the world private providers have contributed effectively to the development of such nonuniversity institutions.

INVESTMENT IN STRATEGIC AREAS OF ADVANCED TRAINING AND RESEARCH. To strengthen competitiveness and protect national interests in key economic areas, low-income countries should consider concentrating on the strategic development of a few targeted disciplines and raising their quality to international standards. The disciplines should be selected for their direct relevance to the nation's potential for economic growth and should be integrated into a coordinated, multisectoral approach to development of a national innovation system. Recent work on the determinants of national innovative capacity points out the importance of specialization in "disciplines and fields congruent with emerging innovation opportunities in the local environment" (Stern, Porter, and Furman 2000: 8). Postgraduate programs in priority areas should preferably be established on a regional basis in order to leverage scarce resources by taking full advantage of economies of scale. For capacity-building purposes, donor support for the development or strengthening of such programs should not be limited to the initial capital outlay but should also include funding (on a declining basis) for long-term maintenance and incentives to attract and retain qualified professionals.

This three-pronged approach should be complemented by the following elements:

- *Quality teaching materials, textbooks, and equipment,* made available to students in the classroom and via library loans, to ensure that their education is current and that their potential is maximized
- *Open or virtual universities and distance education programs* using existing course modules obtained through negotiated concessional rates in order to minimize costs for core disciplines
- *Computer literacy* for all tertiary students to increase information retrieval, communication capacity, academic freedom, and individual productivity and to build the country's general and institutional capacity
- *Information technology,* facilitated by supportive national telecommunications policies, to enhance access to global knowledge
- *Strong humanities courses* for the transmission of local culture and values.

Even when the economic and financial circumstances of a low-income country make it difficult to prepare an IDA credit at a particular time, the World Bank should remain engaged in the tertiary education sector to encourage a systemwide approach to educational development and to assist in the formulation of a national tertiary education reform strategy, as it has done in Tanzania and Uganda and is currently doing in Pakistan. The following instruments can be used to offer effective support in anticipation of, or in lieu of, an IDA credit: (a) analytical work in partnership with well-targeted groups, (b) continued involvement in national and regional policy dialogue, and (c) technical assistance through Institutional Development Fund (IDF) grants.

Small States

Small states, defined as those with populations of 1 million or fewer, confront a unique set of challenges in their efforts to develop the skilled human resources needed to support their economic growth and social development. First, small states can rarely marshal sufficient resources to establish and sustain even one national university. To achieve a relatively modest tertiary enrollment ratio of 10 percent of the relevant age cohort, a country of 1 million inhabitants would have to enroll roughly 5,000 students, at an estimated annual cost of about US$5 million. Second, small economies cannot absorb many graduates, resulting in high graduate unemployment and significant brain drain. Third, small states frequently lack suitably trained nationals who can teach the basic range of university disciplines. Staffing is a chronic problem, and reliance on international recruitment is an expensive solution.

The following approaches are proposed for small states:

- Subregional partnerships with neighboring small states to establish a networked university along the lines of the University of the West Indies, the University of the South Pacific, and the University of the Indian Ocean. The Portuguese-language economies of the African Atlantic region (São Tomé and Principe, Cape Verde, and the Azores) recently began discussing a similar step. A significant new initiative in Africa is the introduction by the African Economic Research Consortium (AERC) of a collaborative Ph.D. program in economics that draws on the strengths of several universities, building on the success of an earlier collaborative master's program. This development could have important implications for doctoral training in other fields.
- Strategically focused tertiary education institutions that address a limited number of the nation's critical human skill requirements for economic growth (e.g., in tourism and international finance) and seek to provide this training at an internationally competitive level.

- Negotiated franchise partnerships between the national government and external providers of tertiary education to offer specified services. The government of Eritrea, for example, contracted the U.K. Open University in 1998 to educate 200 senior civil servants in an MBA program.
- Government-negotiated provision of tertiary distance education by a recognized international supplier. Since much of the cost of distance education is for up-front investment in the development of course materials, collaboration with a well-established program could be very cost-effective for a small country.

Tailoring Options to Country Needs

To assist countries in defining an appropriate approach to tertiary education reforms, the matrix shown in Table 5.2 presents a preliminary list of salient issues and a menu of reform options for different types of countries. (Appendixes J and K provide useful data on selected country conditions.) The matrix is intended merely to exemplify a range of priorities and degrees of emphasis that a country might consider in making its policy choices. Because different economies generally face different problems of varying degrees of urgency, policymakers should regard the matrix as a generalization that may help simplify deliberations and accelerate dialogue in the four major groups of countries discussed in this chapter: middle-income countries, transition economies, low-income countries, and small states. (The entries for OECD countries are provided for comparison only.)

For example, on the issue of coverage, lack of institutional diversification (an underdeveloped nonuniversity sector; low enrollment in private tertiary education) is more likely to be a serious concern in middle- and low-income countries than in the other groups. These countries will probably need to focus more on increasing enrollments than would be the case in transition countries, where higher levels of enrollment are the norm. For small countries, where a diversified tertiary education system is hardly a viable proposition, the policy options will be different. Similarly, the options for increasing diversification in low-income countries and small states differ from those for other countries because of the limited resources available for expanding enrollment. Low-income and small countries are therefore more likely to rely on open and virtual universities than would middle-income and transition economies.

Operational Implications

Drawing on lessons from recent experience as to the relative effectiveness of different forms and types of support, it is possible to formulate

Table 5.2 Issues and Policy Options, by Country Group

Issues and Options	OECD	Middle Income	Transition	Low Income	Small States
ISSUES AND COUNTRY SITUATION					
Coverage					
Diversified system in place	x	xx	xx	xxx	xx
System not yet diversified	xx	xxxx	xxx	xxxx	xxx
Equity					
Cost sharing in place but no student aid	n.a.	xxx	xxx	xxxx	xxxx
Tuition required for poorer-performing students	n.a.	xxxx	xxxx	xxxx	n.a.
Quality					
Accreditation system in place	x	xx	xx	xx	xxxx
No accreditation system	xxx	xxxx	xxx	xxxx	n.a.
Relevance					
Diversified system in place	xx	x	xx	xx	xx
System not yet diversified	x	xxx	xxx	xxxx	xxx
Financing					
Cost sharing in place	x	xx	xx	xx	xx
Insufficient public financing	xx	xxxx	xxxx	xxxx	xxxx
Internal efficiency					
Access based on selection	x	x	xx	xx	x
Open access	xx	xxxx	n.a.	xxxx	n.a.
Governance					
Accountability mechanisms in place	xxx	xx	xx	xx	x
Autonomy without accountability	xx	xxxx	xxxx	xxxx	xxxx
POLICY OPTIONS					
Formulation of strategic vision					
If no reform has taken place yet	xxx	xxx	xxx	xxxx	xxxx
If first-generation reforms have taken place	x	x	x	xx	xx
Institutional diversification					
Short-duration programs	xx	xxxx	xxx	xxxx	xxx
Open or virtual universities	x	xx	xx	xxx	xxxx
Private institutions	xxx	xxx	xxxx	xx	x
Science and technology development					
Capacity for strategy formulation, monitoring, and evaluation	x	xxxx	xxxx	xxxx	xxxx
Competitive funding	x	xxx	xxx	x	x
Promotion of research in priority areas	x	xx	xx	xxxx	xxx

Table 5.2, continued

Issues and Options	OECD	Middle Income	Transition	Low Income	Small States
Capacity for metrology, standards, quality testing; intellectual property rights	xx	xxx	xxx	xx	xx
Improvement in quality and relevance					
Strengthening of existing programs	x	xxx	x	xxx	xxx
Evaluation and accreditation system	xx	xxxx	xxxx	xxxx	xxx
Innovation in program content and delivery	xx	xx	xxx	xx	xx
Innovation in academic organization	xx	xxx	xxx	xxx	xx
Expansion of equity mechanisms					
Scholarships	x	x	x	xx	xxxx
Student loans	xx	xxx	xxx	x	n.a.
Affirmative action programs	xx	xx	x	xxx	
Sustainable financing					
Formula funding	xxx	xxx	xxxx	xx	xx
Cost sharing	xxx	xxx	xxx	xx	xx
Resource mobilization (institutional level)	xx	xxxx	xxxx	xxx	xx
Strengthening of governance structure and management capacities					
National policy body	x	xxx	xxx	xxx	xx
National management information system	x	xx	xx	xxx	x
Boards with outside representation	xx	xxx	xxxx	xxx	xx
Development of ICT infrastructure					
National access and pricing policy	x	xxx	xxx	xxxx	xxx
Support for institutional-level investment	xx	xx	xx	xxx	xxx

n.a. Not applicable.

Note: The gravity of the problem or the urgency of reform is indicated as follows: X, lowest gravity or urgency; XX, low; XXX, high; XXXX, highest.

basic operating principles for Bank intervention in client countries. Bank support should be:

- Appropriate to a country's specific circumstances
- Predicated on strategic planning at the national, local, and institutional levels
- Focused on promoting autonomy and accountability
- Geared toward capacity enhancement and facilitation of the cross-fertilization of relevant regional experiences

- Sequenced in accordance with the time requirements of the capacity enhancement objectives
- Sensitive to the political dimensions of tertiary education reform.

In countries where the need for reform is acute, and depending on country circumstances, the following lending instruments will be applied to support tertiary education reform and development: adaptable program loans, programmatic loans, poverty reduction strategy credits, technical assistance loans, learning and innovation loans, and International Finance Corporation (IFC) loans and guarantees. The choice of lending instrument depends on the specific circumstances:

- Adaptable program loans (APLs) should be the preferred instruments for lending for tertiary education reforms because they facilitate a systemwide, holistic, longer-term approach than traditional lending instruments and investment projects. In countries where a coherent national vision and medium-term reform policies have been established and where political stability is anticipated, an APL with clearly defined successive phases and monitorable performance indicators offers a longer, more appropriate time horizon to accompany tertiary reform efforts. When necessary, the first phase of the APL would focus on consolidating the strategic framework and on building consensus among all stakeholders. In the context of an APL, competitive funds could be used in a programmatic lending mode, serving as grants for quality improvement projects at the institutional level and disbursed in tranches against the grant agreement rather than against individual expenditure items. The tranches would be released only when the grantholders met established targets. This approach could greatly enhance project performance and would place accountability for reform with the parties to the grant agreement.
- Where the tertiary education reform agenda is high on the government's priority list and where, as a result of government efforts to build consensus and raise public awareness, there is a clear commitment by all stakeholders to carry out the proposed reforms, Bank resources would be channeled through budget support in the context of sectorwide programs.
- In low-income countries involved in the preparation of a poverty reduction strategy credit (PRSC), assistance to tertiary education would focus on three dimensions: (a) resource rationalization measures to ensure balanced development of the entire education sector; (b) the effective contribution of tertiary education to the country's Education for All program, especially through teacher training institutions; and (c) the capacity-building role of tertiary education in

promoting the achievement of the other MDGs (agriculture, health, environment) and facilitate economic diversification efforts. These three areas of intervention would be complemented by targeted support for capacity building in a small number of postgraduate programs of excellence in chosen areas of comparative advantage for the country.

- Where there is government interest in initiating change in the tertiary education sector but the technical or political conditions for implementing a reform or starting an innovation are not fully present, the use of technical assistance loans (TALs) or learning and innovation loans (LILs) would be preferable for assisting governments in moving the reform agenda forward. Countries should use TALs to help formulate a comprehensive reform strategy and build a national consensus in favor of it. LILs should be used to try out innovations before replicating them on a larger scale. In Chile a LIL is being used to pilot new types of incentives for science and technology development within the framework of the Millennium Science Initiative. It is thereby paving the way for the launch of a large-scale operation incorporating the results of the pilot experience. Chile's experience has had positive spillovers in science and technology operations in Brazil, Mexico, and Venezuela.

- In countries that have established a positive regulatory and incentive framework to promote the development of private tertiary education, IFC loans and guarantees in support of individual private institutions would complement other World Bank Group sector support in an effective way. In Argentina, for instance, the International Bank for Reconstruction and Development (IBRD), part of the World Bank Group, has supported the launching of evaluation and accreditation mechanisms to ensure educational quality in both public and private institutions as part of the overall tertiary education reform, while the IFC has financed several individual private universities with accredited programs. In conformity with the purpose and focus of recent operations in South Asia and Latin America (see Appendix G), IFC operations in the tertiary education subsector could include supporting the establishment of new private institutions, strengthening existing private institutions (through expansion, introduction of new programs, and improvement in relevance and quality), and developing student loan schemes to help students attend private institutions (IFC 2001). Currently, in India the IFC, in cooperation with Citibank and with NIIT, one of India's largest and most reputable information technology education firms, is assisting in the creation of the country's first large-scale private sector student loan program, amounting to US$90 million. The NIIT student loan program will help fill an urgent need, since very few Indian financial institutions currently provide such loans. Elsewhere, IBRD lending in support of private tertiary education institutions is focusing on systemwide interventions for quality improvement and accreditation through competitive funding and on the establishment of student loan schemes for the entire private sector, on the model of the current IBRD lending operation in Mexico.

Promoting an Enabling Framework for Global Public Goods

Globalization and the growth of borderless education raise important issues that affect tertiary education in all countries but that are often beyond the control of any one government. Among the challenges of particular concern to countries seeking to build up their advanced human capital capacity are new forms of brain drain that result in a loss of local capacity in fields critical to development; the absence of a proper international accreditation and qualifications framework; the dearth of accepted legislation regarding foreign tertiary education providers; the lack of clear intellectual property regulations governing the content and distribution of distance education programs; and barriers to access to information and communication technologies, including the Internet (the "digital divide"). The World Bank is uniquely positioned to work with its partners in the international community—international organizations, bilateral donors, and foundations—to help facilitate or create a discussion platform and promote an enabling framework for the global public goods that are crucial for the future of tertiary education in the developing world.[3] This section briefly reviews the issues surrounding global public goods that are important for tertiary education and outlines actions the World Bank can take.

BRAIN DRAIN. An inevitable consequence of an increasingly integrated global economy and an internationally linked knowledge society is a rise in the worldwide mobility of skilled human resources. Circulation of human capital is seen by many economists as promoting global welfare and as representing a certain efficiency in the world labor market. For developing countries, however, this mobility is frequently viewed as a threat to national welfare and as an inefficient use of domestic public resources—as a loss of funds specifically allocated to educate citizens for the local market and of local capacity for satisfying development needs. The flight of human capital from developing countries, commonly referred to as brain drain, is a multifaceted phenomenon that is driven by much more than pure market forces and concerns about employability. It stems from the complex motivations and calculations of highly skilled individuals who choose to leave their families, communities, and homelands and is complicated by national-level pull (attraction) and push (expulsion) considerations. The motives that enter into educated citizens' decisions about studying or working abroad include the degree to which individual rights and protections are guaranteed at home, prevailing local incomes and employment benefits, the level of basic social services required or desired, the degree of indigenous institutional stability, the amount and type of recognition or affirmation accorded to deserving professionals, the specific work and community environment, and opportunities for professional growth and advancement. Typically, it is the most affluent students, who are the best prepared and can afford to study abroad with their own funding, who choose to emigrate. This is a concern only in that their potential contribution to local capacity may be lost. More troublesome is the human capital flight of individuals educated with local public funds. This represents a double loss to the local economy: loss of locally trained human resources and of human capital investment by the state.

In countries that are concerned about depletion of high-level human capital, governments, institutions, and employers have used both positive and negative interventions and enticements in an attempt to persuade skilled individuals to stay in the country, but usually with only marginal success. Examples of such interventions include salary supplements for professions at risk of brain drain; special reentry packages for graduate students who have completed their studies abroad; free return airfare and shipping and short-term salary guarantees for emigrant professionals who are willing to return home; and the contractual bonding of persons leaving for studies abroad to their employing institutions. Korea, Taiwan (China), and Turkey have implemented successful programs to bring back thousands of experts living overseas. It has been suggested that low-income countries might levy a "departure tax"on professionals who have benefited from highly subsidized local education but wish to leave the country for foreign employment. Some governments require departing professionals with outstanding debt, such as student loans, to repay their debt in full before they are allowed to leave their country.

Human capital emigration is not always a net loss to a country. Emigrants acquire new knowledge and skills while maintaining contact with their home countries, serving as information conduits, and contributing to national development through knowledge sharing. Today's diaspora of national scholars can promote a forging of new institutional partnerships among tertiary institutions abroad and facilitate the flow of knowledge back to their countries of origin. Electronic communication media have made it easier than ever before for intellectual and professional colleagues to remain in touch over distance and time. This professional and social interconnectedness eases not only the circulation of ideas but also the circulation of skilled human capital.

Despite the possible benefits, tertiary institutions and research centers are often at great risk of losing their highest-level human capital to brain drain. The loss of key staff may even generate an institutional crisis. Such hardship can, however, be the impetus for making constructive changes in the organization and remuneration of teaching and research, enhancing working conditions and improving the local climate for scholarship and productivity. Losing key staff, painful as it is, may impel governments to plan for more efficient use of skilled human resources. Another critical requirement for enticing highly skilled individuals to remain in the local labor market is full, unrestricted academic freedom.

As industrial nations face the problems of aging populations and, in many instances, a compression of the labor force, they are likely to become ever more aggressive in recruiting skilled labor from developing countries. It is important that donor agencies, development banks, and national governments not contribute directly to the brain drain through their development assistance projects, especially those supporting tertiary education. Although study and research abroad are critical to intellectual and professional development in many fields, agencies must be cautious about indiscriminately financing multiyear sojourns by local professors and students at tertiary education institutions in industrial countries. Program and project components that include staff development activities based on long-term graduate studies in a high-income country are likely to be vulnerable to staff defections. Evidence is mounting that shorter courses abroad are less likely to result in human capital flight. "Sandwich" or joint-study graduate programs, short tenures, and intensive courses may reduce the risk of staff defections by supporting and nurturing tighter linkages with the home institution. Another mitigating strategy would be to include, as part of scholarship funding, resources for the purchase of the minimum equipment and materials needed by returning scholars, as well as travel funds to allow regular return visits to the hosting institution abroad to regularly update skills and knowledge as needed.[4] Reliance on training institutions in countries that have an oversupply of skilled labor may also serve as an incentive against human capital flight and as a strategy for government-funded programs aimed at building and retaining local capacity. For example, under a recent World Bank project in Eritrea, the University of Asmara has made extensive use of universities in India for cost-effective staff development, with relatively low risk of brain drain.

A worrisome dimension of the brain drain problem that occasionally arises in the low-income countries with the weakest institutional capacity is the deliberate skimming of locally trained human capital by some industrial country governments. Countries as diverse as Jamaica, Senegal, and Tanzania, which themselves acutely need well-trained primary and secondary school teachers, have lost many qualified teachers to aggressive recruitment efforts by European countries faced with teacher shortages. The risk that industrial countries will become more forceful in their recruitment practices to compensate for their aging labor pools makes the issue all the more pressing. The World Bank can work with the OECD, the International Labour Organization (ILO), and the governments of developing countries concerned about brain drain to help devise ways of supporting and protecting professions critical to development objectives.

QUALITY ASSURANCE. The rapid development of virtual providers of tertiary education programs on a global scale, the increasing mobility of professionals across national borders, and the absence of quality assurance infrastructure and capacity in many developing countries make it important to establish an international framework that sets out minimum common standards worldwide. Such international accreditation systems are already being developed in some regions. For instance, the tertiary education policies of transition economies in Eastern Europe are greatly influenced by the coordinated international efforts to promote mobility, employability, and competitiveness being undertaken in Europe as a result of the 1999 Bologna Declaration, the 2001 Prague Declaration, and the 2001 Salamanca Convention. In South America the ministers of education of the Mercosur countries (Argentina, Bolivia, Brazil, Chile, Paraguay, and Uruguay) have established a minimum accreditation framework to facilitate the circulation of professionals from all member countries in their common labor market.

In addition to the support provided to accreditation projects in individual countries, the World Bank will contribute toward the goal of establishing an international qualifications framework through consultations with partners in the donor community and specialized professional associations, as well as through the Development Grant Facility. Two sets of complementary initiatives can be envisaged. First, the Bank could provide technical and financial assistance to groups of countries that wish to set up regional quality assurance systems. For example, the six Spanish-speaking countries of Central America (Costa Rica, El Salvador, Guatemala, Honduras, Nicaragua, and Panama) are constructing a regional accreditation system rather than have each country create its own quality assurance mechanism. Second, the Bank could support global quality assurance initiatives in particular disciplines, similar to the current efforts by the World Federation for Medical Education to establish a body of international standards in medical education.

With HIV/AIDS taking its toll on communities, institutions, and local capacity, the World Bank should help promote the pivotal leadership role that tertiary institutions can have in understanding the impact of the disease, through data collection and research and by educating communities about risks and care options. In addition, the Bank can help miti-gate the tragedy by working with tertiary institutions on the implemen-tation of awareness programs, related curricula, sensitive managerial practices, and community engagement.

TRADE BARRIERS. In the past few years the World Trade Organization (WTO) has spearheaded international efforts to reduce national trade barriers. The inclusion in these negotiations of an increasing number of goods and services is now raising concerns among public officials and in the academic community, especially in developing countries, that WTO rules for tradable goods and services might extend progressively to ter-tiary education services. The threat of increased competition by virtual and other nontraditional providers is leading some governments to take protectionist stands against foreign suppliers. In this context, the World Bank will work at both international and national levels to help define rules of conduct and appropriate safeguards to protect students from low-quality offerings and fraudulent providers, but without erecting rigid entry barriers. The following criteria could serve to guide govern-ments, licensing bodies, and tertiary education institutions in evaluating foreign providers that are not yet accredited by an internationally recog-nized agency: (a) minimum infrastructure, facilities, and staffing require-ments; (b) appropriate, transparent, and accurate information on policies, mission statements, study programs, and feedback mechanisms of foreign providers, including channels for complaints and appeals; (c) capacity-building partnerships between foreign providers and local institutions; (d) comparable academic quality and standards, including the full recognition in the home country of degrees and qualifications delivered by the foreign providers in a developing country; and (e) preservation of national culture.

INTELLECTUAL PROPERTY RIGHTS. A related issue faced by tertiary education institutions in developing countries is that of intellectual property rights for online programs and courses and for access to digital libraries and digital information. The current debate involves two opposing views. On one side, many universities in industrial countries favor enforcing strictly commercial rules for protection of the intellectual ownership of digital courses and materials, on behalf of the university itself or of its professors as intellectual authors. On the other side are the partisans of a public-good approach who, following MIT's recent initiative to offer all its course materials free of charge on its Website, advocate low-cost access to digital courses, textbooks, and journals for tertiary education institutions and scholars in low-income countries. The World Bank will play a brokering role to help create and nurture dissemination partner-ships among publishing companies, universities in advanced nations, and tertiary education institutions in developing countries. This could be done on the model of the recently announced agreement among six leading publishers of medical journals to give free access to their journals to more than 600 institutions in the poorest 60 countries of the world and low-cost access to an additional 30 low-income countries (Galbraith 2001).

BRIDGING THE DIGITAL GAP. The 2001 strategic framework paper, which outlines the World Bank's strategic directions at the corporate level, lists access to digital technologies as one of the main areas to which the World Bank is committed, viewing access to these technologies as a global public good. Many developing countries, especially low-income nations and small states, have limited resources for building up their ICT infrastructure and lack the economic and political leverage to negotiate favorable access and price conditions with international telecommunications firms. The ILO warned in its 2001 *World Employment Report* that the poorer countries may be unable "to reap the advantages that the new technologies could bring at any time soon. This is a worrisome dynamic and is the strongest argument for not letting markets alone dictate the course of the communications revolution" (ILO 2001). On the positive side, the experience of Bangalore, India, shows that a strong telecommunication and information technology infrastructure can stimulate employment growth not only through the development of a local IT industry but also through provision of offshore services for overseas firms and agencies.

As part of its strategic commitment to global public goods, the World Bank will contribute to decreasing the digital divide between industrial and developing countries by supporting investments in ICT infrastructure for tertiary education within countries, or even in a multicountry framework, as is happening under the Millennium Science Initiatives in Latin America and the African Virtual University in Sub-Saharan Africa.

Notes

1. The Operations Evaluation Department (OED) of the World Bank conducted a review of tertiary education projects that had begun in the 1980s and 1990s and had been completed by 2000. The review confirms the importance of considering the political economy of reforms and of relying on positive incentives to induce change in tertiary education systems. The study did not show a clear correlation between the comprehensiveness of reforms and outcomes. The sample, however, did not include some recent tertiary education operations (in, for example, Argentina, Chile, and Indonesia) that support a comprehensive set of reforms and appear at this time to have generated encouraging results. Moreover, many of the projects reviewed in the OED exercise were focused on modern-

ization rather than reforms. A more complete understanding of comprehensive approaches and their effectiveness will be possible only after additional reform projects have been completed and fully evaluated.

2. See Appendix D for a detailed description of the types of intervention under each category.

3. The development agencies include UNESCO, the OECD, the European Union, the International Labour Organization (ILO), the Association for the Development of Education in Africa (ADEA), and the Northern Policy Research Review and Advisory Network on Education and Training (NORRAG).

4. This approach has been successfully pioneered in East Africa by the German Academic Exchange Program (DAAD).

Appendixes

Appendix I. Promoting Science and Technology for Development: The World Bank's Millennium Science Initiative

Appendix J. Statistical Tables on Tertiary Education

Appendix K. Socioeconomic Inequities in Tertiary Education: Enrollment and Government Expenditure by Income Quintile

Appendix A. New Issues Facing Tertiary Education Systems and Institutions

The profound changes sweeping the world—globalization of labor and other markets, the information and communication revolution, and sociopolitical transformations—pose challenges and open opportunities for tertiary education systems in all countries, including developing and transition countries. This appendix, organized according to aspects of the tertiary education system, outlines the questions education policymakers may want to consider as they plan for the future of tertiary education in their countries.

Nature of the Education and Training Experience

- How can sufficient direct communication and human interaction on wired campuses and in Web-based courses be promoted in order to build up critical thinking and social learning? What is an appropriate mix of face-to-face and online teaching?
- With so many program configurations and course options to choose from, how can students construct an adequate academic path on their own?
- Is there too much emphasis on science and technology programs? What are the prospects for humanities and social sciences? How can students acquire the values needed to live as responsible citizens?
- How can online students benefit from the international dimension of foreign studies (immersion in a different culture)?
- How can a strong sense of identity and community be maintained in institutions that serve a heterogeneous student population?

Academic Management

- What types of mechanisms and arrangements are desirable and effective for introducing flexibility and strengthening the system's capacity to change, adapt, and innovate rapidly? How can stability be maintained in an ever-changing environment?
- How can interdisciplinarity and multidisciplinarity be promoted across traditional faculty and program boundaries?
- How should programs and courses for part-time students and returning graduates be organized? Should they be integrated into regular programs or organized as separate programs? Should pedagogical approaches be adapted for use with these students?
- Will the prestige of programs be based on that of the offering institution or on the reputation of individual faculty members? What is the future of tenure?

Use of Technology

- How can technologies be identified that are best suited to the curricular and pedagogical objectives of the programs?
- What is the appropriate balance between "high tech" and "high touch" (the degree of human interaction as a counterbalancing human response to the use of technology)?[1]
- How can overreliance on technological gimmicks and loss of hands-on training opportunities be avoided?
- How can linguistic and cultural identity be preserved as communication in a major world language becomes increasingly imperative?

Financing

- How can new educational technologies and the related infrastructures be financed sustainably?
- How can the growth of a digital divide between institutions and countries be prevented?
- How can tertiary education institutions remain viable as financial support shifts to consumers, faculty members become more independent, and degrees fade in importance?

Governance

- How can universities with a decentralized setup (that is, with autonomous faculties and departments) undertake the type of comprehensive change required by the new challenges?
- How can a sense of academic mission be maintained in an environment of emerging corporate behaviors and the risk of corporate takeover?
- How can academic freedom best be preserved as corporate financing of research programs grows?

Quality Assurance

- What evaluation and accreditation mechanisms and methods are appropriate for online and distance education programs?
- What evaluation methodology should be used to assess programs that involve heavy use of information technology?
- Should standards for part-time students be different from those for regular students?

1. The concepts of "high tech" and "high touch" were introduced by John Naisbitt in his 1982 book *Megatrends: Ten New Directions Transforming Our Lives.*

- How can national authorities exercise quality control over foreign institutions established in their countries? How will rulings by the World Trade Organization (WTO) and decisions under the General Agreement on Trade in Services (GATS) affect national governments' ability to regulate these institutions?
- Should governments have different policies for not-for-profit and for-profit private institutions?
- How can students access current information on the quality of online institutions and programs?
- How are credit transfer arrangements between campus-based and virtual universities and among virtual tertiary institutions to be organized and regulated?
- How should the competencies and qualifications of students taking a multi-institutional academic path be assessed?
- How is the demand for rapid program and course development to be reconciled with the need for careful quality review?

Intellectual Property

- How should intellectual property rights be defined and protected in the case of educational materials prepared specifically for online use? Who owns online courses—the university or the professor? How should their use be regulated?
- How are the intellectual property rights and academic freedom of professors to be reconciled with the rights and interests of their home institutions? Are professors undermining their own academic freedom in their search for protection of intellectual property rights for courses?

Appendix B. Benchmarks for Measuring the Quality of Internet-Based Programs

The new learning technologies made possible by the Internet require different quality measurement standards from those used for conventional programs—or at least call for modification of the traditional standards. This appendix suggests some guidelines for assessing Internet-based educational programs. Benchmarks are suggested for each aspect of the education system.

Institutional support
Security
Reliability of technology delivery system
Centralized support system for distance education infrastructure

Course development
Guidelines for minimum standards in course development,
    design, and delivery, based on desired learning outcomes
Periodic review of instructional materials
Engagement of students in analysis, synthesis, and evaluation

Teaching and learning
Student interaction with faculty
Timely and constructive feedback for student assignments and
    questions
Instruction in research methods

Course structure
Motivation and basic technology knowledge checked before
    registration
Clear course information
Sufficient library resources
Agreement by faculty and students on expectations for completion of
    student assignments and for faculty response

Student support
Full information on programs and student support services
Hands-on training for information research
Access to technical assistance
Accurate and timely response to student queries, including
    complaints

Faculty support
Technical assistance in course development
Training in the transition from classroom teaching to online
    instruction
Continuing assistance during course delivery
Written resources

Evaluation and assessment
Evaluation of effectiveness of teaching and learning
Use of data on enrollment, costs, and innovative applications of
    technology
Review of intended learning outcomes

Source: Phipps (2000).

Appendix C. Resource Diversification Matrix for Public Tertiay Institutions by Source and Category of Income

	Source of income				
Category of income	*Government (national, state, municipal)*	*Students and families*	*Industry and services*	*Alumni and other philanthropists*	*International cooperation*
Budgetary contribution					
General budget	X				
Dedicated taxes (lottery, tax on liquor sales, tax on contracts)	X				
Payroll tax			X		
Fees					
Tuition fees					
Degree programs		X			
Nondegree programs		X	X		
Advance payments		X			
Chargeback	X				
Other fees (registration, labs)		X			
Affiliation fees (colleges)			X		
Productive activities					
Services					
Consulting	X		X		X
Research	X		X	X	X
Laboratory tests	X		X		
Patent royalties, share of spinoff profits, monetized patent royalties deal			X	X	
Operation of service enterprises (television, hotel, retirement homes, malls, parking)			X		
Financial products (endowment funds, shares)			X		
Production of goods					
Agricultural products			X		
Industrial products			X		
Rental of facilities (land, classrooms, dormitories, laboratories, ballrooms, drivethrough, concert halls, mortuary space)			X	X	
Sale of assets (land, residential housing)			X	X	

Category of income	Government (national, state, municipal)	Students and families	Industry and services	Alumni and other philanthropists	International cooperation
Donations					
Direct donations					
Monetary grants			X	X	X
Equipment			X	X	
Land and buildings	X			X	
Scholarships and student loans	X		X	X	X
Indirect donations (credit card, percentage of gas sales income, percentage of stock exchange trade)		X	X		
Tied donations (access to patents, share of spinoff profits)			X		
Concessions (products sold on campus, names)			X		
Loans	X		X		X

Source: Compiled by Jamil Salmi.

Appendix D. World Bank Tertiary Education Projects by Type of Intervention and by Region, Fiscal 1995–2001

Area of support	Sub-Saharan Africa	Eastern Europe and Central Asia	Latin America and the Caribbean	Middle East and North Africa	South Asia	East and Asia and Pacific
Vision development, strategic planning, and consensus building						
National level	Guinea Mozambique Senegal	Bulgaria Hungary Romania		Egypt, Arab Rep. Jordan Tunisia		China Indonesia Vietnam
Institutional level	Eritrea Mauritius Mozambique	Hungary Romania Russian Fed.	Argentina Chile	Egypt, Arab Rep. Jordan		China Indonesia Vietnam
Financing reforms						
Allocation of recurrent budget	Madagascar Mozambique	Hungary Romania	Argentina	Egypt, Arab Rep. Jordan Tunisia		China Indonesia Philippines
Competitive fund (investment)	Madagascar	Romania	Argentina Chile			China Indonesia
Cost sharing		Hungary				
Student loans		Bulgaria Hungary	Mexico Jamaica Venezuela, Rep. Bol. de			

Scholarships		Romania	Jamaica			
Governance and management reforms						
National policy body		Hungary Romania		Jordan		Indonesia
Adoption of academic credit system		Hungary Romania			India	
Management information system		Hungary	Argentina	Egypt, Arab Rep. Jordan Tunisia		Vietnam
Quality improvement						
Strengthening of existing programs	Cameroon Mauritius	Russian Fed.			India	Thailand
Evaluation/accreditation system		Romania	Argentina Chile	Jordan	India	
Innovation in program content/delivery	Madagascar	Hungary Romania	Argentina Chile	Egypt, Arab Rep. Jordan Tunisia		China Indonesia
Innovation in academic organization		Hungary Romania		Jordan		
Information and communication infrastructure		Hungary	Argentina			

Appendix D, *continued*

Area of support	Sub-Saharan Africa	Eastern Europe and Central Asia	Latin America and the Caribbean	Middle East and North Africa	South Asia	East and Asia and Pacific
Institutional diversification						
Establishment or strengthening of polytechnic and technical institutes	Ghana Mauritius		Chile	Egypt, Arab Rep. Jordan Tunisia	India	Malaysia Philippines Thailand
Science and technology development						
Strategy development; capacity for monitoring and evaluation			Brazil			
Reform of allocation mechanism/competitive fund		Romania	Chile Venezuela, Rep. Bol. de			
Promotion of research in priority areas	Mauritius	Romania	Brazil Chile Venezuela, Rep. Bol. de			
Joint public–private sector technology development			Brazil Mexico			
Capacity for metrology, standards, quality testing; intellectual property rights			Brazil Mexico			

Appendix E. Analytical Work in Tertiary Education by the World Bank, Fiscal 1995–2001

Table E.1 Tertiary Education Sector Studies

Country or region and fiscal year	Title; main themes and conclusions	If followed by project, year of project
Romania, 1995	*Strategy Note for Higher Education Reform* Diversification of higher education programs Development of accreditation Development of academic credit system New employment status for academic staff Expansion of postgraduate education Increased cost recovery Improved budget allocation	1996
China, 1996	*Higher Education Reform* Creation of enabling environment by state in which universities can plan their destinies within policy framework set by state Changes in internal university management that include the governing bodies and computerized management information system Financing of higher education through diversification of resources; requires improvement of operating efficiency of system, enhancement of capacity for resource generation, and continuation of cost-recovery policies, complemented by financial assistance system Quality improvement in instructional programs to cover curriculum, teaching and research, quality assurance, and educational inputs and facilities	1999
Jordan, 1996	*Higher Education Development Study* Provision of regulatory environment for dealing with public and private institutions; governance, policymaking, and management practices Improvement of financing mechanisms through private resource mobilization and improved efficiency of public expenditure Increased labor market linkages through collection of data on graduates and labor market surveys Reduction of internal inefficiencies and improvement of quality in education Revision of community college system Mobilization of use of private institutions to reduce the public burden Capacity building for advanced scientific training and research	2000

Table E.1, *continued*

Country or region and fiscal year	Title; main themes and conclusions	If followed by project, year of project
Cambodia, 1997	*Higher Education Development* Governance Credit system Cost recovery	1999
Tunisia, 1997	*Higher Education: Challenges and Opportunities* *Problems identified:* low internal efficiency, linked to channeling of students into compartmentalized fields of study; institutional organization and resource allocation that leave educational establishments with little responsibility and that discourage openness and private initiative; inefficiency in teaching profession stemming from antiquated promotion system; financing almost entirely by public sector and not capable of covering costs of system expansion *Recommendations:* modular style of academic organization that eliminates rigid channeling of students; decentralization in decisionmaking; results-oriented resource allocation and greater autonomy in funding management; separation of teaching and research functions, as well as educator training and evaluation services; financing of expansion of system through recovery of service costs and increased private participation	1998
Brazil, 2000	*Higher Education Sector Study* *Problems identified:* Low standards for quality of instruction and relevance of curriculum; public system provides high-quality education but is marked by inefficiencies as compared with private system *Government strategy for improvement of system:* (a) changes in legal framework; (b) changes in funding system for higher education through greater autonomy with accountability; and (c) evaluation of quality of instruction and performance of institutions Continued trend toward expansion and diversification in the system *External efficiency:* expansion of system needed to ensure long-term economic growth and long-term competitiveness in regard to quality of labor force *Internal efficiency:* high per-student costs, especially in federal university system; high compensation of nonacademic staff; generous pension provisions	

Table E.1, *continued*

Country or region and fiscal year	Title; main themes and conclusions	If followed by project, year of project
	Recommendations: increased access through improved financial assistance; improved quality through rigorous internal quality assurance mechanism; increased relevance through changes in curriculum and identification of national needs; increased efficiency through changes in the civil service system	Not yet decided
India, 2000	*Scientific and Technical Manpower Development* *Problems identified:* overcentralization and lack of autonomy and accountability owing to multiple controls at the central and state government levels; resource constraints and wastage due to internal rigidities; poor quality and relevance of program content in relation to labor market demands; difficulties in retaining S&T personnel in education due to noncompetitive salaries; poor technology/infrastructure support; issue of limited access of disadvantaged groups and regional disparities *Reform strategies:* empowerment and accountability of individual institutions (and faculty) through decentralization of authority and establishment of responsive, accountable management culture; optimal utilization of resources and encouragement of larger private investments; mobilization of additional financial resources from a variety of sources; establishment of effective quality assurance mechanisms for teaching and curriculum reform; networking with other educational institutions, R&D laboratories, and industry establishments to enhance capacity, improve quality, and achieve excellence; increased access to S&T education; reduction in regional imbalances To implement reform, action at the systemic and institutional levels toward improved performance and self-reliance required	2003
Venezuela, Rep. Bol. de, 2000	*Higher Education Sector Profile* Expansion of the higher education system, especially in the private and nonuniversity sectors Inequity in access through the centralized admission system *Governance and financing:* inefficient allocation of public resources	Not yet decided

Table E.1, *continued*

Country or region and fiscal year	Title; main themes and conclusions	If followed by project, year of project
	Quality: professor salaries and advancement in the university system; accreditation of new institutions and of curricular changes *Internal efficiency:* variation across institutional types as reflected in number of graduates and dropouts *External efficiency:* decrease in rate of return to higher education	
Yemen, Rep., 2000	*Higher Education Sector Work* Access and equity Quality and relevance Governance and management Fiscal sustainability	Not yet decided

Note: R&D, research and development; S&T, science and technology.

Table E.2 Sections on Tertiary Education in Education Sector Studies

Country and fiscal year	Title of work; main themes and conclusions
Tunisia, 1996	*Private Provision of Education Services* Development of private higher education
Vietnam, 1996	*Education Financing Sector Study* Enrollment trends in higher education compared with primary and secondary education Unit costs and internal efficiency: economies of scale and scope in tertiary education External efficiency and equity: earnings of higher education graduates Future direction for education finance: enhanced cost recovery in tertiary education through government policies and complementary measures
Lao PDR, 1997	*Public Expenditure Review: Improving Efficiency and Equity in Spending Priorities* Small section on expanding and rationalizing higher education
Philippines, 1998	*Education for the 21st Century* Skills for competitiveness; need to expand S&T fields and recruit qualified teachers Higher education system constrained by efficiency (internal, external), quality level in state university or college, equity in access *Policy options:* develop a reliable set of performance indicators comparable to international best practice; rationalize the structure and management of the Commission on Higher Education; introduce a comprehensive program of student financial assistance; improve the quality of teaching and research to international standards; further deregulate the curriculum to foster innovation; improve and expand the output of university S&T programs *Management issues:* strengthen the Commission on Higher Education's oversight responsibility for higher education; raise institutional standards to those of accredited universities in other countries
Thailand, 1998	*Education Achievements, Issues and Policies* Development of universities to meet demand for high-level manpower in economy; widening of the mandate of the Rajabhat Institutes *Access and equity:* social and regional equity issues addressed through education loan scheme, expansion of regional quota in regional universities, changing role of the Rajabhat Institutes *Role of private institutions:* government encouragement of expansion of private sector through enabling legislation and financial incentives; quality of new private higher education institutions ensured through accreditation process

Table E.2, *continued*

Country and fiscal year	Title of work; main themes and conclusions
	Universities: need for greater institutional autonomy and budgetary self-sufficiency; cost-recovery mechanisms for public institutions; staffing policies to introduce incentives for teaching staff to conduct research and to receive advanced training abroad in areas lacking well-developed postgraduate programs; change in enrollment structure through measures to increase enrollment in S&T fields

Note: S&T, science and technology.

Table E.3 World Bank Publications on Tertiary Education by Year of Issue

Country or region and publication year	Title; main themes and conclusions	Originating department
Worldwide, 1995	*Developing Capacity for Research and Advanced Scientific Training: Lessons from World Bank Experience* World Bank lending strategies for higher education and S&T development; lessons from project experience. Capacity building must address the need to reform the financing and management of higher education and research systems. Efforts to increase the efficiency of government and donor investments in higher education and research must combine strengthening of accountability with increased institutional autonomy. Investment in capacity building needs to be combined with fostering the use of such capacity by enterprises, producers, government, and society as a whole.	Education and Social Policy
Worldwide, 1995	*Reforming Higher Education Systems: Some Lessons to Guide Policy Implementation* Variety of country experiences in establishing mechanisms to coordinate development of higher education systems, in diversifying institutional financing, and in increasing efficiency of public investments. Need for effective policy structures to manage higher education, to link costs of reforms to benefits such as increased opportunity, to take account of institutional constraints on change, and to carefully articulate educational reforms with other public policies that influence the performance of higher education systems.	Education and Social Policy
Worldwide, 1998	*The Financing and Management of Higher Education: A Status Report on Worldwide Reforms* Context of higher education reform: expansion and diversification; fiscal pressure, market orientation, accountability, quality, and efficiency. Trends and reforms in finance and management: supplementation of government with nongovernment revenues; reform of public sector financing; restructuring of higher education institutions.	Human Development Network, Education

Table E.3, *continued*

Country or region and publication year	Title; main themes and conclusions	Originating department
Worldwide, 1998	*Higher Education Relevance in the 21st Century* Massification of higher education and research. Collegiality, managerialism, and the fragmentation of knowledge. Globalization and international competitiveness. Use of new technologies in knowledge production and dissemination. Transition to knowledge industries. Diversification in provision of higher education.	Human Development Network, Education
Worldwide, 1998	*Opciones para Reformar el Financiamiento de la Enseñanza Superior* Challenges to higher education financing include the political challenge of democracy, technological challenges, and the strong social challenge that demands responsiveness of higher education. Exploration of alternative financing mechanisms to generate resources outside public financing while increasing access and quality. Questioning of innovative efforts to reverse past experiences, as well as the possibility of overcoming the current crisis in higher education. Recommendations suggest a strategic, institutional approach in the definition of excellence, reinforced by specific financial measures to build institutional capacity in higher education.	Latin America and the Caribbean Human Development
Worldwide, 1998	*Quality Assurance in Higher Education: Recent Progress; Challenges Ahead* Growing government interest in establishing policy mechanisms to ensure quality and accountability in higher education. Trends toward expansion have brought institutional diversification; shift toward formal systems of quality assurance in higher education. Public reporting component is a key element in many models. Dispute about quality review of academic institutions versus academic programs and the appropriate use of quantitative information in monitoring operations of institutions of higher education. Quality assurance must address both the increased use of educational technology and the interest in global delivery of educational services.	Human Development Network, Education

Table E.3, *continued*

Country or region and publication year	Title; main themes and conclusions	Originating department
France, 1998	*The Organization of Studies in the French University System* Theoretical organization of university studies: the state defines global framework; within this framework, universities are responsible for organization; suggestions by universities to the state are evaluated. Autonomy of university professors in defining the contents of degree programs and course materials is extensive and is reinforced by the lack of assessment procedures. Recent attempts have been made to find equilibrium between national framework set by the state and the autonomy of each university.	Latin America and the Caribbean Human Development
Philippines, 1998	*Higher Education in the Philippines* Rationalization of the system by delineating the role of the public sector and concentrating resources on a few institutions to achieve desired quality. Reduction of financial constraints and inefficiencies: granting greater financial autonomy to higher education institutions and removing credit market failures in student loan scheme. Introducing a variety of strategies for quality improvement. Making external governance effective through changes in the Commission on Higher Education.	Asian Development Bank and World Bank
Bulgaria, 1999	*Higher Education: Policy Design and System Management Legal framework.* National evaluation and accreditation system. Resource management. Quality assurance: internal self-assessment and external evaluation. Improvement of (teaching and learning) quality in a competitive context.	Europe and Central Asia Human Development
Ecuador, 1999	*The Financing of Higher Education in Ecuador* Overview of overfunding of higher education includes the budget process, public and private expenditures on higher education, and trends and patterns. Policy options might address the inequity in public resource allocation and the inefficient use of public resources.	Latin America and the Caribbean Human Development

Table E.3, *continued*

Country or region and publication year	Title; main themes and conclusions	Originating department
Ghana, 1999	*Tertiary Education Policy in Ghana: An Assessment 1988–1998* Assurance of educational quality and relevance. Financial sustainability of the tertiary education system. System expansion and differentiation. Role of the polytechnics. Institutional capacities necessary for system management.	Human Development Network, Education
South Africa, 1999	*Poverty and Inequality in the Distribution of Public Education Spending in South Africa* (includes higher education) Distribution of public spending on primary, secondary, and tertiary education by socioeconomic group.	Africa Region, Country Department I
Uganda, 1999	*Financing Higher Education in Africa: Makerere, the Quiet Revolution* Alternative financing strategies; demand-driven academic reform; decentralization and participatory management; the impact of financial and administrative reforms. Reasons for success; the virtue of necessity; macroeconomic reforms and economic growth; political stability, trust, autonomy; local government reform and decentralization; institutional leadership; ownership. Issues and unfinished business: limits of privatization; quality: teaching and research; internal efficiency; external efficiency; equity; sustainability.	Human Development Network, Education
Worldwide, 2000	*Innovation Funds for Universities* Use of innovation funds to promote and finance improvements in university quality. Policy tools to help university systems improve academic and management quality, introduce innovations aimed at greater academic relevance, and increase university cost-effectiveness. Organization and management of innovation funds.	Latin America and the Caribbean Human Development
Worldwide, 2000	*Higher Education in Developing Countries: Peril and Promise* Higher education and the public interest: need for state policies to protect and promote the public interest in higher education, with the critical principle of autonomy; short-term political interest versus long-term national needs in higher education.	World Bank–UNESCO Task Force on Higher Education and Society

Table E.3, *continued*

Country or region and publication year	Title; main themes and conclusions	Originating department
	Systemwide coordination needed to ensure balance of diversity, autonomy, and competition in both the public and private sectors. Task Force has identified a set of basic principles and tools that promotes good governance across a wide variety of institutions. Strong international leadership for sustained intellectual and financial support for strengthening the S&T capacity of developing countries, as well as efforts to link higher education institutions in developing countries with centers of S&T excellence worldwide.	
Worldwide, 2000	*Tertiary Education in the Twenty-first Century: Challenges and Opportunities* New challenges to the role of higher education: economic globalization; the growing importance of knowledge; the information and communication revolution. Implications for higher education: changing training needs and demand patterns; new forms of competition; changes in structures and modes of operation.	Latin America and the Caribbean Human Development
Argentina, 2000	*Argentina: Fondo de Mejoramiento de la Calidad Universitaria (FOMEC) Evaluación Preliminar y Metodología para la Evaluación de Impacto* Pioneering efforts to introduce competitive financing for quality improvement in higher education. Preliminary evaluation of FOMEC, the Competitive Fund for Enhancement of Educational Quality: characteristics, program execution, and general assessment of evaluation process. Analytical framework for FOMEC and change in higher education institutions.	Latin America and the Caribbean Human Development
Sub-Saharan Africa, 2000	*Tertiary Distance Education and Technology in Sub-Saharan Africa* Benefits of tertiary distance education in providing greater access, improved quality, and cost-efficiency. Institutional models of distance education.	Human Development Network, Education

Note: S&T, science and technology.

Appendix F. World Bank Lending for Tertiary Education: Graphical Overview

Figure F.1 World Bank Lending for Tertiary Education Worldwide, Fiscal 1990–2000

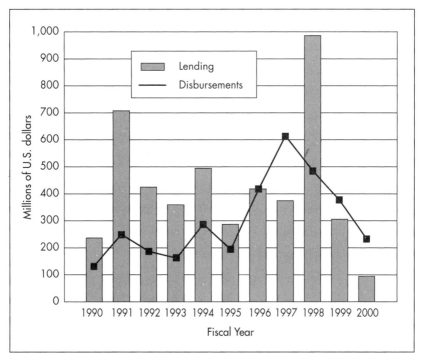

Figure F.2 World Bank Lending for Tertiary Education by Subsector, Fiscal 1963–2000

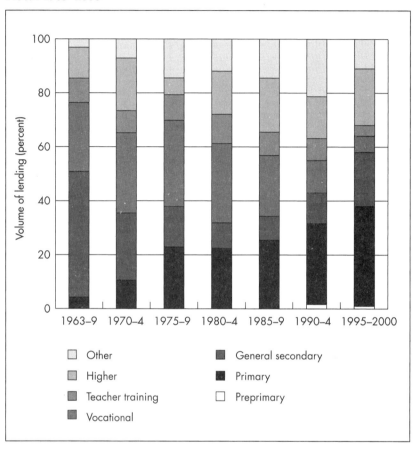

Figure F.3 World Bank Lending for Tertiary Education by Region, Fiscal 1990–2000

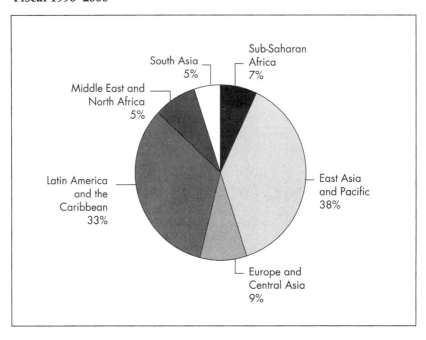

Figure F.4 Ten Largest Borrowers for Tertiary Education, Fiscal 1990–2000

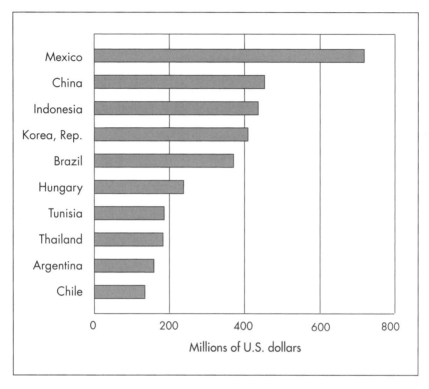

Appendix G. World Bank Group Tertiary Education Projects: Descriptions and Lessons

Table G.1　IBRD Loans and IDA Credits by Fiscal Year and Recipient, Fiscal 1995–2001

Country and fiscal year	Project name; main components	Amount (millions of U.S. dollars) and source
Argentina, 1995	*Higher Education Reform* Institutional strengthening Competitive Fund for Enhancement of Educational Quality (FOMEC) Establishment of national accreditation system Systemwide management information system Formula funding for allocation of public resources	165 (IBRD)
China, 1995	*Technology Development* Transformation of R&D establishment into market-responsive technology development and service-oriented elements of existing research institutions to create new market-oriented entities, the engineering research centers Complementary investments in improving techno-logical public services, including the National Institute of Metrology and technical assistance for a Productivity Center	200 (IBRD)
Guinea, 1995	*Higher Education Management Support* Support of institutional reorganization by financing analysis and reform of university governance, finance, management, female participation, student services, user fees, and other areas in context of decentralization and institutional autonomy; financing for ministry-level develop-ment of accreditation and evaluation procedures Upgrading of information and communication sys-tem by overhauling data collection and dissemina-tion procedures at central ministry level, creating institutional information system, and improving communications Improvement of budgetary programming and moni-toring capacities by supporting ministry-level as well as institution-level financial management	6.6 (IDA)
India, 1995	*Agriculture Human Resource Development Project* Improvement of quality and relevance of higher education and in-service training in agriculture Strengthening of capacity to develop and manage human resources	59.5 (IDA)

Table G.1, *continued*

Country and fiscal year	Project name; main components	Amount (millions of U.S. dollars) and source
Mauritius, 1995	*Higher and Technical Education Project* Strengthening the University of Mauritius: improving the quality of education at the university by upgrading staff and facilities; increasing the number of quality graduates in all fields, with particular emphasis on science, engineering, and management; improving links with employers in order to make curriculum more relevant to national needs and increase the marketability of graduates; developing a viable postgraduate education and research program to attract and retain faculty and produce new knowledge in areas strategic to the country's development; enhancing the efficiency of the university's operations Rationalizing polytechnical education: improving the quality of faculty, curricula, and facilities; supporting the development of key nonengineering programs and strengthening linkages between the polytechnics and both the university and the private sector; strengthening the capacity of the Management Trust Fund, which runs the polytechnics, to formulate policies, monitor labor markets, and consult with employers	16 (IBRD)
Indonesia, 1996	*Higher Education Support: Development of Undergraduate Education* University development program: block grants to six universities for strengthening of undergraduate education Institutional capacity building for Board of Higher Education Implementation of national accreditation system for higher education: consolidation of the National Accreditation Board (BAN) and strengthening of its capacity to establish accreditation systems Competitive domestic fellowship program for recent graduates and present teaching staff Project administration: financing of Central Project Coordinating Unit	65 (IBRD)
Jamaica, 1996	*Student Loan* Restructuring of Student Loan Bureau Expansion of student loan program; loans to be disbursed and collected by commercial banking system	28.5 (IBRD)

Table G.1, *continued*

Country and fiscal year	Project name; main components	Amount (millions of U.S. dollars) and source
	Establishment of grant-in-aid program for poorest students Public awareness campaign to disseminate information about policy changes in cost recovery and about financing options available through the expanded student loan scheme	
Romania, 1996	*Reform of Higher Education and Research* Management capacity improvement: support for improving performance of semiautonomous councils as part of government reform to replace centralized control by the Ministry of Education Undergraduate and continuing education: support for new program development, especially in fields of high student and labor market demand; selection of new programs on a competitive basis according to agreed evaluation criteria Postgraduate education and research centers: development of advanced courses of instruction and research needed for next generation of academic staff and professionals, with advanced training in the new fields required by the market economy; support of research grants program for individual and team research of master and doctoral students	50 (IBRD)
Senegal, 1996	*Higher Education* Improvement of library services through expansion and rehabilitation of the central library of the Université Cheikh Anta Diop de Dakar (UCAD), acquisition of books, and periodicals/library management Upgrading of teaching and research: reinforcement of applied science teaching; development and pilot testing of accreditation system; management of a university research fund; study of alternative models for teaching and financing; installation of computerized information service Strengthening of management capacity; includes reorganization of student services, development of maintenance system, and project administration Refinancing of three Project Preparation Facility (PPF) advances	26.5 (IDA)

Table G.1, *continued*

Country and fiscal year	Project name; main components	Amount (millions of U.S. dollars) and source
Brazil, 1997	*Science and Technology Reform Support* Technology development to stimulate R&D&E activities in the private sector, focusing on innovations by small and medium-size enterprises, on ways of streamlining public incentives for R&D, and on greater productive use of scientific and technological resources by firms S&T research to increase and improve the stock of high-level human capital, focusing on investments in scientific research and graduate training under improved procedures and policies, including incentive mechanisms aimed at shifting scientists' and technicians' focus toward areas more relevant to the productive sector Sectoral support to improve efficiency and quality throughout the S&T system (improved monitoring and evaluation systems)	155 (IBRD)
Eritrea, 1997	*Human Resources Development* External technical assistance: recruitment of foreign nationals from selected high-quality universities Foreign training for Eritrean nationals, mostly at M.A. level but also some Ph.D. and B.A Institutional strengthening and project administration through human resource development, provision of computer equipment, and technical support	15.2 (IDA)
Indonesia, 1997	*Quality of Undergraduate Education* Improvement of educational quality through competitive grants to undergraduate programs at private and public universities Improvement of discipline service centers through direct investment and performance awards Support for Central Project Coordinating Unit	9.5 (IBRD)
Russian Federation, 1997	*Education Innovation* (with higher education component) Higher Education Innovation Fund to encourage reform of selected higher education institutions; includes three complementary "windows" for capacity building in social science institutions, for governance reform, and for social sciences academic support	71 (IBRD), of which 50 for higher education

Table G.1, *continued*

Country and fiscal year	Project name; main components	Amount (millions of U.S. dollars) and source
Thailand, 1997	*University Science & Engineering Education* Improve quality of undergraduate science and engineering programs through financing for institutional development program: (a) short-term overseas training for selected academic and technical support staff in the educational use and maintenance of project-financed equipment, and (b) technical assistance and academic support services	143.4 (IBRD)
Cameroon, 1998	*Higher Education Technical Training* Strengthening of existing disciplines through introduction of new training options requested by local industries Addition of new disciplines and system coherence Institutional development, evaluation and follow-up, and sustainability of policy initiatives	4.8 (IDA)
Chile, 1998	*Higher Education Improvement* Policy framework and capacity building: (a) enhancement of the legal and regulatory framework, including development of appropriate roles of the tiers involved in higher education institutions, establishment of policies and mechanisms for transfer of students and graduates between institutions, and proposals for amendments to present and future laws; and (b) development of policies in urgent areas, establishment of networking procedures between various types of higher education institutions, capacity building for planning and management at various higher education institutions, design of a management information system, and implementation of a marketing campaign to promote technical education Quality assurance: (a) consolidation of the national system for quality assurance through creation of a National Board for Accreditation and Evaluation; (b) establishment of a qualification framework for study programs with specifics for undergraduate, graduate, and technical programs; (c) design and implementation of a quality awareness campaign Financing: (a) in institutional funding, increase in institutional accountability by establishing a coherent policy as foundation for funding methodology, increasing accountability and developing a funding methodology, and establishing	145.45 (IBRD)

Table G.1, *continued*

Country and fiscal year	Project name; main components	Amount (millions of U.S. dollars) and source
	Competitive Fund for Quality and Relevance; (b) in student aid, revision of student loan and scholarship schemes by identifying causes of existing inequalities and by revising policy instruments that target students' needs, in light of stated national policy	
Hungary, 1998	*Higher Education Reform* Policy and institutional development through reforms in allocation of students and finance, administration of higher education, teaching programs and structures, tuition charges and student loans, private higher education Introduction of Higher Education Institutes Investment Program by government for integration of single-purpose institutions into multifaculty colleges and universities Management information system: includes expert services for development of strategy and process redesign, software development, upgrading of information technology networks, and training support Management capacity development in areas of planning, financial management, information systems, academic reform, and policy analysis Development of a national guaranteed student loan program Project Management and Project Preparation Facility	150 (IBRD)
Madagascar, 1998	*Education Sector Development* (with higher education component) Three project components, one each for primary, secondary, and tertiary education Reform of higher education by assisting institutions to modernize and diversify through financing of subprojects under a Fund for the Development of Higher Education	65 (IBRD/ IDA) of which 5 for higher education
Mexico, 1998	*Knowledge and Innovation* S&T research: improve the quantity, quality, and relevance of research and human capital formation through field development to stimulate research in new and lagging fields of scientific, social, and economic relevance; research projects to promote research quality, improve peer review; institutional strengthening of National Council for Science and Technology (CONACYT)	300 (IBRD)

Table G.1, *continued*

Country and fiscal year	Project name; main components	Amount (millions of U.S. dollars) and source
	Industry-university linkage: support joint action between universities/research institutes and the private sector by restructuring public S&T institutes, providing matching grants for joint industry-academic projects, funding technical assistance to universities to strengthen outreach Enterprise technology enhancement: financing of technology modernization program to upgrade small and medium-size enterprises; private regional/sectoral technology support centers; special pilot programs to foster consultation among government, academia, and the private sector; pilot venture capital fund	
Mexico, 1998	*Higher Education Financing* Establishment of private student loan agency for students in private universities (nationwide) Strengthening of Sonora State student loan agency	180.2 (IBRD)
Tunisia, 1998	*Higher Education Reform* Supply response: extension of academic and nonacademic public facilities in both existing and new sites to absorb additional students; upgrading of scientific equipment in existing institutions to avoid widening gap between these and new institutions; establishment of new libraries and restocking of existing libraries; development of private sector interest in higher education sector in pedagogic service provision, as well as ancillary service provision Quality and relevance: support for implementation of reforms already started by the government for reducing repeater and dropout rates in first cycle, introducing flexibility in second cycle, modernizing pedagogic methods; improvement of faculty development and management through quantitative (recruitment) and qualitative (productivity) means Governance and management: decentralization of management responsibility; capacity building at central and decentralized levels	80 (IBRD/IDA)

Table G.1, *continued*

Country and fiscal year	Project name; main components	Amount (millions of U.S. dollars) and source
	Intensified use of new technologies: equipment of computer centers for use by students and faculty and provision of computers for management and administration; technology training and support for pedagogy; technology training and support for management Financing: global financing strategy; equitable participation of students in education costs; cost recovery for nonacademic services	
Vietnam, 1998	*Higher Education* Capacity building, institutional development, computerization Grants on competitive basis to support quality improvement in selected higher education institutions and universities Provision of coordination, implementation, procurement, contract management, and accounting functions needed for project implementation	83.3 (IDA)
Chile, 1999	*Millennium Science Initiative (MSI)* Management structure for the MSI: (a) establishment and operations of Board of Directors, Program Committee, and Implementation and Management Unit; (b) technical assistance for selection of science institutes and science nuclei; (c) proposal to scale up and institutionalize the project; and (d) monitoring and evaluation studies Competitive Fund for Scientific Excellence: science institutes, and science nuclei Network for the Promotion of Scientific Excellence: networking activities, including research visits to establish formal and informal connections with high-level international institutions; coordination of appropriate initiative-wide activities with directors of science institutes, science nuclei, and principal investigators; programs for exchange of researchers and of graduate and postgraduate students; design and delivery of international advanced courses; dissemination of lessons learned	5 (IBRD)

Table G.1, *continued*

Country and fiscal year	Project name; main components	Amount (millions of U.S. dollars) and source
China, 1999	*Higher Education Reform* Renewal and restructuring of science and engineering disciplines; adoption of student-centered learning strategies and increase in access to laboratories, computer facilities, and library resources; upgrading of teachers and staff in support of reform Funding of innovative forms of cooperation, including partnerships and networks Funding of project activities that support institutional capacity for change	50 (IDA), 20 (IBRD)
Bulgaria, 2000	*Education Modernization* Improvement of efficiency and effectiveness in resource management in higher education institutions through reform of allocation process and establishment of a National Higher Education Management Information System Maintenance of high levels of access to and improvement of equity in higher education institutions through establishment of student loan system and reform of the stipend system Improvement of quality of teaching and learning as well as internal management structure in higher education through creation of a Competitive Teaching and Management System Strengthening of capacity of Ministry of Education and Science for project management and communication	14.39 (IBRD)
Jordan, 2000	*Higher Education Development* Improvement of infrastructure for inter- and intra-university information technology networks, management information system, modern library systems, and faculty training Support of Higher Education Development Fund for allocation of investment funding for subprojects, information technology, proposals, and faculty development centers Reform of community college system Support of project implementation capacity	34.7 (IBRD)

Table G.1, *continued*

Country and fiscal year	Project name; main components	Amount (millions of U.S. dollars) and source
Venezuela, Rep. Bol. de, 2000	*Millennium Science Initiative (MSI)* Capacity building: (a) capacity building for new Ministry of Science and Technology, with technical support in setting up national S&T policies; (b) establishment and operations of Board of Directors, Program Committee, and Implementation and Management Unit; (c) technical assistance for selection of centers of excellence (CEs) and nuclei for excellent research (NERs); (d) development of a proposal to scale up and institutionalize the project; and (e) monitoring and evaluation studies Competitive Fund for Scientific Excellence: (a) centers and nuclei of scientific excellence, and (b) Network for the Promotion of Scientific Excellence—networking activities include research visits to establish formal and informal connections with high-level international institutions; coordination of initiative-wide activities with directors of CEs, NERs, and principal investigators; programs for exchange of researchers and of graduate and postgraduate students; design and delivery of international advanced courses; and dissemination of lessons learned	5 (IBRD)
India, 2001	*Technician Education Project* Assist remote and economically underdeveloped states to expand capacity and improve quality and efficiency of technician education Increase access of some disadvantaged sections of society to technical education and training	64.5 (IDA)

Note: IBRD, International Bank for Reconstruction and Development; IDA, International Development Association; R&D, research and development; R&D&E, research and development and engineering; S&T, science and technology.

Table G.2 Institutional Development Fund (IDF) Grants by Fiscal Year and Recipient, Fiscal 1995–

Country and fiscal year	Project name; main components	Amount (U.S. dollars)
Cambodia, 1995	*National Higher Education Action Plan* Restoration of higher education sector through ten-year plan Priority needs: system and institutional human resource development; review and revision of academic programs; rehabilitation of institutional physical plant and facilities Legislation and structure: formulation of a national policy on higher education; establishment of a national coordinating body for all higher education; establishment of a permanent forum for heads of all higher education institutions Academic programs: review/revision of existing academic programs and creation of new programs; coordination of the systematic development of academic instructional materials; commissioning of a feasibility study on the introduction of a credit system in the management of academic programs Access and output: development of policies and procedures to increase participation of females in higher education; review/revision of existing student financial assistance policies and procedures in favor of poor students, provincial students, women, handicapped persons, and veterans; reform of admission criteria and revision of student recruitment process Language: preparation of legislation on use of the national language as a medium of instruction in education at all levels; creation of a national language institute Resources: establishment of financial management system and of training program for financial services staff in institutions; commissioning of a study on the feasibility of introducing a system of fees in public institutions; establishment of a new legal status within the civil service system for academic staff in higher education Institutional management: introduction of an institutional strategic planning service and a management information system; review/revision of the organization, regulations, and responsibilities of the various institutional management functions; development of an administrative manual governing operation management functions	295,000

Table G.2, *continued*

Country and fiscal year	Project name; main components	Amount (U.S. dollars)
Morocco, 1996	*Strengthening Government Capacity to Design and Implement Higher Education Reform* Strengthening the institutional capacity of the Ministry of Higher Education and Scientific Research to effectively carry out the analysis, diagnosis, and reform formulation process necessary to address key issues in the system Reform agenda covers design and implementation of reform that integrates all segments of the higher education system; introduction of full management autonomy at the institutional level; diversification of higher education supply, elimination of duplication, and rationalization of existing system; improvement of academic research and its linkage to private industry; support of the development of private higher education institutions; definition of a new role for the ministry, focusing on accreditation, evaluation, and provision of incentives	199,300
Cambodia, 1999	*Legal/Regulatory Framework for Higher Education* Technical assistance to advise government on legal and regulatory framework for management of public and private higher education, to strengthen financial management system in higher education, and to develop a system of financial accreditation and a framework for quality assurance in higher education Training and workshops to build consensus and share information on the issues addressed above	252,200
Bosnia and Herzegovina, ongoing	*2000 Education Development Project* Develop a common framework for the fragmented system of legislation and governance Strengthen professional coordination and governance via establishment of a Higher Education Coordination Board Establish a higher education fund for institutions of higher education to strengthen institutional authorities and management, develop institutional strategy, and implement institution-wide development plans Develop mutual recognition and accreditation processes	3,500

Note: The IDF is a Bank grant facility that finances discrete, generally innovative, upstream capacity-building activities that are identified during and closely linked with the Bank's policy dialogue and its economic and sector work. The IDF is considered a fund of last resort, financing eligible activities for which no alternative financing (Bank/IDA lending, United Nations Development Programme financing, or other loans or grants) is available. The amount of a grant does not exceed $500,000.

Table G.3 International Finance Corporation (IFC) Operations in Support of Tertiary Education Institutions by Fiscal Year and Country, Fiscal 1998–2001

Country and fiscal year	Project name; main components	Amount (U.S. dollars)
Argentina, 1998	*Universidad de Belgrano* Construction and furnishing of new building ("the Tower") to help modernize instructional facilities, alleviate the university's shortage of space, and upgrade computing facilities with latest technology Refinancing of high-interest medium-term debt Capitalization of Student Loan Financing Program Improvement in quality of education and services	22
Argentina, 1998	*Universidad Torcuato Di Tella* Expansion plan to maintain the university's reputation as a top-quality, community-oriented learning institution and to meet the growing demand for its services; includes increase in total enrollment by over 50 percent; renovation of old building to increase university's total space per student, to provide adequate space for professors to conduct research, and to accommodate a bookstore, library, museum, and community auditorium; and increase in scholarships to attract a diverse applicant pool of students from all socio-economic backgrounds	9
Argentina, 2000	*Asociación Civil Universidad del Salvador* Goal of maintaining the university's reputation as a top-quality, community-oriented learning institution and to meet the growing demand for its services Expansion project of the university's Pilar Campus includes construction of new classrooms, a large auditorium, a library, student dormitories, a veterinary clinic, and three outpatient clinics	10
Argentina, 2000	*Instituto Tecnologico de Buenos Aires* Construction of new campus on outskirts of Buenos Aires to complement the university's old main building downtown Accommodation of undergraduate studies on new campus and of graduate programs, part-time classes, technical assistance, and consulting services in existing main building Development impact through improvement in quality of one of the country's leading universities, as well as demonstration effect for commercial lending in the sector	7

Table G.3, *continued*

Country and fiscal year	Project name; main components	Amount (U.S. dollars)
Peru, 2000	*Universidad Peruana de Ciencias Aplicadas (UPC)* Goals: accommodation of rapid growth; rationalization of educational facilities; enhancement of reputation for academic strength San Isidro Campus: completion of building to house UPC Business School and Cibertec Monterrico Campus: construction of new building to accommodate new classrooms and laboratories Computer systems: upgrading of computer network and internal systems to support a distance education program Fire safety systems: implementation of corrective action plan based on fire safety audit of facilities Working capital: funding of student loans and scholarships for students from lower socioeconomic levels	7
Uruguay, 2000	*Asociación Instituto de Estudios Empresariales de Montevideo (Universidad de Montevideo)* Goal: increase university's capacity to accommodate the increasing demand for private, university-level education Expansion of classroom facilities Expansion of library Growth of student loan program Debt refinancing Project implementation in three stages to correlate with student enrollment	5
India, 2001	*National Institute of Information Technology (NIIT), Student Loan Investment* Student loan program: financing for students participating in GNIIT, NIIT's flagship graduate education program, which is modular, computer based, and off campus Introduction of new type of student loan, which could provide a working model for a student loan system that could be replicated throughout the country	9

Table G.4 World Bank Tertiary Education Projects under Preparation by Fiscal Year and Country or Area, 2000–

Country or area and fiscal year	Project name; main components	Amount (millions of U.S. dollars) and source
Bosnia and Herzegovina, 2000	*Education Development Project* (with higher education component) Develop a common framework for the fragmented system of legislation and governance Strengthen professional coordination and governance via establishment of a Higher Education Coordination Board Establish higher education fund for institutions of higher education to strengthen institutional authorities and management, develop institutional strategy, and implement institution-wide development plans Develop mutual recognition and accreditation processes	10.6 (IDA), of which 3 for higher education
Guinea, 2000	*Guinea Education for All (EFA) Program* (with higher education component) Government priorities for higher education include establishing gender equity, improving quality and relevance of teaching and research, and ensuring financial sustainability Expansion of access to education primarily refers to primary and secondary education, but might provide for tertiary level as well Improving quality of education by developing and testing strategies for teaching and learning, including the development of a university central library to restore a positive learning environment for students and professors, higher education curriculum reform to review all university programs of study, research and innovation facility through matching grants on a competitive basis to professors or groups of professors, and upgrading of faculty through twinning arrangements with outside universities Strengthening capacity for decentralized management to provide support for central ministries and national institutions in changing to a role of setting policies and establishing effective monitoring and evaluation systems while shifting resources and responsibilities to local administrations; financing of private provision of higher education	70 (IDA), of which 32.24 for higher education

Table G.4, *continued*

Country or area and fiscal year	Project name; main components	Amount (millions of U.S. dollars) and source
Kosovo (Yugoslavia), 2000	*Education and Health Project* (with higher education component) Strengthen governance and institutional capacity of the University of Pristina Define legal statute Strengthen organization Develop management capacities Develop legal and medical accreditation system	5 (special financing), of which 0.5 for higher education
Bolivia, 2001	*Education Sector Reform* (with higher education component) Institutional strengthening of ministry and universities Establishment of National Accreditation Agency Establishment of Competitive Quality Improvement Fund	5 (IBRD)
Chile, 2001	*Lifelong Learning and Training Project* (three components, of which one addresses students in grades 11 and 12 of secondary education and the first two years of tertiary education in the technical track) Increase in coverage and improvement of quality: link technical training at secondary and tertiary levels by strengthening institutional framework and formation of networks Preservice and in-service teacher training: assist design and implementation of teacher training Complete the curriculum reform (only for grades 11 and 12): assist change in pedagogical practices through new curriculum to facilitate curriculum implementation Support for the absorption of graduates in the labor market: improve quality and relevance of instruction and labor market accommodation of graduates while improving labor market practices regarding training of youth and improved transition to initial employment	200 (IBRD)

Table G.4, *continued*

Country or area and fiscal year	Project name; main components	Amount (millions of U.S. dollars) and source
Egypt, Arab Rep., 2001	*Higher Education Enhancement* Improved efficiency through reform of governance and management: reform of legislation governing higher education; rationalization of funding allocation mechanisms; establishment of National Quality Assurance Council; capacity building; development of management information system and management training; establishment of Higher Education Enhancement Fund Improvement of quality and relevance of university education: establishment of integrated computer and network infrastructure; development of interuniversity library system Improvement of quality and relevance of midlevel technical education: consolidation of middle technical institutes into technical colleges; curriculum redesign and instructor training; strengthening of academic management and administration	50 (IBRD)
Cambodia, 2002	*Higher Education Development* Upgrading/training of staff Incentives for reform of higher education system Establishment of credit system	To be determined
India, 2003	*Subsector Development Program in Technical Education (Phase I)* Competitive grant scheme to support excellence in engineering colleges and polytechnics through institutional autonomy; networking for quality, competence, and impact enhancement; enhancing of services to industry and community; and management capacity development	110 (IDA), 50 (IBRD)
Mozambique, 2003	*Higher Education Project* Strengthening of institutions of higher education: support of academic quality and relevance of training; improvements in efficiency; infrastructure rehabilitation/construction at institution level Sector-level management reform and improved coordination and external linkages: analysis of policy issues; design and testing of funding formulas and resource allocation mechanisms and revised financing policies; development and introduction of human resource management policies in public higher education; building of planning, budget,	80 (IDA)

Table G.4, *continued*

Country or area and fiscal year	Project name; main components	Amount (millions of U.S. dollars) and source
	and financial management capacity; establishment of management information system for national higher education	
	National academic excellence program: design and development of quality assurance mechanisms and monitoring and accreditation system; creation of national program for faculty academic excellence awards; design of national program for student academic excellence awards; design and introduction of student-oriented learning	
	Higher education scholarship fund (national pilot): financing of design, start-up, initial operation, and evaluation of Higher Education Scholarship Fund to serve as pilot instrument for allocation of public funding to higher education institutions on capitation basis, improvement of responsiveness to student and employer demand, and improved targeting of public funding to vulnerable groups	
	Program implementation: technical assistance to ministry for coordination, administration, and management of national higher education system; technical assistance in the area of procurement; technical assistance for setting up monitoring and evaluation mechanisms; support for program development	
Nigeria, 2003	*University System Innovation* Improved teaching and learning quality: support of innovation and modernization of teaching and learning activities with the aim of improving quality and relevance to graduate employment Improved management capacities: strengthening of management capacities necessary for institutions with newly received autonomy; development of strategic plans for each university Electronic networking: e-mail communication capacities for teaching, learning, research, management, and performance monitoring of system National Universities Commission (NUC): support of NUC with staff skills and institutional resources necessary to carry out responsibilities and with funding for strategic planning exercise; capacity building in quality assurance and monitoring performance; establishment of other support services	90 (IDA)

Table G.4, *continued*

Country or area and fiscal year	Project name; main components	Amount (millions of U.S. dollars) and source
	Special initiatives include prevention and control of HIV/AIDS within university community; initial capacity building for tertiary distance education; graduate fellowship program for women; higher education policy studies and related skills development	
Sri Lanka, 2003	*Tertiary Education* Building institutional capacity in the tertiary education system through improvement of national planning, monitoring, and evaluation systems and connectivity; establishment of Board for Quality Assurance; strengthening of management of public and private universities and faculties Improving quality and relevance: establishment of competitive fund to allocate resources to improve undergraduate degree programs in public and private universities; subcomponent to support quality improvement interventions in universities and faculties to enhance the quality and relevance of undergraduate degree programs; competitive fund to support program selected by transparent and objective procedures; faculties to be invited to submit development plan elaborated by faculty degree programs	40 (IDA)
Brazil, to be determined	*Higher Education Improvement* Increase access to tertiary education through student loan program for qualified needy students Facilitate transition to a more diverse and efficient high-quality system through new funding system and regulatory framework under which resource allocation is tied to performance	120 (IBRD)
Ghana, to be determined	*Ghana Education Sector* Tentative dialogue with government about broad sector development program that would encompass various subsectors and would have several phases under adaptable program lending (APL), with the first phase possibly devoted to tertiary education and institutional management capacity	To be determined

Table G.4, *continued*

Country or area and fiscal year	Project name; main components	Amount (millions of U.S. dollars) and source
	Provisional agreement with National Council for Tertiary Education (NCTE) that the development objective would be to improve the training of human resources in order to enhance national capacities to generate and share knowledge and to adopt technologies, for national growth and development Six tentative components: improve quality and relevance of selected postgraduate programs, with an emphasis on science and technology; upgrade the quality and relevance of polytechnic education; strengthen system and institutional governance and management; expand the use of information and communication technologies within the tertiary system; initiate distance learning programs within the main universities; restructure the student loan scheme into a self-sustaining program of targeted assistance to needy students	
Tanzania, to be determined	*Education Rationalization Credit* (with higher education component) Management of higher and technical education sector Cost-effectiveness: reduction in number of institutions; reallocation of funding; privatization Coordination of institutions in education sector through transfer of executive authority to one agency Improvement of relevance of higher education to labor market Equity: increase enrollment and expand access to education and training	100 (IDA)
Venezuela, Rep. Bol. de, to be determined	*Second Student Loan and Higher Education Improvement* Student loan program (undergraduate and graduate): increase access to tertiary education for academically qualified but financially needy students through modifications in FUNDAYACUCHO student loan program Technical assistance for quality assurance: promote improved quality and efficiency of both undergraduate and graduate education through creation of new quality assurance mechanism; support for quality assurance process; strengthening of capacities of Ministry of Education and of individual institutions; linking of resource allocation to performance; pilot investments for improvements in teaching and research	50 (IBRD)

Table G.5 Lessons Learned from World Bank Project Completion Reports by Year of Completion and Country

Country and fiscal year	Project name; main components
China, 1995	*Second University Development Project* Reform of the higher education sector is most feasible within a supportive policy environment in which all participants, both within and outside the education sector, are in fundamental agreement on the scope, pace, and direction of reform. The government recognized that to reform the economy it had to change the way it trained its economists and administrators. International technical assistance in education projects can provide vital and important educational inputs into a reform process that is under way and is fully supported by the education policy structure.
Indonesia, 1995	*Professional Human Resource Development Project* It would be helpful to estimate the economic rate of return at project appraisal in order to assess the possibility of long-term development results commensurate with project costs and to have benchmarks to consult during design, implementation, and supervision. The government's long-term policy for meeting high-level manpower needs was to support the growth of domestic graduate education while using overseas education in the short term. To conclude that an expensive overseas fellowship makes economic sense requires a finding that the typical fellow will have a substantial impact on the economy that will be sustained over a long period of time.
Jamaica, 1995	*Education Program Preparation and Student Loan Project* In pursuing the goal of increasing the financial sustainability and administrative efficiency of student loan programs, enforceable covenants and monitoring provisions should be included in the loan agreement.
Indonesia, 1996	*Second Higher Education Development Project* Key project inputs will be more available if the project is developed with rather than for universities. Little consideration was given during project preparation to how investments were to be utilized and sustained. It would have been more efficient if the project had relied financially at least in part on existing sources of funding at the university level and if the planning of the project had been based on specific objectives as spelled out by the universities themselves.
Nigeria, 1997	*Federal Universities Development Sector* Higher education projects are unusual in that their beneficiary institutions—the universities—are generally stronger, better endowed, and more capable than other public institutions. In addition, they possess an organized and influential constituency of staff, students, and alumni, which can act as powerful interest groups. Broad consultation in the process of project preparation is essential. Project performance can often be enhanced through the decentralization of certain implementation responsibilities.

Table G.5, *continued*

Country and fiscal year	Project name; main components
	Higher education project objectives should promote not only cost-efficiency and effective resource allocation but also the parallel need to establish mechanisms and procedures for quality assurance.
	When compared with user fees, the potential for university income generation from entrepreneurial activities is limited. Efforts to develop it may not be cost-effective and may undermine the main university mission of teaching and research.
Ghana, 1999	*Tertiary Education Project*
	Managed expansion of tertiary enrollments is critical for maintaining educational quality, yet political demands make it very difficult for governments to exercise this control. World Bank staff should make this key project variable a permanent part of dialogue with the government and should use total recurrent expenditure per student as the main performance indicator for monitoring balance between expansion and quality.
	In projects that have quality of tertiary education as an explicit objective, relevant performance indicators should be identified to effectively monitor project impact.
	A close working relationship among the arms of government involved in higher education, and especially between the Ministry of Education and the Ministry of Finance, is necessary to ensure implementation of sector priorities in the allocation of public resources.
	It is imperative to establish essential infrastructure before launching a management information system (MIS), to familiarize managers early on with computer technology, and to obtain institutional commitment to cover system maintenance costs.
	To ensure the quality of research, research funds should be managed by an institution with a mandate for research rather than the project implementation unit or parent ministry, and research proposals should be invited from university departments rather than from individuals.
Kenya, 1999	*Universities Investment Project*
	The successful achievement of development objectives requires the formulation of indicators that can be monitored throughout project implementation.
	The implementation experience of previous and ongoing projects should be reflected in project design and appraisal.
	Institutional continuity and memory are important factors in successful implementation.
	Project design should provide for an appropriate balance between decentralization of responsibilities to universities and central coordination.
	Universities are large-scale, complex organizations with increasing market orientation, which requires careful attention to managerial training at all levels.

Table G.5, *continued*

Country and fiscal year	Project name; main components
Korea, Rep., 1999	*Environmental Research and Education Project* Frequent and detailed supervision, as well as good relationships with the borrower, can save a project.
Mauritius, 1999	*Higher and Technical Education Project* Achieving consensus on difficult sector policies requires transparency of approach and the building of confidence among all stakeholders.
Venezuela, Rep. Bol. de, 2000	*Student Loan Reform Project* The rationale for undertaking the project lacked the sector analysis data necessary to demonstrate how the project was to be integrated within overall sectoral policies. The project objectives did not attach sufficient importance to the specific requirements of the sector, which resulted in overlooking flaws in the country's university system that affected higher education financing. The institution under reform suffered from institutional and financial inefficiency prior to project launch. The fact that it functioned as the executing agency for the project compounded existing problems and resulted in recurrent project funding and management problems. Performance indicators should not just measure short-term inputs; indicators that measure outputs with long-term impacts are also necessary. Student loan projects require excellent financial management and reporting capacity from their inception. If these are lacking, they should be improved through technical assistance before resources are committed to lending.

Appendix H. Knowledge-Sharing Initiatives of the World Bank Aimed at Bridging the Digital Divide

This appendix describes recent global initiatives by the World Bank designed to enhance and expand country capacity in information technology and communications and to foster knowledge sharing.

Global Development Learning Network (GDLN)

The GLDN was created to harness the latest technology in the fight against poverty by facilitating the simultaneous provision of courses, seminars, and discussions from a variety of global sources to participants linked by interactive video, electronic classrooms, satellite communications, and Internet facilities. The GDLN initiative is being led by the World Bank as part of its commitment to serve as a Knowledge Bank. It involves beneficiaries in client countries, who will have access to a wide range of new cost-effective learning opportunities through the latest distance learning technology and through distance learning centers that will become independent and self-sustaining, and charter partners such as multilateral and bilateral agencies and private companies that will participate in content provision, delivery, use, innovation, evaluation, and initial funding of the GDLN.

African Virtual University (AVU)

The AVU is a technology-based distance education network that began in 1997 as a pilot project in the Africa Education Department of the World Bank, in partnership with 12 African, European, and North American universities. It has since evolved and was recently established as an independent nonprofit organization with headquarters in Nairobi. The AVU is a "university without walls" that uses modern information and communication technologies to enhance access of postsecondary students in Sub-Saharan Africa to tertiary education opportunities in the fields of science and engineering through direct access to high-quality academic faculty, curricula, and learning resources throughout the world. It aims to bridge the digital divide by training scientists, engineers, technicians, business managers, and other professionals who will promote economic and social development and help Africa leapfrog into the Knowledge Age. The AVU's delivery model combines satellite and Internet technologies that are integrated with the goal of providing high-quality educational content from all over the world at an affordable cost to existing universities, while taking into account the technological and infrastructure limitations currently prevailing in African countries.

In the pilot phase, the AVU teaching-learning model consisted of a mixture of videotaped and live lectures delivered by one-way video, two-way audio digital satellite broadcasts, and e-mail interaction between students and instructors, supplemented by textbooks, course notes, and learner support in the classroom by local facilitators. In addition to courses, the AVU offers a digital library with full-text journals and a catalogue of subject-related Web links. Since the inception of the AVU, 30 learning centers have been established in universities in 15 Sub-Saharan Africa anglophone and francophone countries. The program has delivered approximately 3,500 hours of instructional programs, and more than 24,000 students have registered in semester-long AVU courses. Anecdotal reports on the pilot phase indicate satisfactory academic results and a low dropout rate of about 15 percent.

Having been established as an independent nonprofit entity, the AVU is about to launch full operations that will include assisting partner African universities with upgrading their access to high-speed Internet connectivity and with other technology improvements; building the capacity of partner universities for technology-enhanced distance education; developing a Web-based portal for the African educational community to share information and access new distance learning products and services; facilitating the delivery of accredited programs in computer science, business sciences, and distance education to African students, using Internet technologies, and expanding the scope and scale of the existing AVU digital library. To implement this strategy, the AVU is planning to concentrate initially on the learning sites with the greatest potential and to select content providers on the basis of a transparent international bidding procedure, with full involvement of the stakeholders to ensure ownership.

In the years to come, one challenge for the AVU will be to establish a strong financial scheme that will allow it to expand and will guarantee the sustainability of its activities. Another will be to focus ever more on pedagogy and the development of local capacity. Reduction of per-student cost, expansion of AVU access for disadvantaged students, and indigenization of AVU materials and methods may present greater hurdles than might be anticipated from the initial institutional focus on infrastructure and courseware. The inevitable obsolescence of hardware and materials will require regular infusions of capital.

Global Development Network (GDN)

The GDN aims to enhance the quality and availability of policy-oriented research and strengthen the institutions that undertake this work. The GDN offers tools, services, and networking opportunities to help the institutions and their members join together to fight poverty.

World Links for Development Program (WorLD)

WorLD provides Internet connectivity and training in the use of technology in education for teachers, teacher trainers, and students in developing countries. It then links students and teachers in secondary schools in developing countries with schools in industrial countries for collaborative learning via the Internet. WorLD provides sustainable solutions for mobilizing the equipment, training, educational resources, and school-to-school partnerships required to bring students in developing countries online and into the global community.

Appendix I. Promoting Science and Technology for Development: The World Bank's Millennium Science Initiative

Today, a handful of the world's richest countries produce the overwhelming majority of new scientific and technological (S&T) knowledge. Countries in this exclusive group enjoy the fruits of a virtuous circle. Meanwhile, most of the rest of the world's nations struggle, with varying degrees of success, to establish S&T research systems that can invigorate their economies and provide solutions for their social needs. Countries that want to improve their S&T capacity have to make extra efforts to accumulate and maintain the critical mass beyond which benefits start to accrue.

Despite the difficulties, there are good reasons to hope that aspiring countries can make progress in closing the gaps that separate them from scientifically advanced countries. First, information and communication technologies (ICT) now provide unprecedented access to existing knowledge and virtually erase the disadvantages of physical distance as a factor in research collaboration. Second, more is being learned about the process of innovation and about the policies and practices that make investments in S&T effective. Third, the international science community is marked by an open culture that freely shares basic knowledge to strengthen science throughout the world.

The Rationale for Supporting Excellence in Research

It is widely accepted that knowledge is a critical determinant of economic growth and is transformed into goods and services through a country's national innovation system (NIS). Cutting-edge research is an essential part of an effective NIS in which science and technology are intertwined. A community of trained individuals is the most effective knowledge transfer and adaptation mechanism available, capable of capitalizing on the best science in the world. It is also widely accepted that anonymous peer review and competitive funding enhance research quality and increase productivity in science and technology.

Fostering Development through Support for Research Excellence

The World Bank seeks to assist countries that wish to increase the contribution of S&T to poverty reduction and economic development. One way in which it is doing so is under the Millennium Science Initiative

(MSI), an umbrella for new lending through which the Bank's client countries can borrow to improve their S&T capacity. Projects under the MSI generally take the form of highly selective competitive funds to support research. These funds can differ according to a country's specific needs and circumstances, but they all provide targeted support that focuses on research excellence, human resources training, and linkages with partners in the international science community and in the private sector.

One goal of the MSI is to raise standards for research output and performance by concentrating resources on a selected group of researchers and providing funding and working conditions that approximate those of researchers at the cutting edge of the discipline. The aim is to show that relevant, world-class research can be done anywhere in the world, and within the budgets of most developing countries. More important, MSI projects seek to demonstrate that the process for selecting the best researchers—through open and transparent competition guided by peer review—is also a highly cost-effective way to invest in S&T. Experience shows that, once introduced, such state-of-the-art practices in research funding tend to spread throughout a national research system, further improving cost-effectiveness.

Origins and Benefits of the MSI

The MSI was conceived at a meeting of top-level government officials and distinguished researchers from developing countries convened by Eduardo Frei, a former president of Chile. As a result of the meeting, a number of participants came together to form the Science Institutes Group (SIG), which is dedicated to promoting development by closing the gaps in S&T between the industrial and developing worlds. With the support of the private, U.S.-based Packard Foundation, the SIG has continued to engage scientists and government leaders in garnering support for revitalizing science research in the developing world. The World Bank and the government of Chile cofinanced the first MSI project, in April 1999.

It is expected that MSI projects will yield the following benefits:

- Promoting transparent, merit-based allocation procedures that forge cultures of quality
- Increasing training opportunities for young people and reducing brain drain
- Facilitating global and regional connections among researchers.

Centers of excellence have been established in many countries to focus on research of superior quality.[2] The World Bank itself does not fund individual centers of excellence. Instead, it works as a partner with the national government (or its designated representative) in a client country. The client country and the World Bank agree to the project design, the implementation period, and financing arrangements. The responsibility for implementing the project rests with the borrower. The World Bank provides technical support in the supervision of aspects of implementation.

For a country to participate in the MSI, its government must formally request a project from the World Bank. This normally occurs after intensive dialogue within the country involving the relevant government agencies and civil society (in particular, the science and technology community) and between the country and the World Bank through periodic meetings to discuss the Bank's assistance strategy for the country. Today, MSI projects are under way in four countries—Brazil, Chile, Mexico, and Venezuela.

---

2. The staff, work programs, and resources of such centers are chosen and developed through highly selective processes and bolstered by the presence of the advanced infrastructure required for the area of research. There are several different models of such centers, varying according to their genesis and intended purposes. A center of excellence may be a single independent institution, or a network of laboratories and departments within an institution, or a broader association of institutions. Centers may be national or international, public or private. Recognized centers of excellence include the Consultative Group on International Agricultural Research (CGIAR) system, the Max Planck Institutes, Mexico's Secretariat for Public Education–National Council for Science and Technology (SEP-CONA-CYT) Centers, the U.S. National Science Foundation's Engineering Research Centers (ERCs) and Science and Technology Research Centers (STCs), the Howard Hughes Medical Institutes, the Abdul Salaam International Center for Theoretical Physics in Italy, and the Indian Institutes of Technology. Centers of excellence vary not only in their composition but also in their organizational and administrative structures, legal status, and funding sources. The concentration of high-quality research within centers of excellence is considered an effective counterstrategy against "brain drain" because of the incentives thus created for top researchers to work productively in their countries of origin.

Appendix J. Statistical Tables on Tertiary Education

Table J.1 Gross Tertiary Enrollment Rates, Selected Years, 1980–98, and by Gender, 1998

Economy	1980	1985	1990	1995	1998 Total	1998 Male	1998 Female
Afghanistan			1.8	2.0			
Albania	5.1	7.2	6.9	11.0	12.0	10.1	14.0
Algeria	5.9	7.9	11.4	12.0	14.0		
Angola	0.4	0.7	0.8	1.0	1.0	1.0	1.0
Antigua and Barbuda							
Argentina	21.8	35.7	38.1	36.2	36.2		
Armenia			23.8	13.9	12.2	10.5	14.0
Australia	25.4	27.7	35.5	72.9	79.8	76.9	82.9
Austria	21.9	26.4	35.2	47.4	50.0	48.0	52.0
Azerbaijan	24.0	24.4	24.2	18.0	22.0	23.0	21.0
Bahamas, The	16.7	17.7		24.0			
Bahrain	5.0	12.8	17.7	20.0	25.0	19.0	30.0
Bangladesh	2.8	5.1	4.2	6.0			
Barbados	14.8	19.8	27.2	28.7	32.0	20.0	45.0
Belarus	38.9	44.8	47.6	42.3	47.0	41.0	53.0
Belgium	26.0	32.2	40.2	56.3	56.0	53.0	59.0
Belize				1.0			
Benin	1.4	2.4	2.7	2.6	3.0	6.0	1.0
Bhutan	0.3	0.2					
Bolivia	14.9	19.2	21.3	24.0	28.0		
Bosnia and Herzegovina							
Botswana	1.2	1.8	3.2	5.3	5.8	6.1	5.5
Brazil	11.1	10.3	11.2	11.3	14.5	12.0	15.0
Brunei	0.6	2.9		6.6	11.0	8.0	15.0
Bulgaria	16.2	18.9	31.1	39.4	43.0	41.0	53.0
Burkina Faso	0.3	0.6	0.7	1.0	0.9	1.4	0.4
Burundi	0.5	0.6	0.7	1.0	1.0	1.0	1.0
Cambodia	0.1	0.3	0.7	1.9	1.0	2.0	1.0
Cameroon	1.7	2.2	3.3	4.0	5.0		
Canada	57.1	69.6	94.7	87.8	87.3	80.7	95.3
Central African Rep.	0.9	1.2	1.5	1.0	2.0	4.0	1.0
Chad		0.4		0.6	1.0	2.0	1.0
Chile	12.3	15.6	21.3	28.2	34.0	36.0	32.0
China	1.7	2.9	3.0	5.3	6.0		
Colombia	8.6	10.9	13.4	15.5	21.0	19.0	22.0

Table J.1, *continued*

Economy	1980	1985	1990	1995	1998 Total	1998 Male	1998 Female
Comoros			0.5	0.6	1.0	1.0	1.0
Congo, Dem. Rep.	1.2	1.4	2.4	3.3	2.3		
Congo, Rep.	5.1	6.3	5.4	8.0			
Costa Rica	21.0	22.0	26.9	30.3	31.0	33	28
Côte d'Ivoire	2.8	2.6	3.9	6.2	7.0	11.0	4.0
Croatia	19.0	17.7	23.9	28.3	31.0	28.0	33.0
Cuba	17.3	20.1	20.9	12.7	19.0	16.0	22.0
Cyprus	4.0	6.0	15.0	17.0	23.0	20.0	25.0
Czech Rep.	17.3	15.8	16.0	21.8	26.0	26.0	27.0
Denmark	28.3	29.1	36.5	48.2	55.0	47.0	63.0
Djibouti			0.1	0.2	0.3	0.3	0.2
Dominica							
Dominican Rep.		18.0		22.0	22.9	19.0	26.8
Ecuador	34.9	32.0	20.0	23.0			
Egypt, Arab Rep.	16.1	18.1	15.8	20.2	20.2	24.2	15.9
El Salvador	9.4	16.9	15.9	18.9	18.0	16.0	20.0
Eritrea				1.0	1.0	2.0	0
Estonia	24.5	24.2	26.0	38.1	41.8	38.1	47.5
Ethiopia	0.4	0.7	0.8	0.7	1.0	2.0	0
Fiji	2.5	3.2	8.4	13.0			
Finland	32.2	34.1	48.9	70.4	74.1	68.3	80.0
France	25.3	29.8	39.6	51.0	51.0	45.0	57.0
French Polynesia	0.2		1.5	2.0			
Gabon		6.0	5.7	8.0			
Gambia, The				1.7	1.7	2.2	1.2
Georgia	29.9		36.7	39.6	42.0	39.7	44.4
Germany			33.9	46.1	46.0	47.0	45.0
Ghana	1.6	1.4	1.4	1.4			
Greece	17.1	24.2	36.1	42.3	50.0	48.0	52.0
Guam	28.8			66.0			
Guatemala	8.3	8.6		8.5	8.5		
Guinea	4.5	2.1	1.1	1.2	1.3		
Guinea-Bissau					1.0		
Guyana	2.7	2.4	5.0	9.7	11.4	11.3	11.5
Haiti	0.9	1.1		1.0			
Honduras	7.5	8.8	8.9	11.0	13.0		
Hong Kong (China)	10.3	13.3		26.0			
Hungary	14.1	15.4	14.0	20.7	23.6	21.5	25.7

Table J.1, *continued*

Economy	1980	1985	1990	1995	1998 Total	1998 Male	1998 Female
Iceland	20.4	21.1	24.9	35.4	40.0	30.0	51.0
India	5.2	6.0	6.1	6.6	8.0	10.0	6.0
Indonesia	3.8	6.3	9.2	11.3	11.3	14.6	8.0
Iran, Islamic Rep.		4.6	10.0	17.2	17.6	21.9	13.1
Iraq	8.7	11.5		11.0	13.0	17.0	9.0
Ireland	18.1	22.3	29.3	39.6	48.0	44.0	52.0
Israel	29.4	33.1	33.5	40.9	49.0	40.0	57.0
Italy	27.0	25.5	32.1	42.3	47.0	42.0	53.0
Jamaica	6.7	4.4	6.8	7.8	9.0		
Japan	30.5	27.8	29.6	40.5	44.0	47.0	40.0
Jordan	13.4	13.1	16.1	16.0	17.9		
Kazakhstan	34.1	36.7	40.1	33.3	33.3	29.2	37.5
Kenya	0.9	1.2	1.6	2.0	2.0	2.0	1.0
Korea, Rep.	14.7	34.0	38.6	52.0	67.7	82.0	52.4
Kuwait	11.3	16.6	12.5	19.2	19.3	14.6	24.0
Kyrgyz Rep.	16.4	18.3	14.3	11.9	11.9	11.3	12.5
Lao PDR	0.4	1.6	1.2	2.7	3.0	4.0	2.0
Latvia	23.6	22.7	25.0	27.2	33.3	27.0	39.6
Lebanon	30.0	27.8	28.9	27.0	27.0	27.2	26.8
Lesotho	1.0	1.3	1.3	2.4	2.4	2.2	2.6
Liberia		3.0		3.0	8.0	12.0	3.0
Libya	7.8	9.2	14.6	20.0			
Liechtenstein				28.0			
Lithuania	34.7	32.5	33.8	28.2	31.4	25.3	37.8
Luxembourg	2.6	2.6		9.3	9.7	12.4	7.0
Macao (China)			25.4	27.0	32.0	35.0	29.0
Macedonia, FYR	27.5	24.0	16.8	18.9	24.0	22.0	27.0
Madagascar	2.6	3.9	3.0	2.2	2.0	3.0	2.0
Malawi	0.5	0.5	0.6	0.6	0.6	0.9	0.4
Malaysia	4.1	5.9	7.3	11.7	11.7		
Maldives							
Mali	0.8	0.9	0.6	1.0	2.0		
Malta	3.2	5.8	13.0	26.0	29.3	27.2	31.6
Mauritania		2.8	2.8	3.8	3.8	6.3	1.3
Mauritius	1.0	1.1	3.5	6.1	7.0	8.0	7.0
Mexico	14.3	15.9	14.5	15.3	18.0	19.0	18.0
Moldova	29.7	32.8	35.5	25.3	26.5	23.8	29.2
Mongolia	21.8	21.6	14.0	15.2	17.0	10.4	23.8

Table J.1, *continued*

Economy	1980	1985	1990	1995	1998 Total	Male	Female
Morocco	5.9	8.7	10.6	11.1	11.1	12.9	9.3
Mozambique	0.1	0.1		0.4	0.5	0.7	0.2
Myanmar	4.7	4.5	4.1	5.4	7.0	7.0	8.0
Namibia			3.3	8.1	8.1	6.3	9.9
Nepal	2.7	4.4	5.2	4.4	4.8		
Netherlands	29.3	31.8	39.8	48.0	49.0	49.0	49.0
New Caledonia		5.1		5.0			
New Zealand	27.0	33.1	39.7	59.6	62.6	52.8	72.6
Nicaragua	12.4	8.8	8.2	11.5	11.8	11.3	12.4
Niger	0.3	0.5	0.7	1.0			
Nigeria	2.7	3.5	4.1	4.0			
Norway	25.5	29.6	42.3	58.6	65.0	55.0	77.0
Oman		0.8	4.1	5.3	8.0	9.0	7.0
Pakistan		2.5	2.9	3.0			
Panama	20.8	24.5	21.5	30.0	31.5		
Papua New Guinea	1.8	1.6		3.2	3.2	4.2	2.1
Paraguay	8.6	9.1	8.3	10.1	10.3	10.0	10.7
Peru	17.3	22.4	30.4	27.1	29.0	43.0	15.0
Philippines	24.4	24.9	28.2	29.0	29.0	25.2	32.7
Poland	18.1	17.1	21.7	24.7	24.7	21.0	28.5
Portugal	10.7	12.3	23.2	38.8	38.8	33.4	44.4
Puerto Rico	41.6			42.0			
Qatar	10.4	20.7	27.0	27.5	26.6	13.6	40.9
Romania	12.1	10.0	9.7	18.3	22.5	20.8	24.3
Russian Federation	46.2	53.7	52.1	42.8	42.8	37.3	48.5
Rwanda	0.3	0.4		1.0	1.0		
Samoa					8.0	8.0	7.0
San Marino							
Saudi Arabia	7.1	10.6	11.6	15.8	19.0	16.0	21.0
Senegal	2.7	2.4	3.0	3.4	4.0		
Seychelles							
Sierra Leone	0.8	1.8	1.3	2.0	2.0	2.0	1.0
Singapore	7.8	13.6	18.6	33.7	38.5		
Slovak Rep.				15.6	26.0	25.0	28.0
Slovenia	20.2	21.2	24.5	34.5	36.1	31.1	41.3
Solomon Islands							
Somalia		3.0		2.0			
South Africa			13.2	18.9	17.2	18.0	16.5

Table J.1, *continued*

Economy	1980	1985	1990	1995	1998 Total	Male	Female
Spain	23.2	28.5	36.7	47.8	56.0	51.0	61.0
Sri Lanka	2.7	3.7	4.6	5.1	5.1	5.9	3.7
St. Kitts and Nevis							
St. Lucia							
St. Vincent and the Grenadines							
Sudan	1.7	1.9	3.0	4.0			
Suriname	6.7	5.9	9.3	13.0			
Swaziland	3.6	4.4	4.1	5.4	6.0	5.9	6.1
Sweden	30.8	30.0	32.0	46.7	50.3	43.5	57.4
Switzerland	18.3	21.0	25.7	32.6	35.0	40.0	30.0
Syrian Arab Rep.	16.9	17.1	18.2	15.7	15.7	18.2	13.1
Taiwan (China)							
Tajikistan	23.6	20.0	22.1	20.6	20.4	27.4	13.3
Tanzania	0.3	0.3	0.3	0.5	1.0	1.0	0
Thailand	14.7	19.0	15.7	20.1	22.1		
Togo	2.1	1.9	2.9	3.3	4.0	7.0	1.0
Tonga							
Trinidad and Tobago	4.4	5.3	6.6	7.9	6.0	5.0	7.0
Tunisia	4.8	5.5	8.5	13.0	17.0	17.0	17.0
Turkey	5.4	8.9	13.1	19.5	21.0	26.5	15.2
Turkmenistan	22.5	22.4	21.7	20.0			
Uganda	0.4	0.8	1.2	1.7	1.9	2.6	1.3
Ukraine	41.6	46.8	46.6	41.7	43.0	40.0	46.0
United Arab Emirates	3.1	6.8	9.2	11.0	13.0		
United Kingdom	19.1	21.7	30.2	49.6	58.0	53.0	64.0
United States	55.5	60.2	75.2	80.9	80.9	70.6	91.8
Uruguay	16.7	24.0	29.9	28.0	35.0	25.0	45.0
Uzbekistan	28.5	30.0	30.4	35.0			
Vanuatu							
Venezuela, Rep. Bol. de	20.6	25.3	29.0	26.0	29.5	24.0	35.0
Vietnam	2.1	1.9	1.9	4.1	11.0	12.0	9.0
Virgin Islands (U.S.)							
Yemen, Rep.				4.0	10.0	16.0	5.0
Yugoslavia, Fed. Rep.				20.5	22.0	20.0	25.0
Zambia	1.5	2.0	2.3	3.0	3.0	4.0	2.0
Zimbabwe	1.3	3.9	5.2	6.5	6.6	9.4	3.9

Source: UNESCO and World Bank data.

Table J.2 Current Public Expenditure on Tertiary Education as Share of Total Current Public Expenditures on Education, 1980–98 (percent)

Economy	1980	1985	1990	1995	1998
Afghanistan	18.4		12.4		
Albania				10.3	
Algeria	17.3				
Angola		5.0	3.7		
Antigua and Barbuda	13.8	12.7			
Argentina	22.7	33.9	46.7	19.5	21.0
Armenia				13.2	
Australia	22.6	30.5	32.0	30.5	
Austria	14.5	16.6	19.1	21.6	26.0
Azerbaijan			10.4	7.8	7.5
Bahamas, The					
Bahrain					
Bangladesh	12.9	10.4	8.7	7.9	
Barbados	18.1		19.2		
Belarus	13.9	14.0	14.4	11.1	
Belgium	17.3	16.7	16.5	20.5	22.0
Belize		2.3	8.1	7.2	
Benin				18.8	13.0
Bermuda		21.4	20.2		
Bhutan				20.4	
Bolivia	17.1		2.9	28.7	28.0
Bosnia and Herzegovina					
Botswana		17.2	12.2		
Brazil				26.2	24.0
Brunei	16.7	8.9	9.5		
Bulgaria	13.6	12.4	13.9	15.8	18.0
Burkina Faso	33.7	30.7	32.1		18.3
Burundi	23.8	19.8	22.0	15.6	17.1
Cambodia	.				4.0
Cameroon	24.0	27.4	29.5	13.2	
Canada	29.0	30.7	31.4	38.2	30.4
Central African Rep.	18.7	16.8	21.5	24.0	
Chad		16.3	8.2	9.0	17.0
Chile	33.3		20.3	18.1	17.0
China	18.4	20.3	17.2	15.4	
Colombia	24.1	23.7	21.2	19.2	
Comoros			17.3	17.2	3.0

Table J.2, *continued*

Economy	1980	1985	1990	1995	1998
Congo, Dem. Rep.	30.8	28.7			
Congo, Rep.	24.3	34.4		28.0	
Costa Rica	26.1	41.4	36.1	30.9	17.0
Côte d'Ivoire	14.9	17.1		16.4	24.0
Croatia					
Cuba	6.9	12.9	14.4	15.4	15.0
Cyprus	4.1	4.2	3.8	6.5	
Czech Rep.				14.7	19.0
Denmark	17.6	21.9	18.4	22.8	26.0
Djibouti			11.5		
Dominica		2.6	2.5		
Dominican Rep.	23.9	20.8		9.0	12.4
Ecuador	15.6	17.8	18.3	23.0	9.0
Egypt, Arab Rep.	30.9	28.8	36.0	35.4	
El Salvador	14.2			7.2	7.0
Eritrea					9.0
Estonia				17.6	
Ethiopia	19.0	15.0	12.1	21.1	10.0
Fiji	1.9	10.1	9.0		
Finland	19.7	20.1	26.2	28.8	
France	12.5	12.9	13.8	17.0	18.0
French Polynesia			2.5	1.1	
Gabon					10.0
Gambia, The	10.8	13.8	17.8	10.9	
Georgia				18.5	
Germany				22.6	23.0
Ghana	1.8	18.1	11.0		
Greece	20.4	20.1	19.5		31.0
Guam					
Guatemala	19.7		21.2	15.5	
Guinea		23.5		17.2	
Guinea-Bissau					
Guyana	12.6	17.8		7.7	
Haiti	9.6	10.8	9.1		
Honduras	19.3	21.3	18.2	16.6	
Hong Kong (China)	24.6	25.1	30.0	37.1	
Hungary	20.8	16.9	15.2	18.3	20.0
Iceland			14.9	20.8	31.0
India	15.4	15.3	14.9	13.7	

Table J.2, *continued*

Economy	1980	1985	1990	1995	1998
Indonesia			20.0	23.8	17.0
Iran, Islamic Rep.	7.1	10.7	13.6	22.9	19.0
Iraq			20.6		
Ireland	17.6	17.7	20.4	22.6	26.0
Israel	24.8	18.9	16.2	18.2	
Italy		10.2		15.0	16.0
Jamaica	19.2	19.4	21.1	20.0	
Japan	11.1	21.4	22.5	12.1	
Jordan	24.4	34.1	35.1	34.9	
Kazakhstan				12.5	
Kenya	11.7	12.4	21.2	13.7	
Korea, Rep.	8.7	10.9	7.4	7.6	
Kuwait	16.5	17.5		29.9	
Kyrgyz Rep.		8.8	10.0	8.3	
Lao PDR				5.4	16.0
Latvia	11.2	10.3	11.6	12.3	
Lebanon				32.4	21.0
Lesotho	21.7	22.3	18.3	17.0	22.0
Liberia					
Libya	18.0				
Liechtenstein					
Lithuania				18.0	
Luxembourg	1.5	3.3	3.3	4.8	
Macao (China)					
Macedonia, FYR				22.2	
Madagascar	27.5	27.2	26.8		17.0
Malawi	30.2	23.3	20.2	20.5	14.0
Malaysia	12.4	14.6	19.9	15.4	32.0
Maldives					
Mali	24.9	20.1		17.7	15.0
Malta	9.3	8.2	14.6	10.9	19.0
Mauritania	13.5	27.4	24.9	20.1	38.0
Marshall Islands					6.0
Mauritius	7.7	5.6	16.6	16.8	13.0
Mexico	12.1	17.6	16.5	17.2	20.0
Moldova					
Mongolia					
Morocco	18.3	17.1	16.2	15.8	16.0
Mozambique			9.9		

Table J.2, *continued*

Economy	1980	1985	1990	1995	1998
Myanmar		13.0		11.7	43.0
Namibia				9.4	12.0
Nepal				26.4	13.0
Netherlands	26.5	25.4	31.9	29.9	29.0
New Caledonia	0.4	0.8	1.0	1.3	
New Zealand	28.3	28.3	37.4	29.1	29.1
Nicaragua	10.5	23.2	20.9		
Niger	17.0				
Nigeria	25.0				
Norway	13.6	13.5	15.2	27.1	26.0
Oman		15.3	7.4	3.0	2.0
Pakistan	18.8	18.2	16.6	13.5	4.0
Panama	13.4	20.4	21.3	23.5	26.0
Papua New Guinea					28.0
Paraguay		23.8	26.5	22.4	22.0
Peru	3.1	2.7		16.0	20.0
Philippines	22.1	22.5		16.9	15.0
Poland	23.6	18.2	22.0	16.0	22.0
Portugal	10.5	12.7	16.3	16.4	18.0
Puerto Rico					
Qatar					
Romania			9.6	17.3	
Russian Federation					
Rwanda	9.6	13.0	16.2		
Samoa					40.0
San Marino	2.7	4.2	6.7	14.0	
Saudi Arabia	27.9	27.1	21.2	17.8	17.0
Senegal	25.0	19.0	24.0	23.2	23.0
Seychelles			9.5	13.1	8.0
Sierra Leone		15.1	34.8		28.0
Singapore	17.1	27.9	29.3	34.8	
Slovak Rep.			15.0	16.7	12.7
Slovenia			17.0	16.9	
Solomon Islands			13.7		
Somalia					
South Africa		24.8	21.5	15.4	15.0
Spain			15.4	15.1	20.0
Sri Lanka	8.9	9.8	11.7	12.2	
St. Kitts and Nevis	2.9	2.1	12.2	11.6	

Table J.2, *continued*

Economy	1980	1985	1990	1995	1998
St. Lucia	14.7	4.5	12.8	12.5	
St. Vincent and the Grenadines					
Sudan	20.7			21.1	
Suriname	7.4	7.7	8.8	7.6	
Swaziland	10.7	19.5	26.0	27.5	32.0
Sweden	9.3	13.1	13.2	27.7	26.0
Switzerland	18.6	18.1	19.7	19.7	20.0
Syrian Arab Rep.	48.5	50.6	30.5		35.0
Taiwan (China)					
Tajikistan	9.6	7.7	9.1	10.3	
Tanzania	11.1	12.7	17.1		
Thailand	19.3	13.2	14.6	19.4	24.0
Togo	29.8	22.8	29.0	32.9	22.0
Tonga	14.7	17.9			
Trinidad and Tobago	10.2	8.9	11.9	13.3	
Tunisia	20.5	18.2	18.5	18.8	22.0
Turkey	28.3	23.9		31.6	22.5
Turkmenistan					
Uganda	18.0	13.2			
Ukraine	14.0	13.5	15.1	10.7	
United Arab Emirates					
United Kingdom	22.4	19.8	19.6	23.7	22.0
United States		25.1	24.1	25.2	
Uruguay	16.1	22.4	22.6	27.0	22.0
Uzbekistan				9.7	
Vanuatu			3.4	6.4	7.0
Venezuela, Rep. Bol. de	34.6	37.0		31.8	
Vietnam				22.0	
Virgin Islands (U.S.)					
Yemen, Rep.					
Yugoslavia, Fed. Rep.			18.6	21.8	
Zambia	18.0	18.3	18.4	23.2	
Zimbabwe	7.5	3.8	12.3	17.3	15.0

Note: The new International Standard Classification of Education (ICSED) system was introduced in 1997. Data for 1998 based on the new ICSED system are marked in italics in this table, indicating that the data include the first and second stage of tertiary education (levels 5 and 6).

Source: UNESCO and World Bank data.

Appendix K. Socioeconomic Inequities in Tertiary Education: Enrollment and Government Expenditure by Income Quintile

Table K.1 Enrollment in Tertiary Education by Income Quintile, Selected Countries, Recent Years

Country and year	Income quintile				
	I	II	III	IV	V
Argentina (1998)					
Public	28.5	31.0	23.3	12.0	5.3
Private	51.7	26.2	14.1	6.2	1.7
Brazil (1998)[a]	74.0	18.0	4.0	4.0	
Chile (1998)	65.5	38.8	23.0	13.3	8.7
Colombia (1997)	51.9	23.3	12.9	5.1	6.4
Costa Rica (2000)	55.5	23.4	10.7	7.2	3.4
Dominican Rep. (2000)	24.0	22.0	20.0	18.0	15.0
Ecuador (1996)					
Public	5.2	3.9	13.0	38.4	38.2
Private	25.9	12.2	18.8	27.2	15.5
Guatemala (2000)	47.8	22.6	12.2	12.1	5.3
Mexico (1998)[a]	58.0	25.0	11.0	6.0	
Peru (1998)[a]	50.0	24.0	14.0	12.0	
Turkey (1998)	11.0	11.0	20.0	30.0	25.0
Venezuela, Rep. Bol. de (1998)	23.0	22.0	16.0	13.0	12.0

Note: Quintile I is the highest income group; quintile V is the lowest.

a. Data for the two lowest income quintile groups have been combined.

Source: World Bank data.

Table K.2 Government Expenditure on Tertiary Education by Expenditure Quintile, Selected Countries, Recent Years

Country and year	Expenditure quintile				
	I	II	III	IV	V
Armenia (1996)	34.9	24.7	18.0	16.7	5.7
Côte d'Ivoire (1995)					
Tertiary education students	54.6	18.1	4.5	3.5	19.2
Tertiary technical					
education students	100.0	0	0	0	0
Ecuador (1994)	42.5	22.6	15.3	13.3	6.3
Ghana (1992)	45.2	20.2	19.0	9.5	6.0
Guyana (1993)	65.4	23.1	3.8	7.7	0
Jamaica (1992)					
All tertiary students	39.8	24.5	13.3	13.3	9.2
University students	52.9	23.5	17.6	5.9	0
Kazakhstan (1996)	35.0	24.8	25.6	9.8	4.7
Kenya (1992–93)	44.2	27.5	14.3	11.9	2.1
Kyrgyz Rep. (1993)	30.2	28.9	10.1	14.5	6.3
Madagascar (1993–94)	89.0	9.0	1.0	2.0	0
Malawi (1994–95)	58.0	20.0	13.0	7.0	1.0
Morocco (1991)	46.6	29.9	12.8	4.3	3.4
Nepal (1996)	93.1	5.7	0	0	1.1
Nicaragua (1993)	71.2	24.3	4.5	0	0
Pakistan (1991)	63.1	18.5	7.3	6.0	5.1
Panama (1997)	38.5	36.8	16.7	6.7	1.3
Peru (1994)	46.2	26.5	15.2	9.5	2.7
Romania (1994)	32.1	24.9	20.1	15.0	7.8
South Africa (1993)	32.2	27.8	16.0	13.3	10.6
Tanzania (1993)	100	0	0	0	0
Vietnam (1991)	67.4	16.3	8.5	7.8	0

Note: Quintile I is the highest; quintile V is the lowest.

Source: World Bank data.

Bibliography

The word *processed* describes informally reproduced works that may not be commonly available through libraries.

Abeles, T. 1998. "The Academy in a Wired World." *Futures* 30 (7): 603–13.

ACU (Association of Commonwealth Universities). 2001. "HIV/AIDS: Towards a Strategy for Commonwealth Universities." Report of the Lusaka Workshop, November 7–10.

Adam, D. 2001. "Keeping Up with the Joneses." *Nature* 413 (September 13): 105–6.

Albrecht, Douglas, and Adrian Ziderman. 1991. *Deferred Cost-Recovery for Higher Education: Student Loan Programs in Developing Countries.* World Bank Discussion Paper 137. Washington, D.C.

Altbach, Philip G. 1998. *Comparative Higher Education: Knowledge, the University and Development.* Greenwich, Conn.: Ablex.

Altbach, P., ed. 1999. *Private Prometheus: Private Higher Education and Development in the 21st Century.* Westport, Conn.: Greenwood Press.

Anderson, J. R. 1999. "Institutional Reforms for Getting an Agricultural Knowledge System to Play Its Role in Economic Growth." *Pakistan Development Review* 38 (4, pt. I, winter): 333–54.

Association of African Universities and the World Bank, in collaboration with the African Economic Research Consortium. 1997. *Revitalizing Universities in Africa: Strategy and Guidelines.* Washington, D.C.: World Bank.

Banker, Rajiv D., Hsi-Hui Chang, and Sumit K. Majumdar. 1998. "Economies of Scope in the U.S. Telecommunications Industry." *Information Economics and Policy* 10 (2, June): 253–72.

Barros, R., and L. Ramos. 1996. "Temporal Evolution of the Relationship between Wages and Education of Brazilian Men." In Nancy Birdsall and Richard H. Sabot, eds., *Opportunity Foregone: Education in Brazil.* Inter-American Development Bank. Baltimore, Md.: Johns Hopkins University Press.

Bennell, Paul, and Terry Pearce. 1998. *The Internationalisation of Higher Education: Exporting Education to Developing and Transitional Economies.* IDS Working Paper 75. Brighton, U.K.: Institute of Development Studies, University of Sussex.

Birdsall, Nancy. 1996. "Public Spending on Higher Education in Developing Countries: Too Much or Too Little?" *Economics of Education Review* 15 (4, October): 407–19.

Blom, Andreas, Lauritz Holm-Nielsen, and Dorte Verner. 2001. "Education, Earnings and Inequality in Brazil, 1982–1998: Implications for Education Policy." Policy Research Working Paper 2686. Education Sector Unit, Latin America and the Caribbean Region, World Bank, Washington, D.C.

Bollag, B. 2001. "African Universities Begin to Face the Enormity of Their Losses to AIDS." *Chronicle of Higher Education* (March 2).

Bond, J. 1997. "The Drivers of the Information Revolution: Cost, Computing Power and Convergence." In "The Information Revolution and the Future of Telecommunications." Finance, Private Sector, and Infrastructure Network, World Bank, Washington, D.C.

Bowen, W. G., and Derek Bok. 1998. *The Shape of the River: Long-Term Consequences of Considering Race in College and University Admissions.* Princeton, N.J.: Princeton University Press.

Candy, P. C., G. Crebert, and J. O'Leary. 1994. *Developing Lifelong Learners through Undergraduate Education.* Commissioned Report 28. Canberra: National Board of Employment, Education and Training.

Card, David, and Thomas Lemieux. 2000. "Can Falling Supply Explain the Rising Return to College for Younger Men? A Cohort-Based Analysis." NBER Working Paper 7655. National Bureau of Economic Research, Cambridge, Mass.

Carnevale, D. 2001. "U. of Vermont Considers Intellectual-Property Policy Said to Foster Distance Education." *Chronicle of Higher Education* (May 24). Available at <http://chronicle.com/free/2001/05/2001052401u.htm>.

Carnevale, D., and J. R. Young. 1999. "Who Owns On-Line Courses?" *Chronicle of Higher Education* (December 17).

Carrington, William J., and Enrica Detragiache. 1999. "How Extensive is the Brain Drain?" *Finance & Development* 36 (June): 46–49.

Cervantes, M., and D. Malkin. 2001. "Russia's Innovation Gap." *OECD Observer* (November): 10.

Choi, G. S. 2001. "An Analysis of Economic Returns to Investment in Education" (in Korean). Processed.

Clark, Burton R. 1998. *Creating Entrepreneurial Universities: Organizational Pathways of Transformation.* Oxford, U.K.: Pergamon.

CVCP (Committee of Vice-Chancellors and Principals of the Universities of the UK). 2000. *The Business of Borderless Education: UK Perspectives.* London.

Denmark. 2001. "White Paper to the Danish Government on Tertiary Education Reform." Copenhagen.

Densford, L. 1999. "Motorola University: The Next 20 Years." *The New Corporate University Review* 1 (1, January–February). Available at <http://www.traininguniversity.com/tu_pi1999jf_4.php>.

Dollar, David, and Paul Collier. 2001. *Globalization, Growth, and Poverty: Building an Inclusive World Economy.* New York: Oxford University Press.

Duraisamy, P. 2000. "Changes in Returns to Education in India, 1983–1994: By Gender, Age-Cohort and Location." Discussion Paper 815. Economic Growth Center, Yale University, New Haven, Conn.

Easterly, William, and Ross Levine. 2000. "It's Not Factor Accumulation: Stylized Facts and Growth Models." IMF Seminar Series 2000-12 (March): 1–52. International Monetary Fund, Washington, D.C.

Economist Intelligence Unit. 2001. "Political Risk Outlook: Russia's Institutions." February 15.

El-Khawas, Elaine, Robin DePietro-Jurand, and Lauritz Holm-Nielsen. 1998. "Quality Assurance in Higher Education: Recent Progress; Challenges Ahead." Human Development Network, Education, World Bank, Washington, D.C. Available at<http://www1.worldbank.org/education/tertiary/quality.html>.

Foley, M. 1997. "Labor Market Dynamics in Russia." Discussion Paper 870. Economic Growth Center, Yale University, New Haven, Conn.

Galbraith, K. 2001. "6 Publishers Will Give Poor Countries Free or Discounted Electronic Access to Journals." *Chronicle of Higher Education* (July 10). Available at http://chronicle.com/free/2001/07/2001071001t.htm>.

García Guadilla, C. 1998. *Situación y principales dinámicas de transformación de la educación superior en América latina.* Caracas: UNESCO-Regional Centre for Higher Education in Latin America and the Caribbean (CRESALC).

Gibbons, Michael. 1998. "Higher Education Relevance in the 21st Century." Human Development Network, World Bank, Washington, D.C.

Gibbons, M., C. Limoges, H. Nowotny, S. Schwartzman, P. Scott, and M. Trow. 1994. *The New Production of Knowledge: Science and Research in Contemporary Societies.* London: Sage.

Gladieux, Lawrence E., and Watson Scott Swail. 1999. "The Virtual University and Educational Opportunity: Issues of Equity and Access for the Next Generation." April. The College Board, Washington, D.C.

Glaeser, Edward L., David L. Laibson, and Bruce Sacerdote. 2000. "The Economic Approach to Social Capital." NBER Working Paper 7728. National Bureau of Economic Research, Cambridge, Mass.

Glanz, James. 2001. "Trolling for Brains in International Waters." *New York Times* (April 1).

Hanna, Donald E., and associates. 2000. *Higher Education in an Era of Digital Competition: Choices and Challenges.* Madison, Wis.: Atwood.

Harrison, Lawrence E., and Samuel P. Huntington, eds. 2000. *Culture Matters: How Values Shape Human Progress.* New York: Basic Books.

Hartnett, Teresa. 2000. *Financing Trends and Expenditure Patterns in Nigerian Federal Universities: An Update. Internal Report.* November. Washington, D.C: World Bank. Processed.

Helliwell, John F. 1996. "Economic Growth and Social Capital in Asia." NBER Working Paper 5470. National Bureau of Economic Research, Cambridge, Mass.

Hirsch, Werner J., and Luc E. Weber, eds. 1999. *Challenges Facing Higher Education at the Millennium.* American Council on Education. Phoenix, Ariz.: Oryx Press.

Hopper, Richard. 1998. "Emerging Private Universities in Bangladesh: Public Enemy or Ally?" *International Higher Education* 10 (winter). Boston College, Center for International Higher Education, Boston, Mass.

————. 1999. "The Higher Education Loan Program of Grameen Bank." *International Higher Education* 16 (summer). Boston College, Center for International Higher Education, Boston, Mass.

IDB (Inter-American Development Bank). 1999. "Higher Education in Latin America: Myths, Realities, and How the IDB Can Help." Washington, D.C.

IFC (International Finance Corporation). 2001. *IFC Strategic Directions: Investing in Private Education.* Global Practice Group for Social Sectors, Washington, D.C.

IHEP (Institute for Higher Education Policy). 1998. *Reaping the Benefits: Defining the Public and Private Value of Going to College.* Washington, D.C.

ILO (International Labour Organization). 2001. *World Employment Report 2001: Life at Work in the Information Economy.* Geneva.

Kelly, M. J. 2001. *Challenging the Challenger: Understanding and Expanding the Response of Universities in Africa to HIV/AIDS.* Paris: Association of Donors for African Education.

Kisilevsky, M. 1999. "Circuitos públicos y privados en la universidad argentina: señales desde la encuesta de hogares." *Pensamiento Universitario.* Universidad Nacional de Quilmes, Buenos Aires.

Koswara, J. 1996. "Women in Science and Technology in Higher Education." Country Report: Indonesia. Presented at the Expert Group Meeting on the Promotion of Women in Science and Technology, Southeast Asian Ministers of Education (SEAMED), Bangkok.

Kozma, R., and J. Johnson. 1991. "The Technological Revolution Comes to the Classroom." *Change* (January/February).

Krugman, Paul. 1996. "Of Economists and Liberals." *American Prospect* 7 (29, November–December): 13–15.

Lächler, U. 1997. "Education and Earnings Inequality in Mexico." World Bank, Washington, D.C. Processed.

Lall, Sanjaya. 2000. "Skills, Competitiveness, and Policy in Developing Countries." QEH Working Paper 46. Queen Elizabeth House, University of Oxford, Oxford, U.K.

Lam, D. 1999. "Generating Extreme Inequality: Schooling, Earnings, and Intergenerational Transmissions of Human Capital in South Africa and Brazil." Research Report 99-439. Population Studies Center, University of Michigan, Ann Arbor.

Lamancusa, J., J. Jorgensen, and José Zayas-Castro. 1997. "The Learning Factory: A New Approach to Integrating Design and Manufacturing into the Engineering Curriculum." *Journal of Engineering Education* (April): 103–12.

Larsen, K., R. Morris, and J. P. Martin. 2001. *Trade in Educational Services: Trends and Emerging Issues.* OECD Working Paper. Paris.

Lumina Foundation. 2002. "Unequal Opportunity: Disparities in College Access among the 50 States." Available at <http://www.luminafoundation.org/>.

MacWilliams, B. 2001. "Corruption, Conflict, and Budget Cuts Afflict Academe in Former Soviet Republics: Few Universities Have the Resources or the Will to Reform." *Chronicle of Higher Education* (December 11): A43.

Mangan, K. 2000. "In the Digital Era, Bureaucracies Are a Burden to Business Schools, Educators Are Told." *Chronicle of Higher Education* (April 11).

Maslen, G. 2001. "Australia's Leader Proposes New Student-Loan Program and More Money for Research." *Chronicle of Higher Education* 30 (January).

McCollum, K. 1999. "Cornell University Offers Developing Nations Digital Journals on Agriculture." *Chronicle of Higher Education* (November 30).

Mendels, P. 2000. "Study on Online Education Sees Optimism, with Caution." *New York Times* (January 19).

Milanovic, Branko. 1998. "Explaining the Increase in Inequality during the Transition." Policy Research Working Paper 1935. Development Economics Research Group, World Bank, Washington, D.C.

Mkude, D. J. 2001. "Reforming Higher Education: Change and Innovation in Finance and Administration. A Case Study of the University of Dar es Salaam." March. World Bank, Washington, D.C. Processed.

Musoke, M. 2002. "Maternal Health Care in Rural Uganda: Leveraging Traditional Systems and Modern Knowledge Systems." *Indigenous Knowledge Notes,* no. 40 (January). World Bank, Washington, D.C.

Naisbitt, John. 1982. *Megatrends: Ten New Directions Transforming Our Lives.* New York: Warner.

Nelson, R., ed. 1993. *National Innovations Systems: A Comparative Analysis.* New York: Oxford University Press.

NSF (National Science Foundation). 2000. *Science and Engineering Indicators 2000,* vol. 2. Washington, D.C.

Nzimande, Blade, and Mpumelela Sikhosana. 1996. *Affirmative Action and Transformation.* Durban, South Africa: Indicator Press.

Obwana, M., and D. Norman. 2000. "Status of Agricultural Economics in Selected Countries in Eastern and Southern Africa." Study implemented for the International Food Policy Research Institute (IFPRI). May–June.

OECD (Organisation for Economic Co-operation and Development). 1996. *Lifelong Learning for All.* Paris.

_____. 1998a. *Redefining Tertiary Education.* Paris.

_____. 1998b. "Technology, Productivity, and Job Creation." *Best Policy Practices.* Paris.

_____. 2000. "Science, Technology and Industry Outlook." Paris.

_____. 2001. *Education Policy Analysis: Education and Skills.* Paris.

Olsen, J. 2000. "Is Virtual Education for Real?" *TechKnowLogia* (January–February): 16–18.

Paskey, H. 2001. "Canadian Universities Band Together in a Giant Journal Licensing Deal." *Chronicle of Higher Education* (September 14). Available at <http://chronicle.com/free/2001/09/2001091401t.htm>.

Pessino, C. 1995. "Returns to Education in Greater Buenos Aires 1986–1993: From Hyperinflation to Stabilization." Working Paper 104 (June). Centro de Estudios Macroeconómicos de Argentina, Buenos Aires.

Phipps, R. 2000. "Measuring Quality in Internet-Based Higher Education: Benchmarks for Success." *International Higher Education* 20 (summer). Boston College, Center for International Higher Education, Boston, Mass.

Porter, Michael E. 1990. *The Competitive Advantage of Nations.* New York: Free Press.

Powar, K. B., and V. Bhalla. 2001. "International Providers of Higher Education in India." *International Higher Education,* no. 23 (spring).

Regel, O. 1992. "The Academic Credit System in Higher Education: Effectiveness and Relevance in Developing Countries." PHREE Background Paper Series 92/59. Population and Human Resources Department, World Bank, Washington, D.C.

Ritzen, J. 2000. "Social Cohesion, Public Policy and Economic Growth: Implications for OECD Countries." Presented at the OECD Expert Seminar on Childhood and Social Exclusion, Québec, Canada.

Romer, P. 1990. "Endogenous Technological Change." *Journal of Political Economy* 98: S71–S102.

Ryoo, J. K., Young-Sook Nam, and Martin Carnoy. 1993. "Changing Rates of Return to Education over Time: A Korean Case Study." *Economics of Education Review* 12 (1): 71–80.

Sadlak, J., and P. G. Altbach, eds. 1997. *Higher Education Research at the Turn of the New Century.* Paris: UNESCO Publishing.

Saint, William S. 1992. *Universities in Africa: Strategies for Stabilization and Revitalization.* World Bank Technical Paper 194. Washington DC.

Salmi, Jamil. 2000. "Student Loans in an International Perspective: The World Bank Experience." LCSHD Paper Series 44. World Bank, Washington, D.C. Available at <http://wbln0018.worldbank.org/LAC/lacinfoclient.nsf/d29684951174975c85256735007fef12/d4a6119794fde8be85256792006c55cb?OpenDocument>.

_____. 2001. "Tertiary Education in the 21st Century: Challenges and Opportunity." *Higher Education Management* (OECD, Paris) 13 (2): 5–130.

Schady, Norbert R. 2002. "Convexity and Sheepskin Effects in the Human Capital Earnings Function; Recent Evidence for Filipino Men." Policy Research Working Paper 2566. World Bank, Washington, D.C.

Scott, Peter, ed. 1998. *The Globalization of Higher Education.* London: Society for Research into Higher Education.

Shin, Dong-Ho. 2001. "Emerging Sticky Companies: Local and Institutional Embeddedness of Technology-Intensive Start-ups of Taejon, Korea." CGIRS Working Paper 99-3. Center for Global, International, and Regional Studies, University of California, Santa Cruz. Available at <http://www2.ucsc.edu/globalinterns/wp/wp99-3.pdf>.

Smallwood, S. 2001. "The Price Professors Pay for Teaching at Public Universities." Chronicle of Higher Education (April 20). Available at <http://chronicle.com/weekly/v47/i32/32a01801.htm>.

Smith, D. 2001. "A More Peaceful World?" *Washington Post* (January 27): A13.

Solow, R. M. 2000. "Notes on Social Capital and Economic Performance." In P. Dasgupta and I. Serageldin, eds., *Social Capital: A Multifaceted Perspective,* 6–10. Washington, D.C.: World Bank.

_____. 2001. "What Have We Learned from a Decade of Empirical Research on Growth? Applying Growth Theory across Countries." *World Bank Economic Review* 15 (2): 283–88.

Stern, Scott, Michael E. Porter, and Jeffrey L. Furman. 2000. "The Determinants of National Innovative Capacity." NBER Working Paper 7876. National Bureau of Economic Research, Cambridge, Mass.

Subbarao, K., Laura Raney, Halil Dundar, and Jennifer Haworth. 1994. *Women in Higher Education: Progress, Constraints, and Promising Initiatives*. World Bank Discussion Paper 244. Washington, D.C.

Thurow, L. 1999. *Building Wealth: The New Rules for Individuals, Companies and Nations in a Knowledge-Based Economy*. New York: Harper Business.

Trafford, Abigail. 2001. "Calif. Vintners Put Hopes in Brazilian Labs: Work on Decoding a Devastating Microbe Reveals New Rules of Global Science." *Washington Post* (December 29): A1, A19.

UNDP (United Nations Development Programme). 2000. *Human Development Report 2000*. New York: Oxford University Press.

UNESCO (United Nations Educational, Scientific, and Cultural Organization). 1998. *Higher Education in the Twenty-First Century: Vision and Action*. Final Report of the World Conference on Higher Education. Paris.

———. 1999. Statistical Yearbook 1999. Paris.

———. 2000a. *Science for the Twenty-First Century: A New Commitment*. Final Report of the World Conference on Science. Paris.

———. 2000b. *World Education Report 2000*. Paris.

United Nations. 2000. *The World's Women: Trends and Statistics*. New York.

USDL (U.S. Department of Labor). 2000. *Occupational Outlook Quarterly* (winter 1999–2000).

Van de Walle, Dominique. 1992. "The Distribution of the Benefits from Social Services in Indonesia, 1978–87." Policy Research Working Paper 871. World Bank, Washington, D.C.

Varghese, N. V. 2001. *Economic Crisis and Higher Education in East Asia*. Paris: UNESCO, International Institute for Educational Planning.

Vorozhtsov, Vladimir Petrovich. 1999. "Combating Crime in Russia: The Particular and the Common." In Sergei Oznobishchev and James H. Brusstar, *U.S.-Russia Partnership: Meeting the New Millennium*. Washington, D.C.: National Defense University Press. Available at <http://isuisse.ifrance.com/emmaf2/USRUS/usrp17.html>.

Wagner, A. 1998. *Tertiary Education and Lifelong Learning: Perspectives, Findings and Issues from OECD Work*. Paris: OECD/IMHE.

———. 1999. "Lifelong Learning in the University: A New Imperative?" In W. Hirsch and L. Weber, eds. *Challenges Facing Higher Education at the Millennium*, 134–52. American Council on Education. Phoenix, Ariz.: Oryx Press.

Wolfe, B., and S. Zuvekas. 1997. "Nonmarket Outcomes of Schooling." *International Journal of Educational Research* 27 (6): 491–501.

Woodhall, M. 1997. "The Reform of Higher Education in Developing Countries: Some Implementation Issues." Prepared for Human Development Week. World Bank, Washington, D.C. Processed.

World Bank. 1994. *Higher Education: The Lessons of Experience*. Development in Practice series. Washington, D.C.

———. 1995. *Priorities and Strategies for Education*. Washington, D.C.

———. 1997. *World Development Report 1997: The State in a Changing World*. New York: Oxford University Press.

———. 1999a. *Education Sector Strategy*. Washington, D.C.

————. 1999b. "Hashemite Kingdom of Jordan: Public Sector Review." Washington, D.C.

_____. 1999c. *World Development Report 1998/1999: Knowledge for Development.* New York: Oxford University Press.

_____. 2000a. *Hidden Challenges to Education Systems in Transition Economies.* Washington, D.C.

_____. 2000b. "Reforming Public Institutions and Strengthening Governance. A World Bank Strategy. Executive Summary." Washington, D.C.

_____. 2000c. "Republic of Korea: Transition to a Knowledge-Based Economy." Report 20346-KO. Washington, D.C.

_____. 2000d. *World Development Indicators.* Washington, D.C.

_____. 2000e. *World Development Report 1999/2000: Entering the 21st Century.* New York: Oxford University Press.

_____. 2001a. *A Chance to Learn: Knowledge and Finance for Education in Sub-Saharan Africa.* Washington, D.C.

————. 2001b. "Education Indicators for East Asia and Pacific." Washington, D.C.

————. 2001c. *World Development Report 2000/2001: Attacking Poverty.* New York: Oxford University Press.

World Bank and UNESCO. 2000. *Higher Education in Developing Countries: Peril and Promise.* Report of the Independent World Bank/UNESCO Task Force on Higher Education and Society. Washington, D.C.

Xueqin, J. 2001. "New Reports Add to Picture of Corruption in Chinese College Admissions." *Chronicle of Higher Education* (September 7). Available at <http://chronicle.com/daily/2001/09/2001090706n.htm>.

Yamada Reiko. 2001. "University Reform in the Post-Massification Era in Japan: Analysis of Government Education Policy for the 21st Century." *Higher Education Policy* 14 (4): 277–91.

Young, J. R. 2001. "At One US University, Royalties Entice Professors to Design Web Courses." *Chronicle of Higher Education* (March 30). Available at <http://chronicle.com/free/v47/i29/29a04101.htm>.